Local Organizational Adaptations to Climatic Change

The Last Glacial Maximum in Central Europe and the case of Grubgraben (Lower Austria)

Jeff T. Williams

BAR International Series 698
1998

Published in 2019 by
BAR Publishing, Oxford

BAR International Series 698

Local Organizational Adaptations to Climatic Change

© Jeff T. Williams and the Publisher 1998

The author's moral rights under the 1988 UK Copyright,
Designs and Patents Act are hereby expressly asserted.

All rights reserved. No part of this work may be copied, reproduced, stored,
sold, distributed, scanned, saved in any form of digital format or transmitted
in any form digitally, without the written permission of the Publisher.

ISBN 9780860548843 paperback
ISBN 9781407350110 e-book

DOI https://doi.org/10.30861/9780860548843

A catalogue record for this book is available from the British Library

This book is available at www.barpublishing.com

BAR Publishing is the trading name of British Archaeological Reports (Oxford) Ltd.
British Archaeological Reports was first incorporated in 1974 to publish the BAR
Series, International and British. In 1992 Hadrian Books Ltd became part of the BAR
group. This volume was originally published by Archaeopress in conjunction with
British Archaeological Reports (Oxford) Ltd / Hadrian Books Ltd, the Series principal
publisher, in 1998. This present volume is published by BAR Publishing, 2019.

BAR titles are available from:

	BAR Publishing
	122 Banbury Rd, Oxford, OX2 7BP, UK
EMAIL	info@barpublishing.com
PHONE	+44 (0)1865 310431
FAX	+44 (0)1865 316916
	www.barpublishing.com

TABLE OF CONTENTS

List of Tables	ii
List of Figures	iii
Summary	iv
Acknowledgments	vii

1.0 Introduction 1
1.1 The Last Glacial Maximum 1
1.2 Climatic Change and Cultural Adaptation 2
1.3 Environmental Determinism 4
1.4 Strategy for Research 4
1.5 Outline of Contents 5

2.0 Grubgraben: A Provocative Site 7
2.1 Site Location and Local Geography 7
2.2 History of Activity 7
2.3 Sources of Data 7
2.4 Archaeological Levels and Features 9
    2.4.1 Level AL1 9
    2.4.2 Level AL2 9
    2.4.3 Level AL3 10
    2.4.4 Level AL4 10
    2.4.5 Variability in Site Framework 10
2.5 The Artifact Assemblages 11
2.6 Absolute Dating 12
2.7 Regional Representation 13
2.8 Paleoclimatic Reconstruction 18
2.9 Seasonality 21
2.10 Controls on Variability 21
2.11 Conclusions 23

3.0 How to Research the Problem 24
3.1 Expectations for Variability 24
    3.1.1 Ethnographic Analogy 24
    3.1.2 Actualistic Archaeology and Ethnohistory 25
    3.1.3 Generalizations from Modern Hunter-Gatherers 25
        3.1.3.1 Housing 26
        3.1.3.2 Storage 26
        3.1.3.3 Mobility 26
3.2 A Pattern Recognition Approach 27
    3.2.1 Residential Interassemblage Variability 28
    3.2.2 The Structure of Variability 29
3.3 Conclusions 29

4.0 Quantitative Procedure 31
4.1 Structural versus Classificatory Analysis 31
4.2 The Harpending-Rogers Method 33
    4.2.1 Conducting an Analysis 33
    4.2.2 Data Normalization 33
4.3 Interpretation of Results 34
4.4 Robusticity of the Solutions 35
4.5 Surrogate Scale/Sample Size Effects 35

5.0 Interassemblage Variability at Grubgraben 37
5.1 Analysis Stage 1: General Classes of Remains 38
    5.1.1 Description of the Data 38
    5.1.2 Dimensions of Variability 39
    5.1.3 Case/Variable Relations 43
    5.1.4 Summary 44
5.2 Analysis Stage 2: Classes of Lithic Items 45
    5.2.1 Description of the Data 45
    5.2.2 Dimensions of Variability 46
    5.2.3 Case/Variable Relations 49
    5.2.4 Summary 51
5.3 Analysis Stage 3: Classes of Faunal Remains 51
    5.3.1 Description of the Data 52
    5.3.2 Dimensions of Variability 53
    5.3.3 Case/Variable Relations 57
    5.3.4 Summary 58
5.4 Analysis Stage 4: Lithics and Fauna 58
    5.4.1 Description of the Data 59
    5.4.2 Dimensions of Variability 59
    5.4.3 Case/Variable Relations 65
    5.4.4 Summary 65

6.0 Diachronic Variability in Organizational Properties 67
6.1 Method of Comparison 67
6.2 General Classes of Remains 67
6.3 Classes of Lithic Items 68
6.4 Classes of Faunal Remains 69
6.5 Classes of Lithics and Fauna 70
6.6 General Observations 71

7.0 Explaining Organizational Change 74
7.1 Sources of Variation 74
7.2 Linking Climate and Organization 75
7.3 Intrasite Functional Variation 76
7.4 Climatic Change 77
7.5 Summary 79

8.0 Concluding Remarks 80
8.1 Review of Methods and Results 80
8.2 Discussion 80
8.3 Criticism 81
8.4 Directions for Further Research 83

Bibliography 85

LIST OF TABLES

Table 2.1. C14 Dates from Grubgraben 12

Table 2.2. Radiocarbon Dates between 25,000 BP and 13,000 BP from Archaeological Sites in Central Europe 14

Table 5.1.1. Analysis Stage 1: Frequencies in General Classes of Remains 38

Table 5.1.2. Analysis Stage 1: Scaled Principle Components for General Classes of Remains 39

Table 5.1.3. Analysis Stage 1: Correlation Coefficients between Principle Component Scores and Sample Sizes 40

Table 5.2.1. Analysis Stage 2: Frequencies in Classes of Lithic Items 46

Table 5.2.2. Analysis Stage 2: Scaled Principle Components for Classes of Lithic Items 47

Table 5.2.3. Analysis Stage 2: Correlation Coefficients between Principle Component Scores and Sample Sizes 47

Table 5.3.1. Analysis Stage 3: Frequencies of Skeletal Elements for Reindeer and Horse 53

Table 5.3.2. Analysis Stage 3: Scaled Principle Components for Skeletal Elements for Reindeer and Horse 54

Table 5.3.3. Analysis Stage 3: Sorted Scores on Dimension 1 55

Table 5.3.4. Analysis Stage 3: Sorted Scores on Dimension 2 56

Table 5.3.5. Analysis Stage 3: Sorted Scores on Dimension 3 57

Table 5.3.6. Analysis Stage 3: Correlation Coefficients between Principle Component Scores and Sample Sizes 58

Table 5.4.1. Analysis Stage 4: Scaled Principle Components for Lithic Items, Reindeer and Horse Elements, Quartz, and Cobbles 61

Table 5.4.2. Analysis Stage 4: Sorted Scores on Dimension 1 62

Table 5.4.3. Analysis Stage 4: Sorted Scores on Dimension 2 63

Table 5.4.4. Analysis Stage 4: Sorted Scores on Dimension 3 64

Table 5.4.5. Analysis Stage 4: Correlation Coefficients between Principle Component Scores and Sample Sizes 65

Table 7.1. Correlation Coefficients between Principle Component Scores for Archaeological Levels and an Ordinal Measure of Climatic Severity 76

Table 8.1. Comparison of Interassemblage Variability at Grubgraben Explained by Adaptation to Climatic Change (C) and by Intrasite Functional Variation due to Excavation Sampling Bias (E) 81

LIST OF FIGURES

Figure 2.1. Physiographic map of central Europe showing the location of Grubgraben and selected other Gravettian and Epigravettian sites 8

Figure 2.2. C14 dates from Table 2.1 sorted by level 13

Figure 2.3. Mean C14 dates for Grubgraben AL1–AL4 13

Figure 2.4. Radiocarbon chronology of archaeological sites in central Europe dating between 25,000 BP and 13,000 BP 16

Figure 2.5. Stratigraphy of the loess sequence at Grubgraben 18

Figure 2.6. Total Quartz and Angular Quartz Distributions (Coarse Fraction) 20

Figure 5.1. Analysis Stage 1: General Classes of Remains 43

Figure 5.2. Analysis Stage 2: Lithics 50

Figure 5.3. Analysis Stage 3: Faunal Remains 59

Figure 5.4. Analysis Stage 4: Lithics and Fauna . . . 66

Figure 6.1. Analysis Stage 1: General Classes of Remains 68

Figure 6.2. Analysis Stage 2: Lithics 69

Figure 6.3. Analysis Stage 3: Faunal Remains 70

Figure 6.4. Analysis Stage 4: Lithics and Fauna . . . 71

Figure 6.5. Comparison of 1st Principle Components 72

Figure 6.6. Comparison of 2nd Principle Components 72

Figure 6.7. Comparison of 3rd Principle Components 73

Summary

During the Last Glacial Maximum from 22,000 to 14,000 BP, human groups in central Europe were subjected to dramatic changes in climate and environment as the last major advance of the ice sheets brought about some of the most severe ice-age conditions of the Pleistocene epoch. Climatic conditions became especially severe in central Europe as the northern continental and southern alpine ice masses encroached to within 500–600 km of one another, leaving only a narrow periglacial corridor from central and southern Germany through Poland, Bohemia, Moravia, and Lower Austria.

Early indications of a marked hiatus in the archaeological record from central Europe ca. 18,000 BP motivated the view that conditions of extreme aridity and severe cold during the Last Glacial Maximum rendered much of the region uninhabitable by human groups. More recent archaeological evidence, however, suggests that any regional hiatus in occupation was probably short-lived, and that a human presence persisted in many parts of central Europe despite severe climatic conditions. How did these human groups adapt to climatic and environmental changes during the Last Glacial Maximum? It seems unlikely that strategies for coping with pre-glacial environments would have remained unchanged in the face of full glacial conditions, but this is a view to be evaluated rather than assumed.

The recently excavated Epigravettian site of Grubgraben in Lower Austria is of exceptional significance for investigating the nature of human adaptations in central Europe during the Last Glacial Maximum. A sequence of four archaeological levels, securely dated to the latter half of the Last Glacial Maximum, document an extended period of repeated and intensive site utilization during an episode of local climatic deterioration. The site also offers a previously unavailable degree of experimental control over many potentially confounding sources of variation such as site geography and environment, the timing and direction of climatic change, site type, season of occupation, agents responsible for the archaeological deposits, excavation methodology, and data recovery.

Using Grubgraben as a relevant archaeological test case, the problem is considered of recognizing the variability between archaeological assemblages that is referable to the adaptations of hunter-gatherer systems to climatic change during the Last Glacial Maximum. The focus is specifically on recognizing adaptations that are local in scale and organizational in nature. Local adaptations are modifications expressed at or near the level of the individual hunter-gatherer settlement, in contrast to regional adaptations involving, for example, settlement-subsistence patterns or raw-material procurement networks. Organizational adaptations involve changes in the ways that specific materials and behaviors are integrated, in contrast to absolute changes in the inventories of materials and behaviors. Resolution of these localized, organizational adaptations is achieved by restricting the scale of the study geographically and systemically, and investigating the joint archaeological and climatological variability at a single site representing a single node in the overall network of sites in a hunter-gatherer settlement system.

To describe the structure of the archaeological record in organizational terms, a scaled principle components analysis of normalized frequency data is used to summarize interassemblage variability in terms of a set of composite variables. These composite variables represent covariance relations between different classes of remains and monitor organizational properties of the archaeological record that result from the consistent interaction of specific materials and behaviors. The analysis is conducted in four stages, using a different description of the archaeological record in each stage. In the first stage of analysis, interassemblage variability is summarized using a small number of general classes of remains to obtain an initial impression of the patterned variability between assemblages. The second and third stages of analysis, respectively, examine the structure of interassemblage variability in lithic items and in skeletal elements for reindeer and horse. In the fourth stage of analysis, the lithic and faunal datasets of the second and third stages are combined and the joint interassemblage variability in lithics and fauna is examined.

In each stage of analysis the four archaeological levels enable three principle components to be constructed. The organizational relations implied by the principle components are interpreted by appeal to knowledge and ideas regarding the form and function of stone tools, principles of the economic anatomy of animals, ethnographic analogy, and ethnoarchaeological observation. When the corresponding principle components from each stage of analysis are compared, three modal trajectories clearly emerge in the patterns of diachronic change between archaeological levels. To distinguish any interassemblage variability that is conditioned by the response of human groups to climatic change from variability contributed by other sources of variation, the correlation of the principle components with an ordinal measure of climatic severity is determined.

The first principle components explain on average about 60% of interassemblage variability in each stage of analysis and monitor coarsely defined organizational properties. In stage 1 events involving reindeer are distinguished from events involving all other classes of remains; stage 2 separates formal tools and resharpening waste from blades, bladelets, and primary production debris; in stage 3 the higher utility parts of the reindeer anatomy are separated from all other faunal elements; and stage 4 reiterates the structure found in stages 2 and 3. These organizational relations are weakly correlated with an ordinal index of climatic severity and are argued to represent the intrasite functional variation generated by the differential spatial placement of the large residential camp relative to the fixed excavation units.

The second principle components explain on average about 34% of interassemblage variability in each stage of analysis and monitor finer organizational contrasts. Stage 1 separates events related to tailoring and general outfitting tasks from events related to the subsistence effort; in stage 2 the technology involving endscrapers is separated from the technology involving other kinds of tools; stage 3 monitors the differential use of high- and low-utility parts from both reindeer and horse; and stage 4 reiterates the results from stages 2 and 3. The organizational relations implied by the second principle components are clearly correlated with an ordinal index of climatic severity and are interpreted as monitoring the adaptive response of the hunter-gatherer systems at Grubgraben to the return of severe ice-age conditions following a relatively mild climatic episode.

The third principle component in each stage subsumes the remaining variance in interassemblage variability and is primarily informative of residual stochastic variation in the data on assemblage composition. All stages of analysis give some indication of weak but suggestive organizational structure on the third principle component, but these dimensions of interassemblage variability are confounded with undirected noise in the data on assemblage composition and cannot reliably be interpreted. The third principle components are diachronically unpatterned and exhibit zero correlation with an ordinal measure of climatic severity.

Comparison of the proportions of interassemblage variability explained by the first and second principle components shows that adaptation to climatic change at Grubgraben accounts for 24–41% of the total variability between assemblages, and is 34–78% of the variation attributed to intrasite functional variation and excavation sampling bias. Organizational relations involving classes of faunal remains are the most sensitive monitors of variability due to climatic change, while relations within classes of lithic items are least sensitive. Although the absolute magnitude of the adaptive response to climatic change is appreciable, the nature of the adaptations, as expressed by the organizational relations, is relatively limited. Existing hunter-gatherer systems may already have possessed a degree of behavioral and technological pliancy that was adequate for coping with climatic and environmental stress during the Last Glacial Maximum or, alternatively, the cultural systems at Grubgraben may already have neared their maximum adaptive response.

ACKNOWLEDGMENTS

Many individuals and institutions have contributed in various ways to make possible the research presented here. The participation of the members of my dissertation committee at the University of Kansas is gratefully acknowledged: Anta Montet-White, Jack L. Hofman, Larry D. Martin, Alfred Johnson, and Brad Logan. Comments and suggestions were also offered by David Frayer, John Hoopes, and Dixie West. These individuals gave generously of their time, effort, and ideas, and their comments and criticisms contributed significantly to the development of the arguments presented within. None of these individuals necessarily agrees, however, with the arguments, interpretations, and conclusions I present, and final responsibility for the contents is entirely mine.

Access to the Grubgraben data was provided by Anta Montet-White. Dixie West, Brad Logan, and Patsy Whitney generously allowed me to use their data on the Grubgraben faunal assemblages, and Margaret Beck, Eva Cook, and Matt Hill made available their work with the Grubgraben cobble, shell, and quartz assemblages, respectively. The willingness of these individuals to share their data and results and answer my many questions is greatly appreciated. Clara Maldener was helpful in locating and supplying several old and obscure German-language references concerning the early history of investigation at Grubgraben, and for this I am most grateful.

The Department of Anthropology at the University of Kansas generously provided five semesters of employment as a graduate teaching assistant, without which it is uncertain whether I could have completed my degree program in archaeology. Michael H. Crawford gave selflessly of his time, support, trust, guidance, and counsel during my studies at the University of Kansas, and his influence on my professional development has been considerable. The erudition and sage counsel of Tom D. Dillehay has been invaluable over the years and deserves special acknowledgment. The superb cuisine, good company, and sincere encouragement of Ravindranath Duggirala and family were most welcome and much appreciated. I am especially grateful to Bonnie, Kate, Paul and Gene for keeping me sane during some bleak and difficult times, and to Alana for her support and companionship and for making all the difference when things were at their blackest and most desperate.

The Fulbright Kommission in Bonn made possible a year-long research stay during 1992–93 at the Institut für Urgeschichte, Eberhard-Karls Universität, Tübingen, Germany, where much of the material presented here was first explored. Deserving of special acknowledgment for my Fulbright experience are Mary Elizabeth Debicki, Helmut Huelsbergen, Richard Schowen, John Hoopes, Jack Hofman, Anta Montet-White, Joachim Hahn, Gerhard Bosinski, Stefan Weil, Reiner Rohr, Ulrich Littmann, Jason Wirth, Annika Queitsch, Regina Queitsch, Thomas Gschwend, Almut Nonnenmann, Clara Maldener, Wolfgang Glatz, Robert Schmidt, Susan Strohmeier, and Franz Moser. At Tübingen I had the serendipitous good fortune to meet and learn from both Gerd-Christian Weniger and Hans-Peter Uerpmann, each of whom contributed importantly to my education in Old World archaeology.

I am most grateful to Rajka Makjanić for giving me the opportunity to contribute to the BAR series, for her patience during the preparation of this edition, and for calling to my attention several errors of geography that remarkably had passed unnoticed by all others. Brad Logan also deserves special thanks for his support in this endeavor and for his especially careful reading of and critical commentary on an earlier draft of the manuscript. Robin Williams Brohm and Yvonne Arena of Williams McBride Design in Lexington, Kentucky, gave generously of their time and effort in the preparation of the camera-ready copy of this manuscript. Christopher Williams and Paulette DiFilippo were helpful in locating and reviewing several references for accuracy.

No acknowledgment would be complete without registering my immense intellectual debt to Lewis R. Binford. No other archaeologist has so effectively conveyed the intellectual challenge and excitement of archaeology as a science, and it is certain that I never would have pursued archaeology without the inspiration and enthusiasm engendered by his research and writing. It has been a privilege to study archaeology as his contemporary, and the extent of his considerable influence will certainly be evident to informed readers of this work.

Finally, I thank my parents for their unquestioning support in all that I have done.

J.T.W.
San Antonio, Texas
September 1997

1.0 Introduction

Some people hate the very name of statistics, but I find them full of beauty and interest. Whenever they are not brutalized, but delicately handled by the higher methods, and are warily interpreted, their power of dealing with complicated phenomena is extraordinary. They are the only tools by which an opening can be cut through the formidable thicket of difficulties that bars the path of those who pursue the Science of man.

Francis Galton

This study, then, exemplifies the realities of ongoing research. The reader will thus find me periodically appealing to ethnographic or egographic analogy, and employing anecdotal justification for accepting some propositions as knowledge. I shall also generalize from small samples and even use poorly controlled observations as operational knowledge. These are all appeals to and a use of knowledge of the moment, which is quite variable in quality and quantity.

Lewis Binford

The problem considered in the following research is that of recognizing and estimating the variability between archaeological assemblages that is conditioned by the adaptive response of hunter-gatherer systems to long-term climatic change and increasingly severe environmental conditions during an ice age. Can cultural adaptations to climatic change and an ice-age existence be recognized in the archaeological record, and if so, can these adaptations be quantified and compared with other sources of archaeological variability? The Last Glacial Maximum in central Europe provides the source of climatic change, in the form of an episode of progressively cooler and more arid conditions and an eventual return to full ice-age conditions following a relatively milder and more humid climatic oscillation. The local adaptive responses of past hunter-gatherer systems to the environmental modifications resulting from this episode of climatic change are investigated by examining the organizational properties of interassemblage variability at the recently excavated Epigravettian site of Grubgraben, in Lower Austria (Montet-White 1988b, 1990a, 1991a).

The motivation for the present research is the desire to understand how the individual hunter-gatherer system responded to the protracted and widespread climatic and environmental changes associated with the Last Glacial Maximum. (To avoid confusion and unnecessary repetition the term "climatic change" will be used, unless otherwise indicated, to refer to the climatic dynamics described above: an episode of increasing aridity, decreasing temperatures, and the onset or return of full ice-age conditions). The consequences of the last ice age for human settlements have been examined elsewhere on broad, regional scales (e.g., Otte 1981; Soffer 1985; Hahn 1987; and articles in Soffer 1987a; Gamble and Soffer 1990a; Soffer and Gamble 1990), but the local effects of the Last Glacial Maximum, i.e., the effects on specific hunter-gatherer systems, have been difficult to address directly because of the absence of a suitable archaeological research context. However, with the recent excavation of Grubgraben, a large Epigravettian site in Lower Austria with evidence for repeated occupation during the latter half of the Last Glacial Maximum, an investigation of local hunter-gatherer adaptive strategies in response to the onset of severe ice-age conditions can be seriously undertaken.

The immediate challenge presented by the research is clearly methodological: how are the adaptive responses of past hunter-gatherer systems to long-term climatic deterioration to be recognized and monitored using the archaeological record? Ultimately, however, methodological advancement in this direction will enable certain views of the past to be better evaluated. For example, recent studies have suggested that human groups were less affected by conditions during the last ice age than has been previously believed, and a human presence evidently persisted in many parts of central Europe despite the worsening climate (Gamble 1983; Valoch 1989; Oliva 1989; Weniger 1989, 1990; Svoboda 1990; Kozlowski 1990; Montet-White et al. 1990; Montet-White 1994; Simán 1990; Dobosi 1991a; West 1995). This position is in marked contrast to earlier views that severe periglacial conditions during the Last Glacial Maximum precipitated a hiatus in the human occupation of central Europe that may have lasted several millennia in some regions (Hahn 1976, 1983; Valoch 1980; Gamble 1983, 1986; Jochim 1983, 1987; Soffer 1987b; Weniger 1989, 1990; Kozlowski 1990; Otte 1990; Straus 1991). These scenarios are not entirely mutually exclusive, but they clearly indicate that much remains to be learned about the form and magnitude of any changes that occurred in systems of organized human behavior in response to the last ice age.

The research presented here will also raise the more fundamental issue of precisely what is involved in behavioral or cultural adaptation by human groups to long-term climatic and environmental stress (Dumond 1972a,b; Jelinek 1982; Davis 1985, 1990; Wobst 1990; Sheehan 1995; Straus et al. 1996). Did cultural adaptation to the climatic changes of the Last Glacial Maximum necessarily involve dramatic transformations of technology, subsistence patterns, and settlement strategies, as is implied by the postulated hiatus of portions of Europe at this time? Or will any cultural changes that can be attributed to climatic change prove to be relatively minor, implying that Late Paleolithic cultural systems were relatively stable and able to maintain themselves by means of rather limited adjustments? Perhaps both extremes of adaptation are potentially involved and there exists a critical point at which the pliancy of existing behavioral and cultural patterns becomes inadequate and yields to more comprehensive systemic structural adjustments. Advances in the methods for monitoring the modifications in past cultural systems that are conditioned by climatic change will provide an improved means of exploring these issues and of elucidating the process of cultural adaptation during the Last Glacial Maximum.

1.1 The Last Glacial Maximum

The last global interglacial/glacial cycle, corresponding to the Upper Pleistocene geological epoch, began approximately 128,000 years BP (Crowley and North 1991; Gamble 1986).

Following a brief interglacial period from 128,000–118,000 BP known as the Last Interglacial Maximum (Crowley and North 1991:116), the subsequent glacial period involved two stages of ice volume growth, at 115,000 BP and 75,000 BP, with the main phase of glaciation beginning after 75,000 BP (Crowley and North 1991:110–131; Hammond 1976).

Known in the New World as the Wisconsin glaciation and in the Old World as the Würm/Weichsel, this last glacial period was one of the most severe ice ages of the Pleistocene epoch, with continental ice sheets reaching their greatest extent worldwide in at least 150,000 years (Crowley and North 1991:115–116, Figure 6.9). The event culminated in the Last Glacial Maximum, a period of maximal extension of the ice sheets lasting from about 22,000 to 14,000 years BP [the frequently cited date of 18,000 BP for the Last Glacial Maximum is simply the midpoint of this interval (Crowley and North 1991:47)].

In Europe, annual average midlatitude surface temperatures during the Last Glacial Maximum were depressed by about 10 °C, with estimated winter temperatures for northwestern Europe 15–20 °C below present values (Crowley and North 1991; Denton and Hughes 1981; CLIMAP 1976, 1981; Butzer 1964). Global surface winds increased by 20–50% or more, and precipitation at the poles is estimated to have decreased by 50% (Crowley and North 1991). Parts of western and central Europe were reduced to polar desert, characterized by extreme aridity and cold temperatures and supporting only tundra and mountain vegetation (Kukla 1975, 1977; Flint 1971; Crowley and North 1991; Butzer 1964; Montet-White 1984). Further to the east, the central and eastern European plains were characterized by steppe conditions (Crowley and North 1991: Figure 3.5; Butzer 1964). The characteristic fauna of the period included large mammals such mammoth, horse, reindeer, and ibex, with smaller fur-bearing forms such as hare, fox, and lemming (Kúrten 1968; Kukla 1975, 1977; Flint 1971; Weniger 1982, 1989).

Two regions of Europe were severely affected during the Last Glacial Maximum: northern Europe because of its higher latitude and proximity to the continental Fennoscandian ice sheet, and central Europe because of its position between the Fennoscandian and Alpine ice masses (Butzer 1964:265–284; Jochim 1987; Straus 1991; Crowley and North 1991). In central Europe a southward-reaching lobe of the Fennoscandian ice sheet covered northeastern Germany and northern Poland to about 52° north latitude (approximately the latitude of Berlin and Warsaw), and extended to within 500–600 km of the Alpine glacier to the south. The proximity of these two ice masses created a periglacial corridor from central and southern Germany through Poland, Bohemia, Moravia, and Lower Austria (Andersen 1981: Figures 1-1 and 1-8; CLIMAP 1981: Map 7B; Weniger 1990; Straus 1991; Crowley and North 1991; Hughes et al. 1981). The conditions of severe cold and, more critically, extreme aridity produced by the dry and dessicating winds streaming off of the ice masses may have rendered this section of Europe largely uninhabitable by human groups, or at least unsupportive of any extended human presence. However, isolated but locally stable pockets of moister and warmer environmental conditions more amenable to human occupation probably developed in places where the prevailing winds were shunted by topographical features (Haesaerts 1990b; Montet-White et al. 1990; West 1995).

Significant deglaciation of midlatitude land masses did not begin until 13–14,000 BP, after which the ice receded and the climate warmed very rapidly (Crowley and North 1991:62–67). Retreat of the ice sheets occurred in two stages. The main phase of deglaciation began ca. 13–14,000 BP and was followed by a brief reversal of the process and a return to cooler conditions during the Younger Dryas (10–11,000 BP). The second phase of deglaciation began by 10,000 BP and lasted for perhaps 2000 years, although remnants of the North American and European ice caps may have remained until 6–7000 BP (Ruddiman and Duplessy 1985; Crowley and North 1991).

Although it is convenient for the purposes of discussion to speak of the Last Glacial Maximum as if it were a singular and well-defined climatic occurrence, it is necessary to emphasize that the Last Glacial Maximum was not a monolithic paleoclimatic event, but a complex series of climatic and environmental oscillations of varying intensity and duration. In its entirety the Last Glacial Maximum lasted approximately 8000 years (Crowley and North 1991:47) and comprised periods of increased humidity and reduced ice cover as well as periods of greater aridity and increases in ice volume. Adaptive responses by cultural systems corresponding to these oscillations in climatic and environmental conditions can be expected (Gamble and Soffer 1990b:8; Weniger 1990:179). Ultimately, of course, the scale at which the Last Glacial Maximum should be examined is not an absolute quantity, but depends entirely on the scale at which human adaptations are explored, and the latter is often predetermined by the nature of the archaeological data (see further discussion in chapter 8).

1.2 Climatic Change and Cultural Adaptation

The Last Glacial Maximum is the only time in prehistory during which essentially modern humans (behaviorally and anatomically) have found it necessary to cope with the full glacial conditions of a major ice age (Wobst 1990; Gamble and Soffer 1990b; cf. Frayer 1984; cf. Straus and Heller 1988; cf. Lindly and Clark 1990). This presents a fascinating situation in terms of human-environment relationships during the Upper Paleolithic, for it is difficult to imagine that an ice age as severe as the Weichsel did not have consequences of some sort for the operation of past cultural systems. It seems unlikely that the behaviors and organizational properties of cultural systems that had been successful at coping with pre-glacial environments would have remained adequate responses to the challenges to survival imposed by full glacial conditions during the Last Glacial Maximum (Wobst 1990). The conditions of the last ice age posed a previously unexperienced suite of problems for human populations during the Late Upper Paleolithic and, in response, a variety of coping tactics can be expected to have emerged (Wobst 1990; van Andel 1990; Gamble and Soffer 1990b).

The present research is an effort to recognize and describe the specific local and organizational responses of past hunter-gatherer systems to a particular episode of long-term, monotonic climatic deterioration during the latter half of the Last Glacial Maximum in central Europe. How did these past systems of organized behavior respond to the extreme climatic and environmental modifications accompanying the last major advance of the ice sheets? How are these systemic adaptations manifested archaeologically, and how can they be recognized and studied? How can any observed changes in past systems be convincingly linked to environmental processes such as climatic change and not to other factors such as variability in site function or excavation and sampling bias?

An important feature of the research is the focus on adaptations by past systems that are *local* in scale and *organizational* in nature. This perspective distinguishes the study from the customary regional approach in which patterns of change in various aspects of hunter-gatherer systems, such as settlement patterns, hunting and subsistence strategies, technological organization, and raw material economies, are examined over large geographical areas (Hahn 1977; Otte 1981; Soffer 1985, 1987a; Gamble and Soffer 1990; Soffer and Gamble 1990; Montet-White and Holen 1991; Montet-White 1994).

The importance of examining system responses at a *local* level follows from the fact that adaptation of any sort is fundamentally a response to a local problem:

> Adaptation is always a local problem, and selective pressures favoring new cultural forms result from non-equilibrium conditions in the local ecosystem (Binford 1968:323).

The concern here is therefore with recognizing the responses to climatic change that occur on a highly localized scale, at or near the level at which the modifications made by individual hunter-gatherer systems are expressed. This resolution is achieved by restricting the scale of the study both geographically and systemically, and investigating the archaeological and climatological variability at a single site representing a single node in the overall network of sites in a hunter-gatherer settlement system.

Adopting a local rather than regional approach, however, imposes severe methodological constraints. Whereas a regional approach can make use of geographically separated assemblages to reconstruct large-scale processes, the exploration of local adaptive responses becomes practical only with the availability of a specific archaeological site meeting many requisite conditions, such as discrete archaeological levels with adequate material inventories, evidence for long-term stability of site function, and sufficient chronological depth to have documented diachronic systemic change. Sites at which these conditions, as well as many other requirements for analysis, are met have not previously been known from central Europe.

In addition to the emphasis on a local scale of adaptation, it is expected that the responses by past cultural systems to climatic change are primarily *organizational* in nature. Organization refers to the manner in which materials and behaviors are integrated or coordinated, and changes in the relationships between materials and behaviors constitute organizational changes in a cultural system (Binford 1987a:455, 1989a:270):

> Organization is not just behavior. It is the manner in which behaviors are juxtapositioned and integrated with one another, and these generalizations cannot be seen simply by the identification of discrete behaviors themselves, nor by inventorying the different ones present at different sites (Binford 1987a:503).

The importance of organizational relations as a mechanism for adaptation is suggested by a systemic view of human behavior:

> [Culture] was a system and was characterized by all that the term "system" implied organizationally. One could document the use of stone pebbles to smooth pottery, shells to scrape it, wood to support a vessel being built, even stone tools or antler tools used in procuring clay and decorating pots. The archaeological record was produced in the context of many variable ways of organizing natural materials, including the organization of human labor itself (Binford 1989a:270).

This passage illustrates that events involving a particular object, such as a pottery vessel, may be related to events involving many other classes of remains such as pebbles, shell, and stone and antler tools. In other words, there exists a number of organizational relations between pottery items, other materials, and behaviors, reflecting the variable ways in which these materials and behaviors interacted. These organizational relations do not necessarily operate simultaneously, however, nor do all the materials and behaviors involved (pottery, pebbles, shell, stone and antler tools, digging, smoothing, and scraping) necessarily participate in any single organizational relation.

The adaptive responses of a cultural system are expected to involve changes in these organizational properties (e.g., changes in the relations between pottery and other materials) rather than absolute changes in the inventory of materials and behaviors (e.g., the addition to or deletion from the material inventory of pottery or stone and antler tools). The kinds of materials that participated in the system do not change fundamentally, nor are specific "unit behaviors", with which these materials are integrated, added or deleted from the system, but the ways in which these materials and behaviors are put together, or organized, are expected to be flexible and situationally responsive (Binford 1968, 1980, 1987a, 1989a; Butzer 1982; White 1982; Davidson 1983; Orquera 1984; Wobst 1990; Gamble and Soffer 1990b; Enloe 1993):

> An important distinction should be drawn between material culture, on the one hand, and intangible adaptive strategies, on the other: It appears that tool kits were far less important for human adaptation in a changeable environment than were organizational devices. Yet standard archaeological procedures are almost exclusively focused on the artifactual residues and their patterning (Butzer 1982:301).

...organizational properties of behavior may be a more appropriate framework for understanding the operation of cultural systems, variability between cultural systems, and *evolutionary change with[in] cultural systems* (Enloe 1993:102, emphasis added).

Comparable points of view, with specific reference to climatic change, are found in Wobst (1990) and Gamble and Soffer (1990b) and are similar in suggesting that systemic adaptations to climatic change are likely to involve changes in the relations among existing materials and behaviors rather than additions, deletions, or modifications of specific behaviors or materials.

1.3 Environmental Determinism

The suggestion that climatic change has been responsible for cultural change is not new (Brooks 1922, Childe 1952). Early formulations of the relationships between climate and culture, however, were often deterministic and tended to treat climate and environment as prime movers of cultural change rather than as components in a complex suite of forces that condition cultural adaptation (Watson et al. 1984:113–154; Binford 1968; Orlove 1980; Wright 1993). Nevertheless, if culture is regarded as "the extrasomatic means of human adaptation" (White 1949:23–39; Binford 1962, 1989a), then climate and environment clearly belong among the extrasomatic stimuli to which culture must respond. Comparative studies of the world's contemporary hunter-gatherers, for example, have amply demonstrated the importance of climatic, environmental, and ecological variables for understanding some kinds of variation in cultural systems (Murdock 1967; Lee 1968; Oswalt 1973, 1976; Binford 1989c, 1990, 1991a; Whitelaw 1991; Jochim 1991; Kelly 1995).

The present study acknowledges a role for climate and the environment in the process of human cultural adaptation during the last ice age, but this position does not constitute or necessitate a posture of environmental determinism. Here is is assumed only that the physical variables that condition hunter-gatherer adaptations across space can also condition those adaptations across time (Wobst 1990; Jochim 1991). For the present purposes the position of van Andel (1990) regarding the role of climatic change in human adaptation is especially appropriate for its methodological intuition:

> It is quite unlikely that correlations between palaeoenvironmental and archaeological variables will illuminate all facets of Late Palaeolithic human settlement and resource exploitation. The palaeoenvironment provided a menu of options for exploitation from which humans selected according to social, economic, and technological determinants. Correlations with environmental variables will thus neither fully identify nor explain those choices; their effect will be visible mainly in the form of a residual unexplained variance (van Andel 1990:34).

Van Andel is suggesting that some portion of archaeological variability may be referable to climatic and environmental dynamics, and that in studying human adaptation this variability must be separated from the variance contributed by unrelated factors. Van Andel has a number of ideas and suggestions as to how this might best be accomplished given the nature of archaeological data and the many spatial and temporal constraints on paleoclimatic reconstruction. The task clearly calls for an approach that combines an analysis of variance in archaeological data with inspection of the correlations of the various components of variability with climatic, environmental, and cultural variables. To the extent that other sources of variability can be controlled or accounted for, the ability to recognize and monitor the variance conditioned by climatic change will be significantly improved. Many of these considerations are implemented in the present research.

1.4 Strategy for Research

Assuming that the local archaeological record is sensitive to the development of climatically conditioned organizational responses in hunter-gatherer systems, then the challenge presented by the research is essentially methodological and will involve minimally the following tasks: (i) find or establish a controlled archaeological situation in which climatically conditioned variability in response to the Last Glacial Maximum is likely to be expressed; (ii) determine what are relevant observations of the archaeological record, and whether these observations can be made in the given archaeological context; (iii) develop a procedure for recognizing and monitoring the organizational properties of past systems, and apply the method to the data to elicit the organizational properties of the given archaeological record; and (iv) assess the correlation between changes in these organizational properties and an independently reconstructed pattern of local climatic change. Successful work toward these goals will require careful attention not only to archaeological methodology but also to archaeological epistemology and research design.

The methodological challenge faced here is similar in several important respects to that confronted by Binford (1984b) in his study of the faunal remains from the Middle Stone Age site of Klasies River Mouth in southern Africa. These similarities are instructive, and the logical structure of Binford's research design is helpful in formulating a clear and appropriate strategy for the problem addressed here [for further discussion and development of this approach to research, see Binford (1984b:9–17)].

In his study of the faunal remains from Klasies River Mouth, Binford sought to develop recognition criteria for evaluating the relative roles of scavenging versus hunting in the subsistence tactics of early hominids (Binford 1984b:15). This is an exciting research topic with significant implications for reconstructions of hominid evolution and social organization. Unfortunately, there is no contemporary context available that the archaeologist may study to obtain insights into how a scavenging subsistence strategy conditions the archaeological record differently from a hunting subsistence strategy:

Introduction

> Ideally, I would like to go out and study a group of people who are obtaining a large proportion of their diet by scavenging. ..... Unfortunately, I know of no opportunities for doing this. I face a situation quite common for archaeologists: I cannot gain a firsthand knowledge of many behavioral and dynamic conditions that characterized the human past by studying contemporary homologies or analogies (Binford 1984b:15).

In other words, there are no contemporary or historically documented human groups that subsist mainly by scavenging and that can provide an ethnoarchaeological context for studying the links between a scavenging subsistence organization and its archaeological consequences. Because there are no relevant learning situations available for direct observation and study, accurate recognition criteria for the conditioning roles of hunting versus scavenging subsistence strategies cannot be developed actualistically. Without a secure knowledge of the static, archaeological consequences of dynamic, system-level processes (such as scavenging and hunting), any inferences about the past are reduced to imaginative guesswork and un- or underinformed stipulation. This is the essential message behind Binford's call for middle-range research (e.g., Binford 1977a, 1981, 1987a, 1989a, 1990) and the development of a "science of the archaeological record" (Binford 1983a:19–23, 1983c:413, 1989a:39).

The same dilemma is confronted in the present research. Knowledge is sought about a domain of past human behavior—namely the local and organizational responses of individual hunter-gatherer systems to a deteriorating climate and the development of severe ice-age conditions—about which archaeologists have little knowledge. Direct experience and firsthand knowledge cannot be acquired, because there are no contemporary or historical contexts available in which to study the archaeological variability generated as hunter-gatherer systems respond to climatic dynamics characteristic of those during the Last Glacial Maximum. Because there is no appropriate domain of contemporary experience for learning about these processes, actualistic middle-range research cannot be conducted to identify relevant data and establish accurate criteria for recognizing the organizational changes associated with adaptation to ice-age conditions.

In the absence of an explicitly relevant middle-range research context in which to directly study the archaeological consequences of the adaptation by hunter-gatherer systems to the onset of ice-age conditions, a productive alternative is to engage in directed pattern recognition work. This approach first requires that an archaeological case be sought out that is characterized by some of the properties believed to be relevant to the study of climatically conditioned ice-age adaptations (Binford 1984b:9–17, 1989a:37, 1989a:67). The test case should be chosen not only for certain properties of interest, but also to provide any specific control conditions that are believed to be necessary for researching the problem at hand. In other words, because the archaeological case is to serve as a surrogate, non-actualistic laboratory in which to evaluate ideas and seek insights about the past, it must be chosen to satisfy as many experimental controls as possible. The nature of these controls is dictated by the nature of the research problem, but they serve in general to greatly reduce, if not entirely eliminate, potentially confounding sources of variation in the archaeological record, and thus allow the patterns and causes of any organizational changes to be more confidently assessed. A desirable control for the present research, for example, would be for all archaeological deposits to be exclusively referable (or nearly so) to human agency, rather than to some indeterminate interaction of human, natural, and animal agents. Another useful control would be for all the archaeological deposits selected for investigation to derive from the operation of the same aspect of a hunter-gatherer system (e.g., from a residential site).

Once an appropriate archaeological situation has been identified for study, the archaeological record from the test case is investigated, using descriptive analytical methods and varying representations of the data, to search for previously unsuspected patterns and meaningful regularities (Binford 1984b:15–16). To the extent that the properties of the test case are relevant and the control conditions are reliable, the newly recognized patterns may then suggest new observations, additional analyses or, ideally, implicate certain properties of the archaeological record as diagnostic indicators of the organizational responses of past systems to climatic change.

1.5 Outline of Contents

In summary, the present research represents an effort to elucidate the nature and extent of the locally active and organizationally expressed adaptive modifications in past hunter-gatherer systems that occurred in response to an episode of climatic and environmental deterioration during the Last Glacial Maximum. To what extent did adaptive modifications develop, and what were some of the specific adaptive strategies involved? The principal motivation for the research is the fact that environmental conditions during the Last Glacial Maximum imposed a complex and previously unexperienced suite of selection pressures on human groups in central Europe. In response, a variety of coping tactics of an as-yet-unknown character are expected to have developed.

In chapter 2 the site of Grubgraben in Lower Austria is introduced as a provocative archaeological case with the potential for having documented the local organizational responses of past cultural systems to the selection pressures imposed by the Last Glacial Maximum. The geography of the site, history of activity, sources of data, and features and assemblages recovered during the excavations are briefly reviewed; the dynamics of climatic change at Grubgraben are outlined as they have been reconstructed from sedimentological data; and the properties of the site which make it an exceptional case study in Late Glacial organizational variability are presented. Grubgraben is argued to control, or hold constant, many sources of variation that could otherwise confound the search for climatically conditioned variability, thus making the site the best archaeological context currently available for investigating local systemic change in response to the Last Glacial Maximum.

Chapter 3 treats the general problem of how to approach the

task of recognizing the response of past systems to climatic change and the onset of ice-age conditions. The utility of middle-range research is discussed at greater length, and the possibility is considered of using generalizations from contemporary hunter-gatherer groups to postulate testable expectations for the archaeological variability that would result from adaptation to glacial conditions. Prior knowledge of hunter-gatherer systems and their archaeological properties can be used to anticipate some kinds of changes in response to climatic change, but the observational data mandated by these arguments are not presently available at Grubgraben. The conclusion is reached that available analogical models of climatically conditioned change in hunter-gatherer systems are unsatisfactory for the present research, and that a pattern recognition analysis of residential interassemblage variability, followed by the correlation of recognized patterns with independently monitored sources of variation, offers the best approach for pursuing the stated research goal.

A discussion of the methodology for elucidating organizational variability is provided in chapter 4. The need is emphasized for analytical approaches that explore different dimensions of interassemblage variability rather than methods that consolidate such variability into taxonomic categories. Some guidelines for pattern recognition work in general are discussed, and an appropriate quantitative method for studying the organizational properties of assemblages is introduced. The method is a multivariate descriptive procedure [scaled principle components analysis of normalized frequency data (Harpending and Rogers 1985)] that has been used successfully in several archaeological and many non-archaeological applications.

Chapter 5 reports the results of a detailed pattern recognition study of interassemblage variability at Grubgraben. The goal of the analysis is to recognize some of the multiple and independently operating processes which structure the record of human occupation at the site. The analysis is conducted in four stages, using general classes of remains, lithic data, faunal data, and a composite lithic/faunal data set, to gain some perspective on how the recognized patterns depend on the specific representation of assemblage composition.

In chapter 6 the dimensions of interassemblage variability elicited by the pattern recognition study are used to chart the diachronic change in organizational properties across the sequence of ice-age settlements at Grubgraben. Several recurring trajectories for the variability in organizational properties are observed, irrespective of the particular representation of the data used in the analysis.

The diachronic patterns in organizational properties are correlated in chapter 7 with an independently reconstructed pattern of climatic change at the site, and the causes of variation in the organizational properties are considered. Climatic deterioration during the Last Glacial Maximum is strongly implicated as the causal agent for some organizational changes, while other trajectories appear to be the results of processes unrelated to climatic change such as excavation sampling bias and intrasite functional variability.

The results of the research are summarized and reviewed in chapter 8, and the implications of the findings for reconstructions of human adaptation in central Europe during the Last Glacial Maximum are examined. The effectiveness of the methodology is evaluated, and the extent to which the goals of the research have been met is considered. Several criticisms of the study are voiced, and suggestions for further research are made.

2.0 GRUBGRABEN: A PROVOCATIVE SITE

In the absence of actualistically controlled observations on the assemblages resulting from the adaptations by hunter-gatherer systems to ice-age conditions, an alternative is to seek out an archaeological situation that provides relevant properties and control conditions against which patterns can be projected and changes recognized and studied. The recently excavated Epigravettian site of Grubgraben, located near Krems in Lower Austria (Montet-White 1988b, 1990a, 1991a,b; Brandtner 1989; Montet-White and Williams 1994), is such an archaeological test case. Grubgraben is characterized by several properties believed to be relevant for recognizing organizational modifications in response to climatic change, and offers a previously unavailable degree of control over many alternative sources of organizational and archaeological variability.

Here the local geography and history of activity at the site are briefly reviewed, the sources of data are noted, and the features and artifact assemblages recovered during the recent excavations are described. This is followed by a review of the environmental conditions and the dynamics of long-term climatic change at Grubgraben as these have been reconstructed from sedimentological evidence. The seasonality of occupation at Grubgraben is considered, and the chapter concludes with a summary of the properties of the archaeological deposits from Grubgraben that make the site a provocative test case for the study of local, organizational responses of past systems to climatic change.

2.1 Site Location and Local Geography

The open-air site of Grubgraben is located in Lower Austria, approximately 50 km northwest of Vienna and 10 km north of the Danube (Figure 2.1). Grubgraben is situated near the intersection of three major physiographic zones: the Bohemian Massif to the north, the Eastern Alps to the south, and the open plains of the Carpathian Basin to the southeast. To the west the Danube river valley forms a corridor between the Eastern Alps and the Bohemian Massif leading directly into the Bavarian Basin and southern Germany (Montet-White 1990b: Figure I-1, 1991b: Figures 13.1 and 13.3). The site lies at an altitude of 270 m above sea level, in a southward-opening, basin-shaped valley located at the uppermost end of a sunken road *(Graben, Hohlweg)* that runs from northeast to southwest between the Heiligenstein (360 m) and Geißberg (336 m; also spelled Gaisberg) mountains (Brandtner 1989: Figure 1; Haesaerts 1990b: Figure III-1). The *Hohlweg* also serves as part of the present-day political boundary between the villages of Kammern to the east and Zöbing to the west (Felgenhauer 1962:9). The Kamp river is 1.6 km southeast of the site and flows southward for about 8 km before turning to the east near Grunddorf and joining the Danube in the Tullner Feld south of Grafenwörth. In addition to the Kamp, several smaller streams such as the Fahnbach, Loisbach, Gscheinzbach, and Mühlkamp are also found within a few kilometers of the site.

For hunter-gatherer groups in central Europe during the last ice age, Grubgraben would have been favorably situated between the Moravian plateau to the north and the Danube river valley to the south. The location of the site in a small basin between the Heiligenstein and Geißberg afforded shelter on three sides from the prevailing winds out of the north and west and provided a broad view of the Kamp and Danube valleys to the south (Montet-White 1990b; Montet-White et al. 1990). Water was easily accessible, both from springs in the ravine and from the Kamp river (Spöttl 1890:79; Kießling 1918:233–234; Haesaerts 1990b). The broad valley floors of the Kamp and Danube rivers provided excellent reindeer hunting grounds (Logan 1990a,b; Whitney 1992; West 1995), and the rivers themselves offered fish and other aquatic resources. Some kinds of raw material for lithic production would have been available in the form of Kamp and Danube river gravels (Pawlikowski 1990b; Montet-White 1990d, 1991b; West and Montet-White 1990); other varieties of raw material were obtained from sources at considerable distances from the site (Pawlikowski 1990b; Montet-White 1991b).

2.2 History of Activity

The history of archaeological activity at Grubgraben has been summarized on several occasions since the discovery of the site in the late nineteenth century. The site is mentioned for the first time by Wurmbrand [1879; but see comments by Brandtner (1989:17)], and is discussed briefly by Spöttl (1889, 1890) and Schacherl (1893). The first historical accounts of the site and detailed descriptions of the recovered artifacts appear in Obermaier (1908) and Kießling (1918). The period after about 1915, but prior to the systematic excavations initiated in 1985, was one of comparatively little activity; the events of this period are described by Kießling (1934), Felgenhauer (1962), Brandtner (1989), and Urbanek (1990). A comprehensive treatment of the history of activity at Grubgraben and the numerous artifact collections attributed to the site appeared in the dissertation by Heinrich (1973, 1974–75) on the Upper Paleolithic in Lower Austria.

Modern archaeological excavations were initiated by Montet-White (University of Kansas) following a visit to the site in 1982. Survey and initial testing of the site took place in the summer of 1985, and were followed by four seasons of fieldwork between 1986 and 1990 under the direction of Montet-White, in collaboration with Friedrich Brandtner in Vienna. The results of the first two seasons of fieldwork (1986–1987) are reported in a monograph edited by Montet-White (1990a) and in several brief reports and articles (Montet-White n.d.a, 1988b, n.d.b, 1991a,b; Brandtner 1989; Montet-White and Williams 1994). At the present time the results of the 1989–1990 excavations are not fully reported, but some preliminary information is given in Montet-White (n.d.b, 1991a,b), Brandtner (1989), and Montet-White and Williams (1994).

2.3 Sources of Data

Most of the data used in this study were obtained from Grubgraben databases assembled by the author and by Dixie West (University of Kansas) over a period of several years from data, field notes, and other materials provided by Montet-White. These databases are maintained at the Museum of Anthropology, University of Kansas, Lawrence, Kansas.

Figure 2.1. Physiographic map of central Europe showing the location of Grubgraben and selected other Gravettian and Epigravettian sites. [From Montet-White (1994: Figure 1). With permission, from the Annual Review of Anthropology, Volume 23, © 1994, by Annual Reviews.]

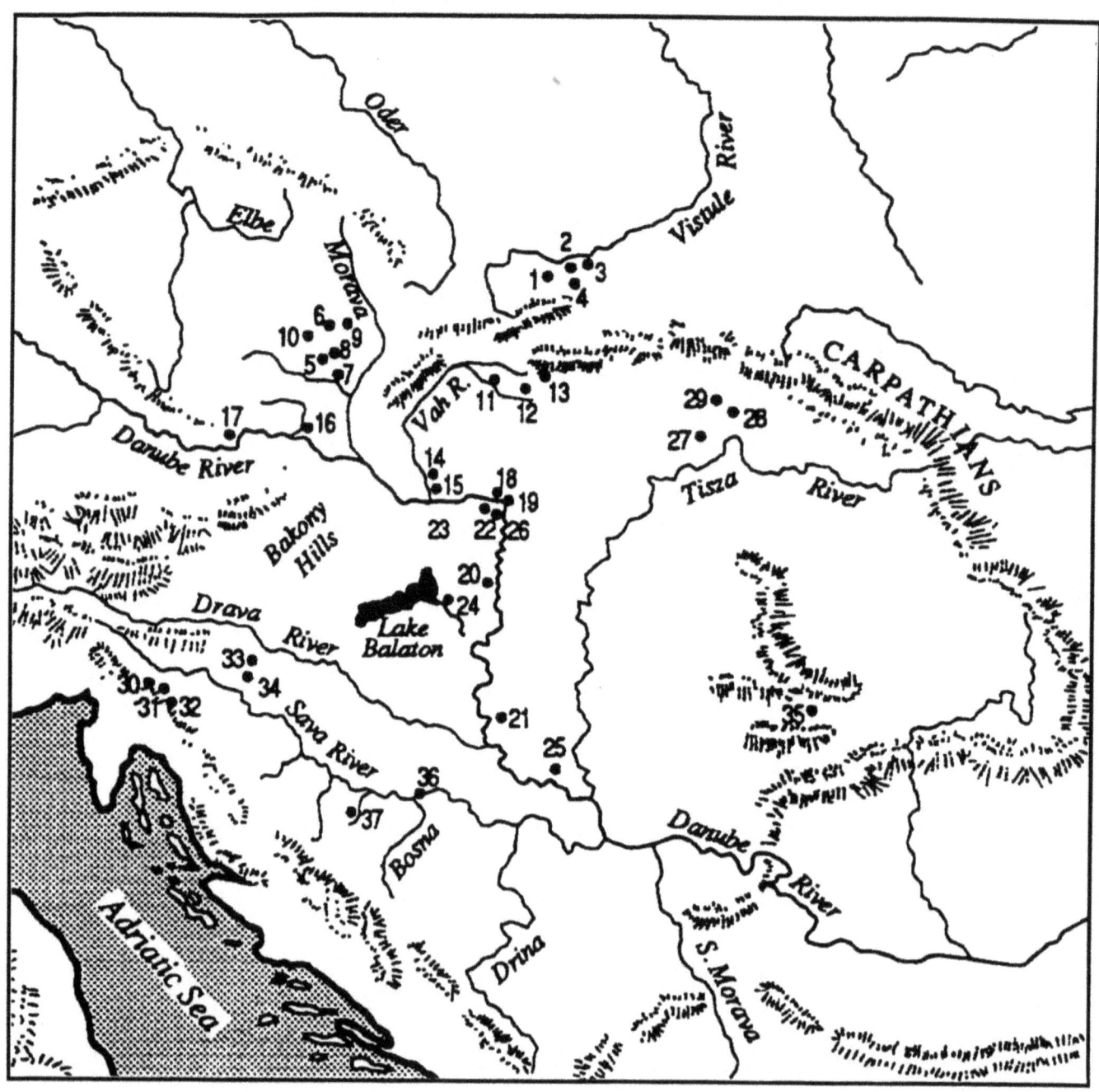

1. Mammutowa; 2. Spadzista; 3. Wójcice; 4. Wolowice; 5. Dolní Vestonice; 6. Kulna; 7. Milovice; 8. Pavlov; 9. Pod Hradem; 10. Stránská skála; 11. Vedrovice; 12. Cejkov; 13. Kasov; 14. Moravany; 15. Nitra-Cermán; 16. Grubgraben; 17. Willendorf; 18. Pilismarót-Diós; 19. Dömös; 20. Dunaföldvár; 21. Madaras; 22. Pilismarót-Pálrét; 23. Pilisszántó; 24. Ságvár; 25. Szeged; 26. Zebegeny; 27. Arka; 28. Bodrogkeresztúr; 29. Hidasnemeti; 30. Luplanska; 31. Ovcja Jama; 32. Zupanov Spodmol; 33. Veternica; 34. Vindija; 35. Temnata; 36. Kadar; 37. Zobiste.

Additional data come from a series of unpublished investigations conducted by students at the University of Kansas into specific aspects of the Grubgraben material: Whitney (1992) examined the faunal assemblage from level AL1; Cook (1993) investigated the dentalia collection from the site; Hill (1993) studied a portion of the quartz assemblage; and Beck (1993) examined the collection of cobbles and hammerstones. These studies have proven valuable in formulating the arguments presented in chapter 5. Data on the faunal assemblages from Grubgraben were generously made available by Logan (1990b) for portions of AL2–AL4 and by West (1995) for the remaining faunal inventory. Through their efforts more than 44,000 specimens of bone from Grubgraben have been individually examined, making the Grubgraben faunal collection the most completely reported faunal data set of its kind in central Europe.

2.4 Archaeological Levels and Features

The excavations at Grubgraben disclosed a sequence of five archaeological levels, designated AL5 (lowest level) to AL1 (uppermost level). Level AL5 was exposed only in two small test pits and appears to be in secondary context (Montet-White 1990c:47; Haesaerts 1990b:29). Very little is known of the spatial extent or artifact content of AL5, and material from this level is not included in any of the analyses reported here. The remaining levels (AL4–AL1) contain extensive lithic and faunal assemblages and numerous features such as hearths, pavements and other stone structures, and pits of varying construction and content. Patterns of artifact distribution indicative of discrete activity areas such as antler and shell work and mandible-smashing were also recognized during the excavations (Montet-White 1990c; Montet-White and Williams 1992, 1994). These facilities (Binford 1983a:145) and *structures évidentes* (Leroi-Gourhan and Brézillon 1966, 1972; Leroi-Gourhan 1976b) are key components of the overall site framework (Binford 1983a:145, 1987a:477) at Grubgraben and provide important clues regarding site function and the nature of the occupations that produced the archaeological deposits. The following descriptions of the archaeological levels and their features are summarized from Montet-White (n.d.b, 1988b, 1990c, 1991a,b), Montet-White and Williams (1994), and Montet-White (personal communication 1994, 1995).

2.4.1 Level AL1

Archaeological level AL1 is exposed over an area of approximately 92 m², and may actually represent two main episodes of occupation (AL1a above, AL1b below) depositionally separated by 1–5 cm of loess. Specific features are associated with each episode of occupation, and it appears that some facilities in the earlier occupation (AL1b), such as the main hearth in unit Lf/1 and the stone concentration in the western half of the exposed area, may have been rebuilt and reused during the later occupation (AL1a). Other features in AL1b, however, appear to have become covered during the later occupation and were not maintained or reused. The individual layers AL1a and AL1b are discontinuous and often difficult to distinguish, and for the present purposes AL1 is treated as a palimpsest deposit resulting from an extended period of occupation. This is not an unreasonable approach because the maintenance and reuse of primary features such as hearths and pavements suggests that the basic functions and spatial organization of the site remained relatively stable between the individual episodes of AL1 occupation.

The main hearth in AL1 is located in the north corner of unit Lf (Lf/1). The hearth is built above ground and consists of a solid, circular arrangement of gneiss slabs rather than stones placed to form a protective ring or enclosure (Montet-White and Williams 1994). The layer of soil underneath the hearth is burned, and burned stones are found scattered about the hearth. Several stages of hearth construction and repair are indicated by the arrangement and appearance of the hearth stones. A long and narrow block of sandstone was set vertically in the center of the hearth and, although its function is uncertain, this block is an integral part of the hearth structure.

A second *structure de combustion* (Leroi-Gourhan 1976b) is located in the western corner of unit Lg (Lg/2). The soil underneath this feature was not reddened by heat, and the identity of the structure as a true hearth is not certain. As with the hearth in unit Lf, however, this structure is also surrounded by a scatter of burned rock.

A large sandstone slab, broken into three pieces but measuring roughly 80 × 65 cm when intact, was found covering a small pile of stones in unit Lf. No cultural material was evident underneath the slab. Interpretation of this feature is difficult; it may have served as part of a storage facility. The feature is located in level AL1b, but despite its size it does not appear to have been reused during the later AL1a occupation.

The most extended feature of AL1 is the stone concentration in trenches L, M, and N, covering an area of about 40 m² (Montet-White and Williams 1994: Figure 3). The slabs of sandstone, arkose, and gneiss are not closely joined, however, and the feature cannot be described as a pavement in the strict sense [i.e., when compared with the explicit, well-defined stone structures generally accepted as pavements and *fonds de cabanes* (Gaussen 1980; Koetje 1987; Sackett 1988; Bosinski 1988; Montet-White and Williams 1994:128)]. Among the larger stones is a suggestion of circular or semicircular arrangements, perhaps 2.5–3 m in diameter, that may represent the outlines of tents or other dwelling structures (Montet-White 1990c, 1991b).

Material in AL1 is very sparse in trenches I and J, consisting of scattered stones, lithics, molluscs, and ochre stains. In unit Ic a small cluster of large trimming flakes was recovered, probably representing a single instance of flint knapping rather than a long-term lithic workshop area. The core and useable blanks resulting from the reduction were not present (Montet-White 1990c:51). Several spatially distinct activity areas have been postulated on the basis of scraper and burin distributions (Montet-White 1990c,d; Montet-White and Williams 1992, 1994).

2.4.2 Level AL2

Archaeological level AL2 is exposed over a contiguous area of 92 m². As with level AL1, two episodes of occupation separated by a thin layer of loess were originally suspected for AL2. It now appears, however, that the thin upper scatter of AL2a is the result of post-depositional downslope transport of material rather than a separate phase of occupation (Montet-White, personal communication 1994).

The dominant feature in AL2 is the large, well-constructed stone pavement in units Ic–If covering an area of 10–12 m^2. The western edge of the pavement was not exposed by the excavation, but because corresponding pavement stones were not visible in the eastern wall of the sunken road it can be assumed that the pavement did not extend more than 1–1.5 m west of trench I. More than 500 stones, primarily sandstone, arkose, and varieties of gneiss, were used in the construction of the pavement (Montet-White 1990c:52).

The AL2 pavement is generally rectangular in shape with rounded corners but exhibits interesting internal structure, and the feature may have been constructed in stages over an extended period of time, with different sections of the pavement serving different purposes. Stones were stacked two and three deep at the northern end of the pavement; in the southern half (units Ie–If) the pavement consists of a single layer of stones which are not as closely joined (Montet-White 1990c:51–56, Figures V-6, V-9, and V-10). A roughly circular area at the south end of the pavement (unit If) was relatively free of stones but contained some burned rocks and burned bone pieces, probably marking the location of an above-ground hearth (Montet-White 1990c: Figure V-7).

A second, more diffuse arrangement of stone slabs, possibly a continuation of the main pavement, is located to the east in trenches J and K. The stones used in its construction are again sandstone and varieties of gneiss. Whereas the main pavement is unusually clean and free of artifacts, the eastern pavement is littered with bones and lithics, suggesting that these two stone features may have served different functions at the campsite (Montet-White 1990c:56, Figure V-7).

A small hearth, located in unit Kf, consists of a circular arrangement of fire-reddened slabs of gneiss. Adjacent to the hearth a large T-shaped piece of antler had been rammed vertically into the ground, perhaps having served to support objects over the hearth (Montet-White n.d.b). A second T-shaped antler piece was found resting horizontally across the hearth. Similar use of antler supports is known from other Paleolithic sites; an especially fine specimen was recovered at the late Magdalenian site of Gönnersdorf in the Rhineland (Bosinski 1981: Figure 34).

An extended and diffuse feature in units Jg/Jf and Kg/Kf is defined by large antler pieces, quartz flakes and flint chips, and large stone slabs. The feature is difficult to interpret in terms of specific activities but is clearly associated with the use or modification of antler. A deliberate bone-smashing area is located in the northern corner of unit Jg, where portions of several reindeer mandibles were found resting on large, flat slabs of gneiss. A number of quartz pieces are closely associated with the feature, and may derive from the use of quartz hammerstones to smash the mandibles (Montet-White 1990c: Figures V-7 and V-8).

2.4.3 Level AL3

The third archaeological layer is exposed over a much smaller area (approximately 48–50 m^2) than either AL1 or AL2, and the excavated areas are not contiguous as they are for the upper levels. By and large the material from AL3 presents an undifferentiated sheet of artifacts and bone fragments, without clear indications of internal structure. The density of artifacts in AL3 is considerably greater than in AL1 or AL2 (Montet-White 1990c: Figure V-11). A layer of rocks is present across most of the level, but these are not joined into pavements or other recognizable arrangements.

The most clearly defined features in AL3 are the earthen pits of varying size and construction (Montet-White n.d.b). A series of wide, shallow depressions is located along trenches K and J. These pits vary from 2–3 m in diameter, are filled with artifacts and bone fragments, and are capped by a layer of stones. The stones, bones, and artifacts associated with the pits are covered with a reddish-brown coloring, possibly ochre, that penetrates into the underlying sediment (Montet-White n.d.b). In addition to these large pits, level AL3 also contains a number of small, basin-shaped depressions, 15–50 cm in diameter, covered with limestone slabs (Montet-White n.d.b). The function of these pits is unknown; they may have been used in contexts of processing or storage, or perhaps as boiling pits (West 1995).

2.4.4 Level AL4

Archaeological level AL4, also exposed over an area of 48–50 m^2, is similar to AL3 in its high densities of artifacts and bones. A number of trash- and earth-filled pits are also present, although the pits in AL4 are smaller and deeper than those of AL3 and may have served different functions (Montet-White 1990c: Figure V-12).

The largest such pit is 20 cm wide and 10 cm deep and is located in the north corner of unit Id (Montet-White 1990c: Figure V-14). The pit was cut into the underlying loess and filled with dark humic material, bone fragments, and lithic chips. Two episodes of fill can be identified in the pit material, perhaps as a consequence of separate occupations. A second pit, deeper and narrower than the first but also filled with bone fragments, lithic debris, and dark humic matter, is located in the western corner of unit Jd (Montet-White 1990c: Figure V-13).

Located between the two pits in units Id and Jd are a series of pit-like structures resembling post-molds. These pits contained dark humic material and were relatively free of artifacts (Montet-White 1990c, n.d.b). As with the structures in AL3, the interpretation of these pits and pit-like features is difficult. To judge from their size, construction, and content, however, the pits in AL4 appear to have served functions different from those in AL3. The two larger pits may have provided storage-, disposal-, or maintenance-related facilities, whereas the smaller pit-like features may be related to the use of dwelling structures at the site.

2.4.5 Variability in Site Framework

It is evident from the above summary of the archaeological

levels and their features that the site framework at Grubgraben is most extensive and varied for archaeological levels AL1 and AL2. This situation is certainly referable in part to the considerably greater horizontal exposure of these levels: approximately 92 m² for levels AL1 and AL2, and only 48–50 m² for levels AL3 and AL4. Despite the differences in horizontal exposure, however, it is significant that each of levels AL1–AL4 at Grubgraben has yielded a sizeable artifact assemblage and is characterized by a substantial investment in features such as hearths, pavements, stone structures, and various kinds of pits.

A possible explanation for the differences in site framework among the levels may be that the individual occupations at Grubgraben were differentially integrated within their respective settlement systems, generating deposits of significantly different content and organization (Binford 1978b:482–497, 1982a, 1983a,b; Jochim 1991; Kelly 1995). In other words, the economic function of the site may have changed as a consequence of simple positional changes of the overall settlement system on the landscape. Thus, some deposits may have accumulated during the use of the site as a residential location, and other assemblages may have been created during periods of site use as a hunting station. The deposits do not exhibit the punctuated character, however, or periodicity in the intensity of site use that would be expected from changes in system positioning (Binford 1983b), although it must be acknowledged that such periodicity could be difficult to recognize with only four excavated levels to examine. Furthermore, the obvious investment in site facilities in all levels, and the evidence for maintenance and reuse of some features [most notably hearths and pavements, but also the staged use of a basin-shaped pit in unit Id of AL4 (Montet-White 1990c: Figure V-14)], also suggest that the overall function of the site remained stable from AL4 to AL1 and that system repositioning and economic rezonation of the site are not sources of interassemblage variability at Grubgraben.

The most probable source of the variability between levels in site framework is intrasite spatial sampling variation, with functionally different areas of a large residential site revealed in each level by the common excavation window. For example, portions of a domestic space may have been exposed in one level and areas of butchering and processing activity in another, yet both are simply specialized areas within a much larger residential site. Without further horizontal exposure of all levels, however, or accurate inferences regarding the function of the existing features and the activities represented by the artifact distributions, this source of interassemblage variability cannot be controlled or even quantified accurately.

2.5 The Artifact Assemblages

The artifact assemblages from Grubgraben recovered during the 1986–1987 excavations have been reported in detail elsewhere (Montet-White 1990d, 1991b; West and Montet-White 1990), and preliminary information on the assemblages recovered during the 1989–1990 excavations is available in Montet-White (n.d.b) and Brandtner (1989). Descriptions of the Grubgraben surface finds and inventories resulting from uncontrolled collection before the modern excavations by Montet-White are available in Obermaier (1908), Kießling (1918, 1934), and Heinrich (1973).

The Grubgraben material inventory is especially notable for its "hybrid" appearance, containing not only formal Gravettian and Epigravettian artifacts, but also several classical Magdalenian and Late Upper Paleolithic elements. Typologically the predominant component is clearly Epigravettian, marked by the presence of small backed points and blades, an abundance of dihedral burins, and by short carinate and shouldered endscrapers (Montet-White 1990d, n.d.a, n.d.b; Montet-White et al. 1990). The assemblages are also distinguished by several typically Late Upper Paleolithic characteristics: numerous perforators and endscrapers, and a rich bone and antler industry including eyed needles, a perforated and decorated antler bâton, and several poorly preserved but easily recognizable bone and antler points, at least two of which have quadrilateral cross-section and longitudinal grooves (Brandtner 1989; Montet-White 1990d, n.d.b). These distinctly Late Upper Paleolithic items in an otherwise Epigravettian context are remarkable; Brandtner has aptly described them as follows:

> ...Funde, die nicht nur jeglicher "Aurignacien-Tradition" widersprechen, sondern selbst für das niederösterreichischen Gravettien ein Novum sind und kein Aufsehen erregen würden, wenn sie etwa aus einem Magdalénien-Verband geborgen worden wären (Brandtner 1989:26).

The presence of these Late Upper Paleolithic elements in the Epigravettian assemblages at Grubgraben is not completely without precedent in central Europe. Dobosi has noted, for example, that "traces of classical magdalenian culture" can be found at Gravettian sites in the Carpathian Basin and even into Moravia (Dobosi et al. 1983:298). It is also significant that Grubgraben is intermediately located with respect to the established distribution of Magdalenian, Late Upper Paleolithic, and Gravettian occupations in central Europe. To the north and west of Grubgraben, for example, the sites of Gudenushöhle [Lower Austria (Obermaier and Breuil 1908; Winkler 1987)], Kulna [Moravia (Valoch 1968)], Pekárna [Moravia (Svoboda 1991)], and Barová [Moravia (Seitl et al. 1986)] have yielded evidence of Late Upper Paleolithic occupations. Late Upper Paleolithic material is also found north of the Carpathians at the cave site of Maszycka in southern Poland (Kozlowski 1989, 1990).

Other sites in Lower Austria, Moravia, and Slovakia, however, have yielded typical Gravettian and Epigravettian assemblages: Willendorf [Lower Austria (Felgenhauer 1956–59; Otte 1981)]; Aggsbach [Lower Austria (Felgenhauer 1951; Otte 1981)]; Kamegg [Lower Austria (Brandtner 1954–55)]; Milovice [Moravia (Oliva 1989)]; Stránská skála IV [Moravia (Svoboda 1990)]; Konevova [Moravia (Valoch 1975)]; Moravany and Nitra-Cermán [western Slovakia (Bárta 1966, 1970, 1980; Kozlowski 1990)]; and Kasov, Cejkov, and Hrceli [eastern Slovakia (Bánesz and Pieta 1961; Bárta 1966; Bánesz 1969; Otte 1981; Bánesz and Kaminská 1984; Kozlowski 1990)]. To the south and east of Grubgraben are found the large Gravettian campsites of the Carpathian Basin: Ságvár (Hillebrand 1934; Gábori and Gábori 1959; M. Gábori 1965; Vörös 1982); Arka (Vértes 1962, 1964/65); Pilismarót-Pálrét (Dobosi 1991b;

Dobosi et al. 1983); Bodrogkeresztúr (Vértes 1966); and many undated and ephemeral sites such as Dömös and Dunaföldvár along the Danube bend near Budapest (M. Gábori 1964, 1970; V. Gábori-Csánk 1970, 1984, 1986; Dobosi 1991b).

The material inventories from Grubgraben also share several provocative characteristics with the Badegoulian from western Europe (Hemingway 1980; Dewez 1987; Lenoir 1988; Montet-White 1994). The Badegoulian, or Initial Magdalenian, refers to a highly localized technological tradition known only from a handful of sites [Hemingway (1980:35) admits only 40 as "most acceptable"] in France, Belgium, and possibly Spain (Hemingway 1980:32–33). Available absolute dates place the Badegoulian in the time period from 18,600 to 16,800 BP (Hemingway 1980:43), making it approximately contemporaneous with Epigravettian industries (such as Grubgraben) in central and eastern Europe (Rigaud and Simek 1990:75–76; Montet-White 1994). In contrast to the preference for cave and rock shelter sites in the Solutrean and Magdalenian periods, known Badegoulian sites are almost exclusively open-air stations at which reindeer was the focal fauna. Climatically, the Badegoulian appears to coincide generally with the Lascaux oscillation and a brief shift toward warmer and moister conditions (Schmider 1990:43; White 1987:269–270). Evidence for a similar brief amelioration of the climate, possibly correlated with the Lascaux oscillation, is found at Grubgraben (corresponding to level AL4; Haesaerts 1990b:34) and at Ságvár, in the Hungarian Plain near Lake Balaton (V. Gábori-Csánk 1970).

Technologically the Badegoulian is a crude, flake-based industry, distinguished primarily by its high proportions of raclettes and transverse burins on notch. The quantity of raclettes is typically 10–20% of the total tool inventory and reaches 30–60% in many assemblages (Hemingway 1980:118, Table 4.6). Within the Badegoulian period proper the proportion of raclettes increases with time as transverse burins decline in frequency (Hemingway 1980:92, Figure 4.2). The terminal Badegoulian assemblages exhibit a decrease in raclettes and a corresponding increase in elements such as backed bladelets.

Splintered pieces are also well represented in Badegoulian assemblages, bifacial retouch is generally absent, and microliths and backed bladelets are uncommon. The available bone industry is small but varied, and contains Magdalenian elements such as perforated batôns, abundant sagaies, perforated teeth, and specimens of bone and antler which have been grooved for the extraction of splinters [although no finished needles have been recovered from Badegoulian contexts (Hemingway 1980)]. The presence of thick endscrapers, blades with flat, scalar retouch, and other Aurignacian-like characteristics are often mentioned and have been cited in support of an evolutionary relationship between the Badegoulian and the Late Aurignacian (Cheynier 1939:354; Rigaud 1976; cf. Hemingway 1980:113, 228). Although few raclettes (site total $n=5$; 0.67%) and transverse burins (site total $n=5$; 0.67%) are found at Grubgraben, similarities to the Badegoulian are nevertheless apparent in the representation of splintered pieces (site total $n=23$; 3.1%), the presence of short, thick endscrapers, the relatively small number of backed pieces for the quantity of tools recovered (Montet-White 1988b:217), and the generally crude and blocky appearance of the entire assemblage (Montet-White 1994). The presence at Grubgraben of blades with scalar, Aurignacian-type retouch was also noted by several of the earliest investigators at the site (Obermaier 1908; Kießling 1918, 1934; Heinrich 1973, 1974–75).

2.6 Absolute Dating

Eight radiocarbon dates are currently available for the archaeological deposits at Grubgraben. These dates are listed in Table 2.1 and displayed graphically by archaeological level in Figure 2.2. Mean dates were computed for AL4–AL2 using the procedure of Long and Rippeteau (1974) and are shown in Figure 2.3. The radiocarbon dates indicate that the sequence of Epigravettian occupations at Grubgraben documents slightly more than two thousand years of repeated site utilization during the Last Glacial Maximum in central Europe.

Table 2.1. C14 Dates from Grubgraben.

Level	Date (yr BP)	Laboratory	Reference
AL1b	16,800 ± 280	Lv-1825	Montet-White, personal communication 1994
AL2	18,600 ± 220	Lv-1822	Montet-White, personal communication 1994
AL2	18,070 ± 270	Lv-1823	Montet-White, personal communication 1994
AL2	17,350 ± 270	Lv-1821	Montet-White, personal communication 1994
AL3	18,030 ± 270	Lv-1810	Montet-White, personal communication 1994
AL3/4	18,170 ± 300	Lv-1660	Haesaerts (1990b:27)[a]
AL4	18,960 ± 290	AA-1746	Haesaerts (1990b:27)[b,c]
AL4	18,400 ± 330	Lv-1680	Haesaerts (1990b:27)[d]

All dates were obtained on bone collagen.

a. Several bone fragments from AL3 and AL4, collected in 1985 from Unit P45 on the western wall of the *Hohlweg*.
b. Accelerator date on sample N106-85, a bone fragment collected in 1985 from Unit P45 on the western wall of the *Hohlweg*.
c. This date is reported in Montet-White (1988b:217) as: Level AL3, 18950 ± 250, AA-1746, bone. Stratigraphic evidence suggests that the date may be too recent by 1000–2000 years (Montet-White 1988b:217).
d. Several bone fragments from AL4, collected in 1987 during the excavation.

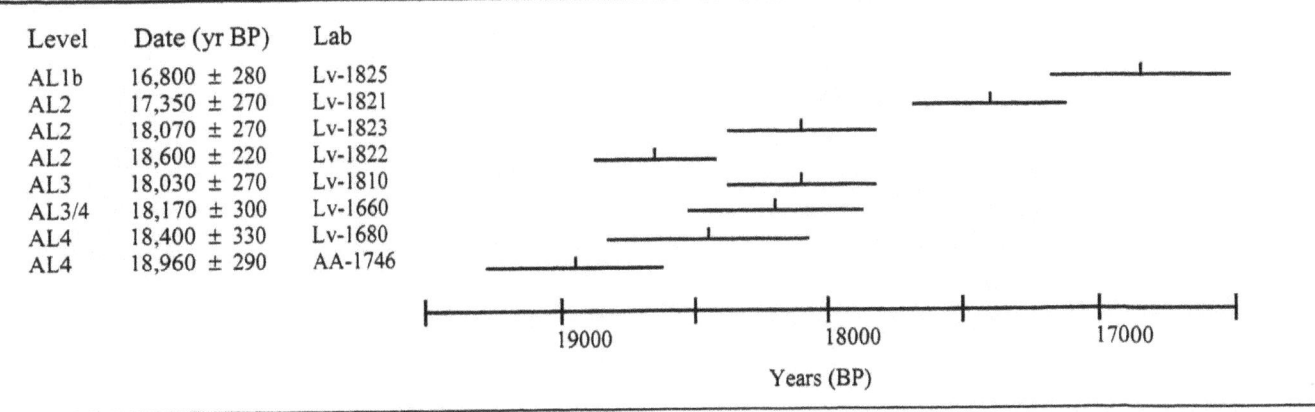

Figure 2.2. C14 dates from Table 2.1 sorted by level. The mean of the C14 date is indicated by the vertical tick, and the horizontal bars extend one standard deviation to either side of the mean.

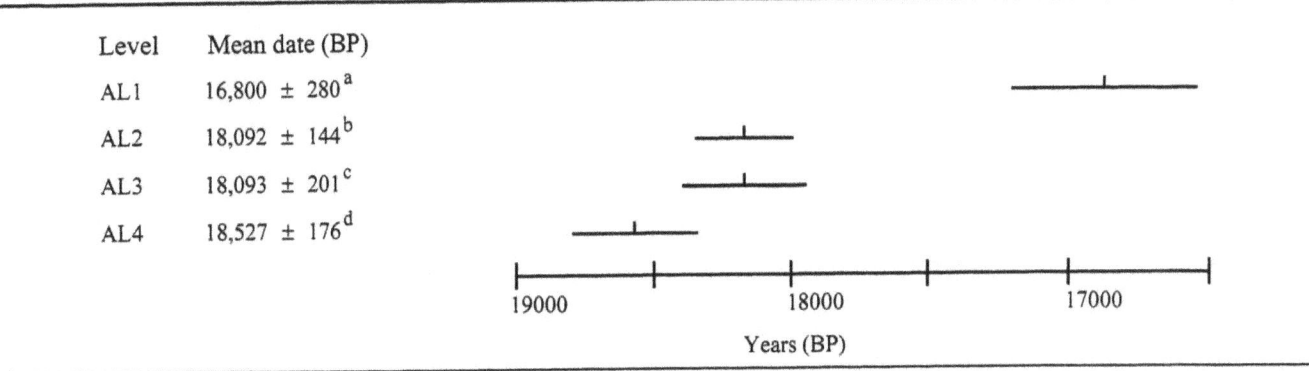

Figure 2.3. Mean C14 dates for Grubgraben AL1–AL4. Mean dates are computed from the dates in Table 2.1 by the procedure described in Long and Rippeteau (1974).

a. Single date only for AL1 (Lv-1825).
b. Mean of $n=3$ dates.
c. Mean of $n=2$ dates, including Lv-1660 (18,170 ± 300 BP) from AL3/4.
d. Mean of $n=3$ dates, including Lv-1660 (18,170 ± 300 BP) from AL3/4.

The large variation between the three dates from AL2 is unusual (Table 2.1). Although AL2 has much less of a palimpsest nature than AL3 or AL4, the dates from AL2 range over more than a millennium, with no overlap of their one-sigma error bars (Figure 2.2). It is possible that the dates are accurate, however, and that the stratigraphically closely spaced older levels (AL2–AL4) have become somewhat intermixed [some evidence for solifluction in level AL2 is suspected (Montet-White, personal communication 1994)]. The mean date for AL2, however, places the time of the AL2 occupation near that for AL3 as would be expected on stratigraphical grounds (Figure 2.5). Approximately 1300 years (between mean dates) elapse between the occupations of AL2 and AL1.

2.7 Regional Representation

Although the concern here is with recognizing the adaptive responses to long-term climatic change that developed locally, i.e., that were specific to the systems that existed at Grubgraben, it is nevertheless the case that the site did not exist in isolation but was integrated into a regional hunter-gatherer settlement-subsistence system. Consequently, activities at the site can be expected to have been conditioned not only by local factors but also by regional constructs such as lithic raw material procurement networks and faunal exploitation ranges. It is therefore important to establish that the situation at Grubgraben was representative of the broader regional circumstances in central Europe during the Last Glacial Maximum.

One means of judging the regional representativeness of Grubgraben might be to compare its lithic or faunal assemblages with the inventories from other Late Upper Paleolithic sites in central Europe. This approach would not be completely satisfactory, however, because the similarity of site inventories is as likely to reflect shared site characteristics (e.g., activities performed, duration of occupation) as to reveal genuine regional affinities (Sonneville-Bordes 1960, 1963, 1966; Binford 1965, 1973; Binford and Binford 1966; Dolukhanov et al. 1980; Kozlowski 1980, 1986, 1991a; Hahn 1981a,b; Otte 1981; Weniger 1981, 1982, 1987a,b, 1989). Because the interest here is with long-term climatic change, it is more instructive to compare the *chronology* of events at Grubgraben with the chronology of occupations at other central European sites dating to the Last Glacial Maximum.

In Figure 2.4 80 radiocarbon dates from 40 sites in central Europe, comprising 59 separate archaeological deposits, are graphically displayed and grouped according to geographical area. Seven regions are represented: Germany (comprising sites in Thüringen, Rhineland, and the Schwäbische Alb), Slovenia and Croatia in former northern Yugoslavia, Moravia, Lower Austria, Poland, Slovakia, and Hungary. The dates used to construct the diagram are given in Table 2.2. Only radiocarbon dates between 25,000 BP and 13,000 BP have been used; these extrema were chosen not only to bracket the duration of the Last Glacial Maximum [from 22,000 BP to 14,000 BP (Crowley and North 1991)], but also to document the slow onset and swift termination of the event. A reference line at 18,000 BP marks the midpoint of the Last Glacial Maximum. Similar usage of radiocarbon dates is found in Weniger (1989, 1990), Simán (1990), and Montet-White (1994).

Some appreciation for the general continuity of settlement in different parts of central Europe is gained by examining the chronology of dated occupations in various regions. A clear change in the frequency and "tempo" of dated occupations in Germany is evident between 22,000 and 17,000 BP. Two problematic dates are those from Aschenstein, in the Rhineland (KN-2712, 18,820 ± 180 BP), and Hohler Fels in the Schwäbische Alb (Layer IIb, H-5120-4569, 17,100 ± 150 BP) (Weniger 1990:171–173). The material from Aschenstein is not well documented and difficult to interpret because the small lithic assemblage lacks unequivocally Gravettian diagnostic forms (Barner 1959, 1962; Thieme 1991). The date from Hohler Fels IIb may be too old, and a second date of 15,760 ± 140 BP (H-5313-4898) comes from the same level (Weniger 1982:20, 1990: Table 9.1). If the dates from Aschenstein and Hohler Fels IIb are omitted from the sequence, then the suggestion of a hiatus in the human occupation of Germany during the Last Glacial Maximum is markedly enhanced (Hahn 1976, 1983; Weniger 1989, 1990).

Most of the radiocarbon dates from Germany for the period surrounding the Last Glacial Maximum come from the southern sites of the Schwäbische Alb, making it difficult to judge how the areas of Rhineland and Thüringen in central Germany differ from southern Germany in their settlement histories. It is interesting to note, however, that the earliest dated occupation in Thüringen is not until 13,700 BP (Bärenkeller, 13,700 ± 380 BP, Bln-220).

Apart from Germany, most areas of central Europe appear to have maintained a more-or-less continuous human presence throughout the Last Glacial Maximum. This is clearly shown

Table 2.2. Radiocarbon Dates between 25,000 BP and 13,000 BP from Archaeological Sites in Central Europe.

Region/Site	Level	Date	Sigma	Laboratory	Reference
Germany					
Aschenstein		18820	180	Kn-2712	Weniger 1990:174–175
Bockstein-Törle	?	24000	?	?	Wetzel 1958:97; Hahn 1977:169
Bockstein-Törle	VI	20400	220	H-4058-3355	Hahn 1977:168
Bockstein-Törle	VI	23440	290	H-4058-3526	Weniger 1990:174–175
Brillenhöhle	VII	>25000		B-492	Riek 1973:156–158
Bärenkeller		13700	380	Bln-220	Feustel et al. 1971:128
Geißenklösterle	Ia	23625	290	H-5117-4568	Hahn 1988b:44
Geißenklösterle	sediment	13110	120	H-7384-7376	Hahn 1988b:44
Geißenklösterle	sediment	14700	120	H-7385-7377	Hahn 1988b:44
Gnirshöhle	II	13050	300	H-6272-5831	Weniger 1982:20
Hohlenstein-Kleine Scheuer	III	13252	98	H-4183-3416	Hahn/Koenigswald 1977:57
Hohlenstein-Stadel	III	13110	160	H-3799-3045	Hahn/Koenigswald 1977:57
Hohlenstein-Stadel	III	13550	130	H-3779-3044	Hahn/Koenigswald 1977:57
Hohler Fels Schelklingen	IIa	15760	140	H-5313-4898	Weniger 1982:20
Hohler Fels Schelklingen	IIa	17100	150	H-5120-4569	Weniger 1982:20
Hohler Fels Schelklingen	IIb	21160	500	H-5314-4899	Weniger 1990:174–175
Hohler Fels Schelklingen	IIb	23000	170	Pta-2746	Weniger 1990:174–175
Hohler Fels Schelklingen	Ib	13085	95	H-5119-4601	Weniger 1982:20
Kniegrotte		13585	165	Bln-1564	Weniger 1990:174–175
Königsaue		13250	280	H-106/89	Mania/Toepfer 1973
Munzingen (Padtberg)		15870	135	H-4156-3373	Albrecht 1979:77, 1981:22
Petersfels (Albrecht)	1.AH4	13030	100	H-7143-7301	Jaguttis-Emden 1983
Petersfels (Albrecht)	1.AH4	13110	90	H-7216-7363	Jaguttis-Emden 1983
Schussenquelle		14470	385	Gro-468	Lang 1962:143–145
Schussenquelle		15900	360	H-860-970	Lang 1962:143–145
Spitzbubenhöhle	2	13840	120	H-4314-3715	Hahn 1984:51
Spitzbubenhöhle	2	15230	100	H-4149-3348	Hahn 1984:51
Teufelsbrücke		13025	85	Bln-1573	Weniger 1990:174–175

Slovenia/Croatia					
Ovcja Jama	lower (4)	19540	500	KN-48	Bailey/Gamble 1990:152
Sandalja	II.c	21740	450	Z-193	Bailey/Gamble 1990:152
Sandalja	II.e	23540	180	GrN-5013	Bailey/Gamble 1990:152
Sandalja	II.f	22660	460	Z-536	Bailey/Gamble 1990:152
Veternica	c	13650	75	GrN-4989	Bailey/Gamble 1990:152
Zakajena	3	17590	510	?	Bailey/Gamble 1990:152
Zupanov	AB	16780	150	GrN-5288	Bailey/Gamble 1990:152
Zupanov	AB/D	13500	175	GrN-5100	Vogel/Waterbolk 1972:65
Moravia					
Dolní Vestonice I		22250	570	Ly-1303	Svoboda 1990:198
Dolní Vestonice II		22368	749	CU-715	Svoboda 1990:198
Konevova		14450	90	GrN-9350	Svoboda 1990:200
Milovice	1 (Basis)	22080	530	ISGS-1901	Oliva 1989:887
Milovice	1 (Basis)	22100	1100	GrN-14825	Oliva 1989:887
Milovice	3	22900	490	ISGS-1690	Oliva 1989:888
Stránská skála	IV	17740	90	GrN-14351	Svoboda 1990:198
Stránská skála	IV	18220	120	GrN-13945	Svoboda 1990:198
Lower Austria					
Aggsbach	B.oben	22450	?	Gr-?	Otte 1981:302
Grubgraben 1986/87	AL1b	16800	280	Lv-1825	Montet-White n.d.
Grubgraben 1986/87	AL2	17350	270	Lv-1821	Montet-White n.d.
Grubgraben 1986/87	AL2	18070	270	Lv-1823	Montet-White n.d.
Grubgraben 1986/87	AL2	18600	220	Lv-1822	Montet-White n.d.
Grubgraben 1986/87	AL3	18030	270	Lv-1810	Montet-White n.d.
Grubgraben 1986/87	AL3	18950	250	AA-1746	Montet-White 1988b:217
Grubgraben 1986/87	AL3/4	18170	300	Lv-1660	Haesaerts 1990b:27
Grubgraben 1986/87	AL4	18400	330	Lv-1680	Haesaerts 1990b:27
Grubgraben 1986/87	AL4	18960	290	AA-1746	Haesaerts 1990b:27
Willendorf	II.5	23830	190	GrN-11194	Otte 1991:47
Poland					
Maszycka	1,2	14600	240	Ly-2453	Weniger 1989:329
Maszycka	3	15490	310	Ly-2454	Weniger 1989:329
Spadzista	B.?	23040	170	GrN-6636	Kozlowski 1986:148
Spadzista	C.II/6a	17400	310	Ly-2541	Kozlowski/Sobczyk 1987:12–14
Spadzista	C1.III/6b	20200	350	OxA-635	Kozlowski/Sobczyk 1987:12–14
Spadzista	C1.III/6b	21000	900	Ly-2542	Kozlowski/Sobczyk 1987:12–14
Spadzista	C1.III/6b	24380	180	GrN-11006	Kozlowski/Sobczyk 1987:12–14
Spadzista	C2.lower	21000	300	Ly-2544	Kozlowski 1986:148
Spadzista	C2.upper	17480	310	Ly-2545	Kozlowski 1986:148
Zawalona		15380	340	?	Kozlowski 1990:208
Slovakia					
Cejkov		19600	340	KN-?	Kozlowski 1990:221
Cejkov		19755	240	Bln-?	Kozlowski 1990:221
Nitra-Cermán		22860	400	GrN-2449	Svoboda 1990:201
Nitra-Cermán		24220	640	GrN-2456	Svoboda 1990:201
Trencianské-Bohuslavice		23700	500	Gd-2490	Svoboda 1990:201
Hungary					
Arka	oben	13230	85	GrN-4218	Vértes 1964/65:105
Arka	unten	17050	350	GrN-4038	Vértes 1964/65:105
Arka	unten	18700	190	A-518	Gábori-Csánk 1970:4
Esztergom-Gyurgyalag		16160	200	Deb-1160	Dobosi et al. 1991:271
Madaras		18080	405	Hv-1619	Gábori-Csánk 1970:4
Pilismarót-Pálrét	K1	16750	400	Hv-1615	Dobosi et al. 1983:310
Ságvár	lower	18600	150	Gro-1783	Vörös 1982:43
Ságvár	lower	18900	100	GrN-1783	Vörös 1982:43
Ságvár	upper	17400	100	Gro-1959	Vörös 1982:43
Ságvár	upper	17760	150	GrN-1959	Vörös 1982:43

Figure 2.4. Radiocarbon chronology of archaeological sites in central Europe dating between 25,000 BP and 13,000 BP. C14 dates are from Table 2.2.

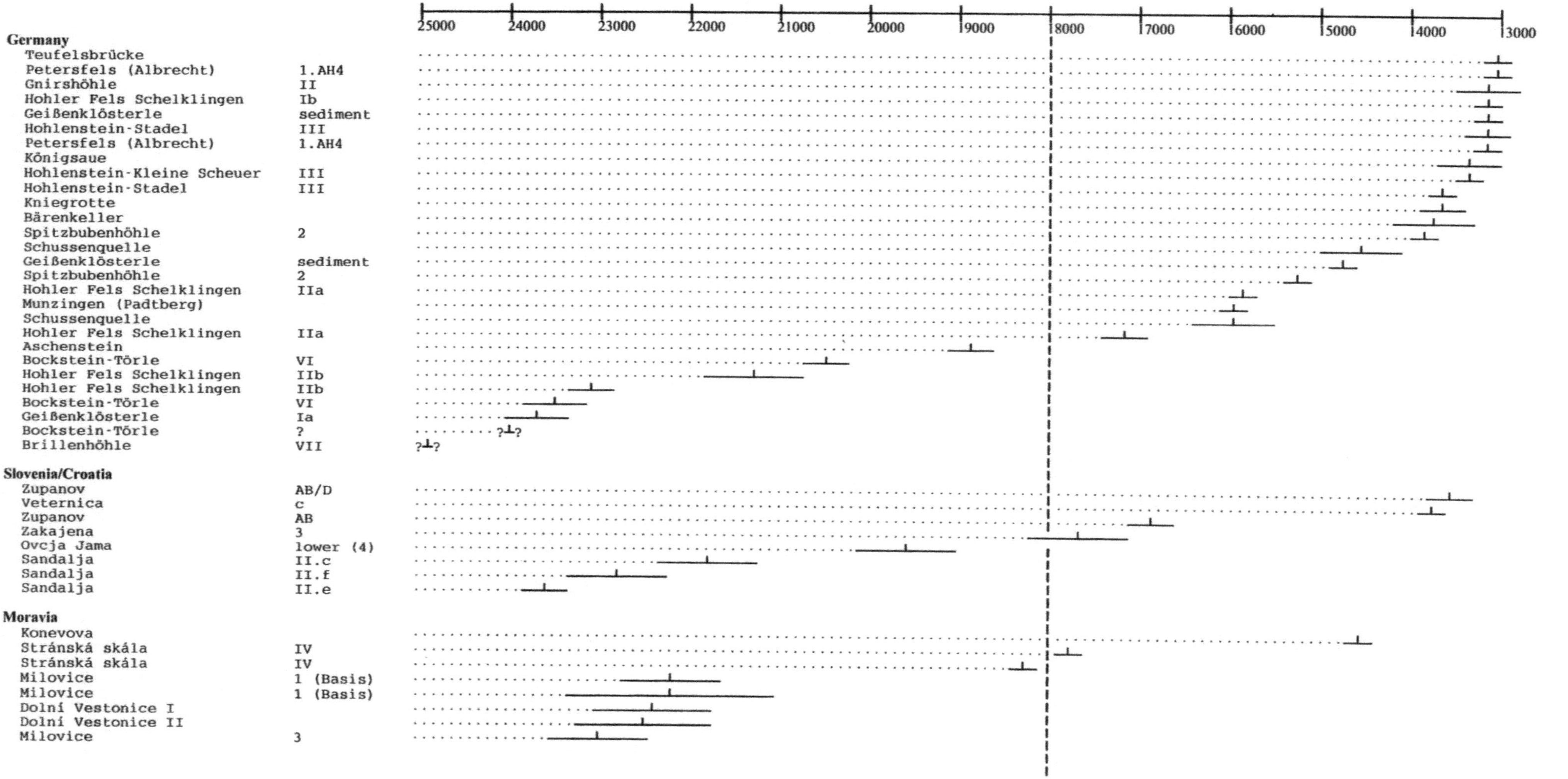
25000
24000
23000
22000
21000
20000
19000
18000
17000
16000
15000
14000
13000
Germany
Teufelsbrücke
Petersfels (Albrecht) 1.AH4
Gnirshöhle II
Hohler Fels Schelklingen Ib
Geißenklösterle sediment
Hohlenstein-Stadel III
Petersfels (Albrecht) 1.AH4
Königsaue
Hohlenstein-Kleine Scheuer III
Hohlenstein-Stadel III
Kniegrotte
Bärenkeller
Spitzbubenhöhle 2
Schussenquelle
Geißenklösterle sediment
Spitzbubenhöhle 2
Hohler Fels Schelklingen IIa
Munzingen (Padtberg)
Schussenquelle
Hohler Fels Schelklingen IIa
Aschenstein
Bockstein-Törle VI
Hohler Fels Schelklingen IIb
Hohler Fels Schelklingen IIb
Bockstein-Törle VI
Geißenklösterle Ia
Bockstein-Törle ?
Brillenhöhle VII
Slovenia/Croatia
Zupanov AB/D
Veternica c
Zupanov AB
Zakajena 3
Ovcja Jama lower (4)
Sandalja II.c
Sandalja II.f
Sandalja II.e
Moravia
Konevova
Stránská skála IV
Stránská skála IV
Milovice 1 (Basis)
Milovice 1 (Basis)
Dolní Vestonice I
Dolní Vestonice II
Milovice 3

(continued page 17)

Figure 2.4. *(continued)*

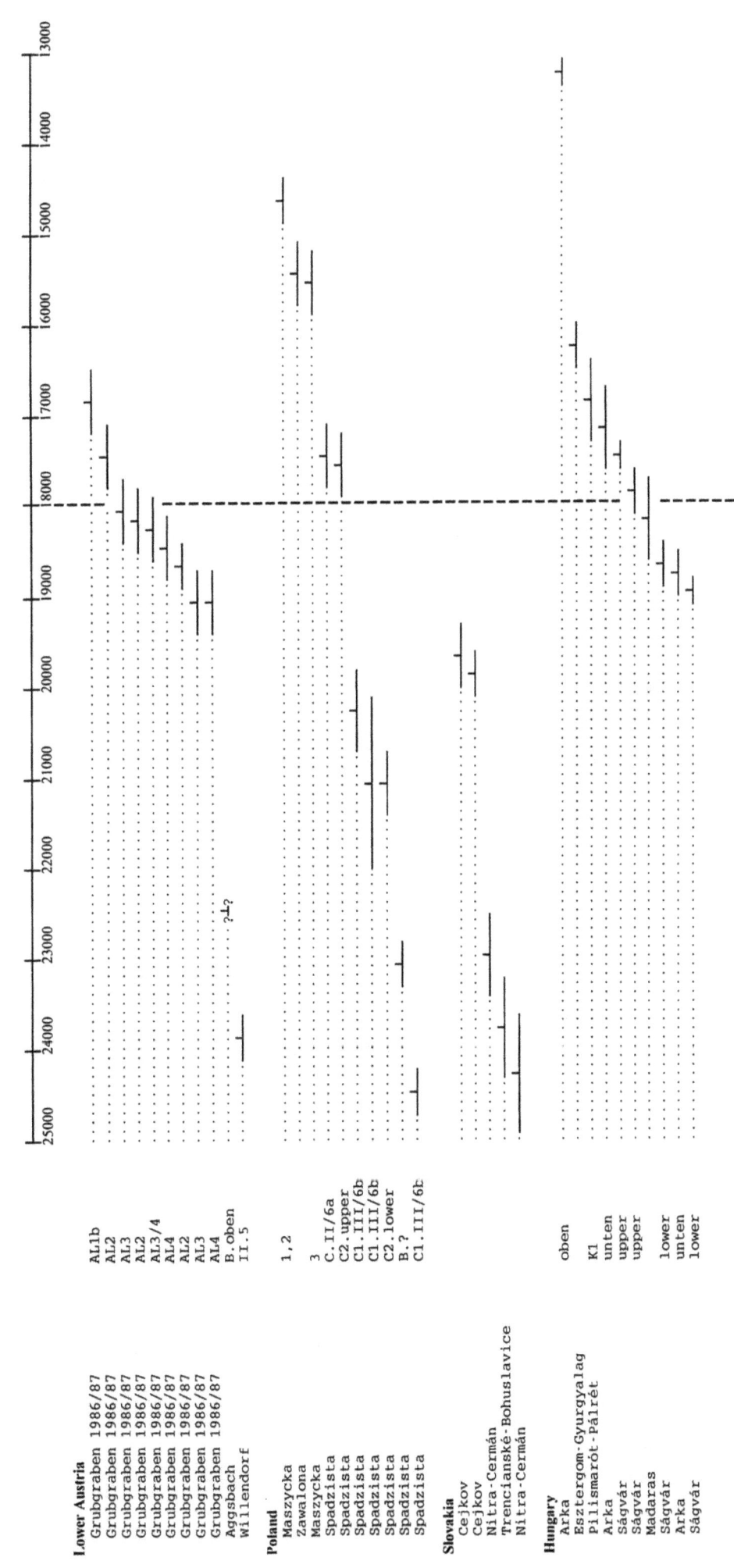

for Hungary by the sites Ságvár, Arka, Madaras, Pilismarót, and Esztergom-Gyurgyalag, and for Lower Austria by the Grubgraben sequence. In Moravia the site of Stránská skála IV has yielded deposits dating to the Last Glacial Maximum, as have Ovcja Jama, Zupanov, and Zakajena in Slovenia. Although the sequences from Moravia and Slovenia contain lengthy gaps, this is almost certainly due to the lack of archaeological deposits that have been dated by radiocarbon methods than to a genuine lack of occupations; many archaeological deposits south of the Carpathians remain undated or have been dated only stratigraphically (Kozlowski 1990; Valoch 1980, 1989).

The evidence for continuous occupation in Poland is equivocal, at least in terms of the radiocarbon dates. The upper layers at Spadzista C are quite close to 18,000 BP, but these deposits may simply represent short-term lithic extraction sites rather than residential locations (Kozlowski 1990). Evidence for the re-establishment of a continuous human presence in southern Poland is not seen until 14,500–15,500 BP at the cave site of Maszycka (Kozlowski 1983, 1989, 1990).

There are no Bohemian sites shown in Figure 2.4. Sites in Bohemia dating to the Second Pleniglacial and Late Glacial are rare, and there are no firmly dated occupations. The site of Praha-Jeneralka probably predates the Stillfried B interstadial at ca. 29–28,000 BP (Kozlowski 1990). There are no C14 dates for either Lubna or Revnice, although both are dated stratigraphically to before 20,000 BP and are also typologically similar to much older sites (Kozlowski 1990:218, Figure 11.4; Otte 1981).

Similarly, there are few occupations in Slovakia dating to the time of the Last Glacial Maximum, and most of these are found in the eastern part of the region (e.g., Cejkov, Kasov, Hrceli). Sites in western Slovakia are considerably older, and "there are virtually no traces of human settlement in western Slovakia between 18.000 BP and the close of the Pleistocene" (Kozlowski 1990:221; Bárta 1966, 1970, 1982).

The comparison in Figure 2.4 illustrates three important facts. First, in terms of chronology and the timing of regional settlements, Grubgraben is one of many sites in central Europe occupied during the Last Glacial Maximum. Although Grubgraben is presently the only well reported site in Lower Austria dating to this period [compare with other Lower Austrian sites discussed in Otte (1981) and Heinrich (1973, 1974–75)], it clearly appears representative of the broader regional situation.

Figure 2.4 also provides compelling evidence of settlement changes during the Last Glacial Maximum in central Europe, although the magnitude of these changes differs from region to region. It appears that inasmuch as there ever was a hiatus in the occupation of central Europe during the last ice age, it was probably highly localized both geographically and temporally and might more accurately be described as comprising only "interruptions in human settlement" (Gamble 1983:208). Some areas of central Europe may well have been devoid of human groups for periods of time during the Last Glacial Maximum—Thüringen, Bohemia, western Slovakia, Poland, and perhaps southern Germany all appear to be good candidates in this regard—but a human presence evidently persisted in most of central Europe during this time despite the changes in climate and environment brought about by the encroaching ice sheets

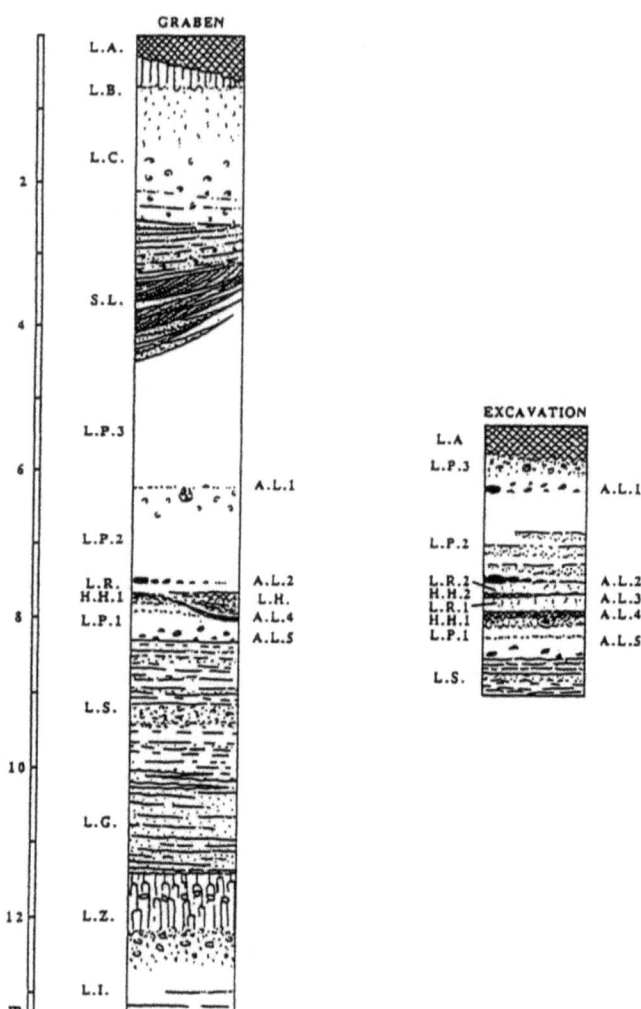

Figure 2.5. Stratigraphy of the loess sequence at Grubgraben [from Haesaerts (1990a: Figure III-9)].

(Kozlowski 1990:223; Svoboda 1990:202; Weniger 1989:329, 1990:173; Simán 1990; Dobosi 1991a; Montet-White 1994).

Of the greatest significance for the present research, however, is the remarkable chronological positioning of the archaeological deposits at Grubgraben. Of the many sites displayed in Figure 2.4, Grubgraben is unique in possessing a sequence of dated occupations centered near the midpoint of the Last Glacial Maximum at 18,000 BP. The deposits at Grubgraben therefore document an extended period of repeated site utilization in central Europe during much of the Last Glacial Maximum, and provide an unparalleled opportunity to investigate the local adaptive strategies of hunter-gatherer groups during the height of the last ice age.

2.8 Paleoclimatic Reconstruction

An extremely important consideration for the present research is the reconstruction of the local paleoclimatic conditions that obtained during the four episodes of occupation at Grubgraben. Because of the poor preservation of pollen and the lack of adequate mollusc and micro-mammal assemblages, paleoclimatic reconstruction must be based almost entirely on sedimentological evidence. Physical characteristics of the loess deposits such as their homogeneity, grain size composition, and mineral content have been used to reconstruct general trends in the Pleistocene climate at Grubgraben (Haesaerts 1985a, 1990b; Pawlikowski 1990a).

The stratigraphy of the loess sequence at Grubgraben (Figure 2.5) has been described in detail by Haesaerts (1985a, 1990b), with supporting sedimentological and mineralogical analyses by Pawlikowski (1990a). The sequence of loess deposits at Grubgraben provides a nearly complete sedimentological record for the Late Pleistocene in the middle Danube basin (Montet-White et al. 1990:159). Most significantly, the lower layers in the loess sequence at Grubgraben have been correlated with the uppermost layers in the well-known loess sequence from Willendorf, thereby filling a long-standing lacuna in the Pleistocene depositional record for Lower Austria and Moravia (Haesaerts 1985a,b, 1990b: Figure III-10; Montet-White et al. 1990).

The stratigraphic and archaeological sequences at Grubgraben are shown in Figure 2.5 [from Haesaerts (1990b: Figure III-9)], and the following outline of stratigraphic relationships and paleoenvironmental conditions at the site is summarized from information in Haesaerts (1985a, 1990b), Pawlikowski (1990a), and Montet-White et al. (1990).

Just prior to the first exposed occupation at Grubgraben (archaeological level AL5) is a homogeneous, fine, laminated loess (unit LS) indicative of dry and cold conditions and characterized by xerophilic molluscs. Events of the AL5 occupation occur at the beginning of unit LP1, a sandy and homogeneous loess deposited under dry conditions.

Events of AL4 took place after the deposition of unit LP1, just prior to and during the formation of a fairly continuous dark brown humic horizon (HH1) of 2–4 cm thickness. Because of its structure and continuity, HH1 is probably related to a short climatic warming trend, possibly correlated with the Lascaux oscillation and the similar development of weak humic horizons at Ságvár in Hungary (Haesaerts 1990b:34; Gábori-Csánk 1970; Montet-White 1994:491). The presence of open woodland conditions dominated by *Pinus cembra* is suggested by the meager pollen record (Haesaerts 1990b:30).

Aeolian activity resumed after AL4, and a thin loess layer (unit LR1), partly reworked by rill wash, covered humic horizon HH1. Events of the third occupation at Grubgraben (level AL3) took place during the development of a second, more discontinuous humic horizon (HH2) of up to 4 cm thickness.

A return of aeolian activity deposited a thin loess layer (unit LR2), also reworked by rill wash, covering humic horizon HH2. Subsequently, events of the fourth occupation (level AL2) took place at the beginning of a thick, homogeneous sandy loess layer (unit LP2). Such a loess is ordinarily indicative of cold and very dry conditions; the upper part of this loess contains a predominance of hydrophilic molluscs, however, suggesting locally more wet and humid conditions in the immediate area of the ravine (Haesaerts 1990b:30).

The final occupation (level AL1) is situated at the interface of two homogeneous, dusty, loess series (units LP3 and LP2) indicative of very cold and dry conditions. The AL1 occupation was later sealed by a one-meter thick loess deposit (unit LP3).

Unit LP3 was subsequently cut by a series of erosional channels that became filled with sand and loess (unit SL). The uppermost sediments of unit SL contain hydrophilic molluscs and are clearly indicative of a warmer and more humid period during which alluvial activity was initiated. The absence of a corresponding well-defined cultural layer indicating an occupation subsequent to AL1 may be a consequence of the extensive terracing and reworking of the upper sediments by vineyard workers (Haesaerts 1990b:18; West 1995).

The last unit of the sequence is a two-meter layer of culturally sterile loess (unit LC), dominated by xerophilic molluscs and indicating very cold and dry conditions. The absence of cultural material in this uppermost loess unit may be an indication that climatic conditions were for a time too severe to support human presence at Grubgraben (Montet-White et al. 1990:160–161).

In summary, there are essentially two different climatic regimes represented by the loess sequence at Grubgraben (Haesaerts 1990b:32; Pawlikowski 1990a:41). The loess just below AL5 (unit LS) and the uppermost loess of the sequence (unit LC) are indicative of very cold and dry conditions. These units are culturally sterile, and human settlement at Grubgraben may not have been possible during these periods.

The intermediate loess layers, containing occupations AL5–AL1, were deposited during relatively warmer and locally more humid conditions. The occupations themselves appear to have taken place during brief pauses in the loess accumulation (Haesaerts 1990b:32).

Within the sequence of occupations from AL4 to AL1 the climatic conditions at Grubgraben, although relatively and locally milder, exhibit a trend toward increasingly cold and dry conditions. Level AL4 is distinguished by conditions sufficiently mild to enable soil formation and the development of a sparse vegetative cover, level AL3 is characterized by a poorly developed and discontinuous humic horizon, and the properties of the sediments from levels AL2 and AL1 continue the trend toward increasing aridity and colder conditions.

Figure 2.6. Total Quartz and Angular Quartz Distributions (Coarse Fraction).

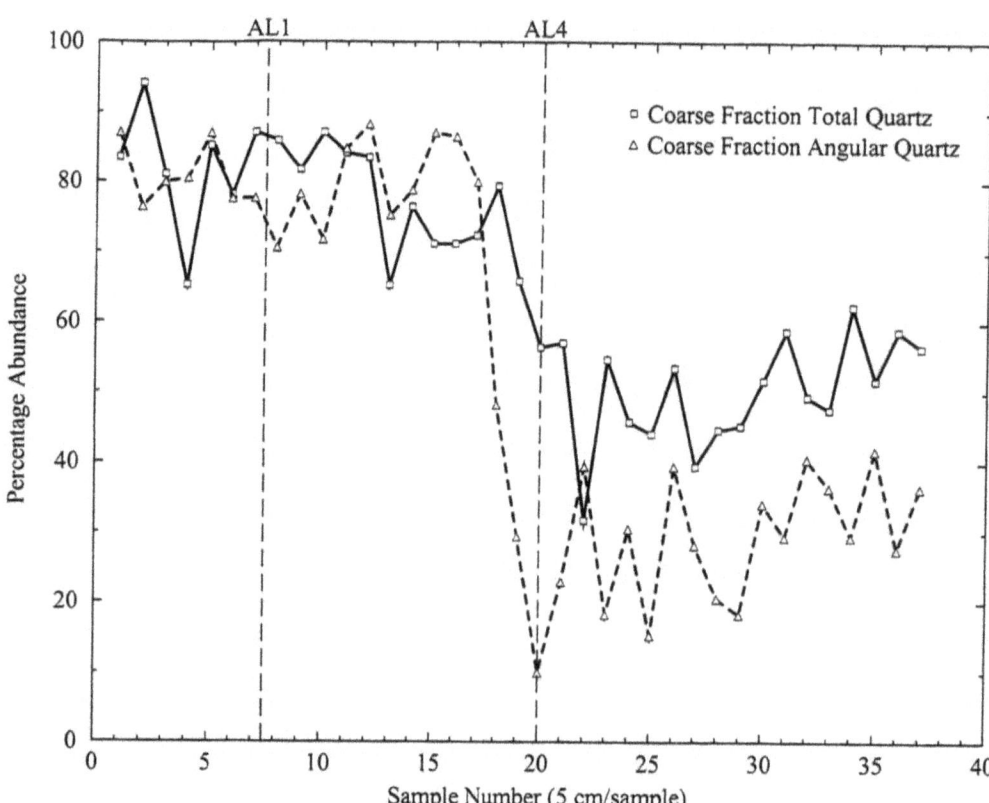

To develop a continuous, "seriational" display of climatic conditions at Grubgraben during the four episodes of occupation, proxy environmental indicators such as pollen, molluscs, or coleoptera are desirable. Unfortunately, pollen at the site is poorly preserved (Haesaerts 1990b:30; Montet-White et al. 1990:160) and cannot be used to monitor the continuous variation in site-specific paleoenvironmental conditions. Malacological analysis [reported in Haesaerts (1990b: Table III-1)] generally confirms the climatic reconstruction based on the physical properties of the loess deposits, and suggests that slightly milder microenvironmental conditions obtained within the Grubgraben ravine proper. Mollusc assemblages were recovered from only four sedimentary units, however, and cannot provide an adequately detailed picture of climatic dynamics at the site.

Despite the inadequacy at Grubgraben of conventional climatic monitors such as pollen and molluscs, the trajectory of climatic change at the site can still be inferred by examining various physical and compositional characteristics of the loess deposits themselves. Properties of the sediments such as the shape, color, orientation (fabric of diamictons), lithology, heavy mineralogy, and magnetic susceptibility of the constituent particles are commonly appealed to as complementary, proxy indicators of paleoenvironmental conditions at the time of formation and deposition (Gale and Hoare 1991; Pye 1987; see also Evans 1978; Chambers 1993). An excellent introduction to the use of the properties of unlithified rocks for environmental reconstruction is available in Gale and Hoare (1991).

Suitable morphological and mineralogical analyses of the loess deposits at Grubgraben are reported by Pawlikowski (1990a) for a two-section column of 37 loess samples from the site. The column begins at the surface with sample number 1, and progresses in increments of 5 cm to sample number 37, taken from the loess units below AL4. The sediment samples were separated into coarse (>100 μm) and fine (70–100 μm) fractions, and in each fraction the percentage composition was determined for total quartz, angular quartz, biotite, and muscovite. The opaque mineral and heavy mineral composition of the coarse fractions are also reported, as are the percentages of the fine and coarse fractions within the total sediment sample (Pawlikowski 1990a: Figures IV-4 and IV-5). In general, the coarse fractions exhibited the greatest variability between stratigraphic samples, and the abundance of angular quartz in the coarse fraction showed the greatest variation of all the measured quantities (Pawlikowski 1990a:41).

The distribution of angular quartz grains in the coarse fraction from loess samples is one of the more efficient quantities for inferring past climatic conditions. The shape of the quartz grains is expected to be rounder and less angular under the increased weathering associated with milder and more humid conditions [Butzer 1964; Smalley and Cabrera 1970; Evans 1978; Pye 1987; see SEM photographs in Pawlikowski (1990a: Figures IV-6 and IV-7)]. The distributions of both the total quartz and angular quartz content in the coarse fractions of the samples from the stratigraphic column of Pawlikowski (1990a) are shown in Figure 2.6. The positions of occupations AL1 (samples 7–8) and AL4 (sample 20) are indicated on the figure; the sample numbers corresponding to occupations AL2 and AL3 are not reported by Pawlikowski (1990a) and are not known. From Figure 2.6 it is clear that a major change in climate, from relatively humid to much drier conditions, is coincident with the AL4 occupation and the development of the thin humic horizon described by Haesaerts (1990b). The same rapid shift is also observed in the distribution of total quartz. In both quantities a slight trend from dry to more humid conditions can be detected prior to AL4.

Following the events of AL4 the proportion of angular quartz fluctuates but does not exhibit a discernible trend. The distribution of total quartz fluctuates as well, but also shows a gradual trend toward drier conditions after the occupation of AL4. A similar pattern—a period of decreasing aridity prior to AL4, a marked increase in humidity coincident with the events of AL4, and gradually increasing aridity following AL4—is also evident in the distribution of biotite in the coarse and fine fractions and, to a lesser extent, in muscovite in the fine fraction (Pawlikowski 1990a: Figure IV-5). These proxy indicators of continuous climatic variation corroborate the reconstructed climatic trend postulated by Haesaerts (1990b).

In summary, the pattern of climatic change at Grubgraben during the period from AL4 to AL1 exhibits the following features: (1) a period of relatively mild and humid conditions, probably corresponding to a brief climatic oscillation or interstadial, during which the events of AL4 transpired; (2) a rapid return to cold and dry glacial conditions soon after the events of AL4; and (3) initiation of a fluctuating but consistent trend toward colder and more arid conditions following AL4 and continuing until after the events of AL1. The diachronic pattern of climatic change is monitored most clearly by the distributions of angular quartz and heavy minerals (biotite and muscovite) in the loess sediments from Grubgraben.

2.9 Seasonality

Grubgraben has been identified in the literature as an Epigravettian winter campsite (Montet-White and Williams 1992, 1994; Montet-White 1991a,b; Logan 1990a,b; Whitney 1992; West 1995). This identification is based primarily on faunal indicators of seasonality discussed by Logan (1990a) for levels AL2, AL3, and AL4, by Whitney (1992) for AL1, and most recently by West (1995) for all four archaeological levels. These investigators have unanimously commented on the difficulty of establishing seasonality because of the generally poor preservation and highly fragmented nature of the faunal material (especially in AL1), but all have arrived at similar conclusions regarding the most likely time of occupation: all levels at Grubgraben appear to represent fall/winter occupations.

Logan (1990a:87–89) identified three indicators of seasonality. Two mandible fragments retaining deciduous molars at the time of death indicated a time of occupation from mid-June to mid-December. This determination was based on the high relief wear patterns on the molars, suggesting that the animals died within their first seven months of life (Logan 1990a:87, Figure IV-2). A third mandible fragment with deciduous and permanent molars indicated the animal's first winter as the mostly likely time of death.

Corroborative evidence for a winter occupation came from the representation of specific faunal elements at the site. Logan (1990a:87) observed that the faunal elements that are most numerous in the assemblages are those with low GUI values [General Utility Index (Binford 1978b:72–75)]. In other words, the animal parts associated with the least amount of useable meat were most abundant in the assemblages (Logan 1990a: Table VI-10). Logan concluded that "the high ratio of low GUI elements and the extreme fragmentation of these remains related to marrow extraction suggests the inhabitants of the structure [i.e., AL2 and AL3] were forced to rely on food sources not necessary during warmer months of the year" (Logan 1990a:87, 90). The absence of wood charcoal at the site, together with the large number of burned bone fragments observed in the faunal assemblages, has been suggested as a further indication of a cold weather occupation and the need to exploit bones as a domestic fuel resource (Logan 1990a:90; Montet-White 1988b:216).

Whitney (1992) attempted to determine the season of occupation of level AL1 using tooth sectioning methods and counts of annual dental cementum rings, as well as tooth eruption schedules and wear patterns (Spiess 1979). Efforts to count annual dental cementum rings were unsuccessful; all tooth sections exhibited patchy cementum along the root margins and distinct annual rings could not be identified (Whitney 1992:40). However, the eruption and wear patterns of two teeth from reindeer under two years of age indicated an occupation between November and May (Whitney 1992:42–43, Table 4.5). Whitney concluded that AL1 "appears to have been a winter and possibly a winter/early spring encampment" (Whitney 1992:58).

Most recently the matter of season of occupation at Grubgraben was investigated by West (1995) using the entire faunal inventory from all levels of the site. The age profiles for reindeer in AL2–AL4 clearly indicated an autumn/winter occupation, but an insufficient number of teeth were recovered from AL1 to accurately infer its season of occupation. The acceptance here of AL1 as a fall/winter occupation is consequently based on the limited evidence of Whitney (1992) and on the similarities in feature inventory and spatial organization between level AL1 and the confirmed fall/winter occupation of level AL2.

Although faunal indicators of seasonality suggest that the site was occupied during the colder months of the year, a longer stay is not excluded (Logan 1990a:89) and is in fact suggested by the considerable investment in site facilities such as pavements and stone structures in AL1 and AL2 and the variety of pits and pit-like features in AL3 and AL4. The effect of longer-term occupation of the site, however, is clearly to increase the probability that the different assemblages were created during similar times of the year, and to increase the stability, or constancy, of the assemblages with regard to seasonally conditioned activities. In other words, evidence for longer-term occupations at Grubgraben also serves to reduce any potential effects of seasonality of occupation on interassemblage variability.

2.10 Controls on Variability

The available published material clearly indicates that Grubgraben is a site of some importance for the study of Late

Glacial adaptations in central Europe. The existence of a site of this size, complexity, and relative stability during the Last Glacial Maximum is especially remarkable in view of the arguments that have been advanced for the depopulation or outright abandonment of portions of central Europe in response to increasingly cold and arid conditions during the last ice age (Hahn 1976, 1983; Valoch 1980, 1989; Gamble 1983; Soffer 1985:247, 1987b; Jochim 1987; Weniger 1989, 1990; Kozlowski 1990; Otte 1990; Simán 1990; Dobosi 1991a; Straus 1991).

The significance of Grubgraben for the present study is as a test case for investigating the local, organizational responses of past systems to the selection pressure of climatic change and the onset of severe ice-age conditions. The site provides valuable control over variables such as geography and physical environment, chronology and timing of climatic change, type of site, season of occupation, agents responsible for the archaeological deposits, and excavation methodology. These controls hold constant many sources of variation in the archaeological record at Grubgraben which could otherwise obscure the evidence for climatically conditioned organizational variability. The success or failure of the pattern recognition approach in chapter 5 will depend critically on the existence and quality of these control conditions.

Geographically, Grubgraben is situated at the southern edge of the Bohemian Massif, near the northwestern margin of the broad Hungarian plain. This places the site near the southeastern periphery of the postulated "abandoned" area of central Europe, and in a region that was clearly subject to the full climatic changes associated with the Last Glacial Maximum. Alternatively, Grubgraben can be seen as "marking the northwestern end of the region in which Epigravettian groups established long term or seasonal base camps" (Montet-White et al. 1990:161), which again points to the environmentally transitional or marginal nature of the site location. Whether or not the periglacial regions of central and southern Germany, Poland, Bohemia, and Slovakia were abandoned or significantly depopulated, Grubgraben was well positioned to have experienced a climatic regime essentially identical to these other regions [apart from microenvironmental variation (Haesaerts 1990b)].

One of the most provocative and, for the purpose of the present research, indispensible controls provided by Grubgraben is climatological: its sequence of four discrete occupation levels is securely dated to the Last Glacial Maximum and records a period of several millennia during which the climate steadily became more severe (Figures 2.4 and 2.6). The lowest level (AL4) is characterized by relatively mild conditions, with sufficient moisture to enable soil formation and the development of a sparse vegetative cover, and the levels above AL4 document a gradual trend toward increasingly dry and cold conditions in the region (Haesaerts 1985a, 1990b; Pawlikowski 1990a).

The importance of working with deposits which derive from a period of monotonic climatic change is emphasized by Wobst:

> If we look at Pleistocene climatic process, we see cycles in the general shape of sine curves. This should alert us. We want to slice time so that climatic process proceeds in the same direction: getting colder and drier, or warmer and more humid, for example. This would imply slicing the pie from the optimum of the interstadial (interglacial) to the temperature minimum of the stadial (glacial), or vice versa (Wobst 1990:338).

This condition is met, as nearly as may be expected, by the sequence of deposits at Grubgraben. Although the rate of climatic change at Grubgraben is not uniform, it is essentially monotonic, proceeding from a mild climatic episode, probably correlated with the Lascaux oscillation, toward increasingly severe glacial conditions (Haesaerts 1990b; Pawlikowski 1990a).

It is also important to achieve some degree of control over the function of the site during its various episodes of occupation if organizational variability in response to climatic change is to be recognized. If some of the assemblages at Grubgraben represent residential occupations, for example, and the remaining assemblages derive from the use of the site as a hunting station, then separating archaeological variability due to long-term climatic processes from variability due to changes in site function would be complicated enormously.

As argued earlier, however, the richness of the lithic and faunal inventories, the presence of many intact features such as hearths, pits of varying content and construction, pavements and other stone structures, and the reuse of many features, all suggest that Grubgraben does indeed provide the desired control over site function. Specifically, the considerable investment in and maintenance of site facilities in each level argues for an interpretation of Grubgraben as a stable residential site, at least during the four episodes of occupation available for study. It is unreasonable, but unnecessary, to assert that these are all residences belonging to a single hunter-gatherer system, but it is practical to accept the deposits as residential palimpsests generated by groups of hunter-gatherers facing common, region-specific environmental pressures.

The relative placement of the hearths, activity areas, debris distributions, and other features could be studied independently to support the claim that the assemblages at Grubgraben are residential in nature, because the establishment and maintenance of the domestic space is believed to be the essential defining characteristic of residential sites (Binford 1983a, 1987a). In other words, at a residential site the domestic area is focal to all other activities, and this organizing principle has immediate implications for the relative spatial positions of different kinds of features within each level (Binford 1983a, 1987a:497–501; Stapert 1989, 1992; Stapert and Terberger 1989; Olive and Taborin 1989). The spatial organization at Grubgraben has already been explored in a preliminary way to address the question of site function (Montet-White 1990c; Montet-White and Williams 1992, 1994), and initial results are consistent with the interpretation of Grubgraben as a sequence of residential occupations.

Despite the evidence for the stable residential nature of Grubgraben, however, the variation in assemblage and feature content across the individual archaeological levels strongly suggests that functionally different areas of the site have been revealed by the common excavation window. Thus, a certain amount of interassemblage variability is expected to be contributed by the intrasite functional variation produced by excavation sampling bias. This source of variation and its contribution to interassemblage variability is considered at length in chapter 7.

Excellent control is also available at Grubgraben over the agents responsible for the character of the assemblages. Because the site is an open-air station, it is reasonable to assume the assemblages are for all intents and purposes primarily referable to human agency. The large faunal assemblage from the site has been well studied (Logan 1990a,b; Whitney 1992; West 1995), and very little evidence for the activity of carnivores or scavengers has been observed (Logan 1990a:90; West 1995); of more than 44,000 bones examined, only 21 exhibited carnivore damage and just 6 displayed rodent damage (West 1995). Taphonomic processes are known to have operated differentially, however, with the quality of preservation of bone decreasing from excellent in AL4 to fair in AL1 (West 1995). Some evidence for solifluction has also been noted in level AL2 (Montet-White, personal communication 1994). The effects of these processes must be seriously considered in studies of butchering patterns (West 1995) or spatial relationships (Montet-White 1990c; Montet-White and Williams 1992, 1994), but they are not expected to compromise the analyses conducted here, which involve only summary assemblage data such as frequencies in various artifact classes [i.e., "facts of assemblage composition" (Binford 1977b)].

Finally, Grubgraben offers many desirable technical advantages. Unlike other relevant sites in the area—Krems-Hundssteig (Laplace 1970; Hahn 1973, 1977:108–109) and Willendorf (Felgenhauer 1956–59; Otte 1981; Haesaerts 1990a) are excellent examples—that were collected or excavated with inadequate controls and have been severely compromised for detailed scientific research, Grubgraben has been minimally disturbed by illicit collection and was recently excavated using modern techniques. Large faunal and lithic inventories were recovered, and data are available for a wide range of artifact classes not always reported in detail for other sites (Cook 1993; Beck 1993; Hill 1993). The availability of a large and well studied faunal assemblage with which to supplement other kinds of data is also a tremendous analytical advantage (Logan 1990b; Whitney 1992; West 1995), because typological summaries of lithic assemblages cannot be expected to reliably monitor general system changes (Vierra 1975; Binford 1978b, 1982a). The recovery of many features such as hearths, stone pavements and other stone structures, and various kinds of pits provides an unusually detailed view of Epigravettian site structure, and the horizontal exposure at the site (92 m^2 for the uppermost archaeological levels AL1 and AL2, and 48–50 m^2 for the lower levels AL3 and AL4) is adequate to give some indications of the intrasite spatial organization in each level (Montet-White 1990c; Montet-White and Williams 1992, 1994).

2.11 Conclusions

In retrospect it can be appreciated that most of the controls discussed above are realistically attained only at a single, multicomponent site at which the climatic conditions during each period of occupation can be independently reconstructed. It is unrealistic to expect that a body of data relevant to the study of climatically conditioned changes in the local organizational properties of past systems could be assembled simply by juxtaposing assemblages from a number of sites from different regions that stand in unknown or uncertain chronological and climatic relationships to one another. Using assemblage information from any and all central European sites that date to the Last Glacial Maximum would yield poorly controlled data, because there is no assurance that these sites monitor a period of monotonic climatic change. Even supposing that the sites could be shown to date to some common episode of unidirectional climatic change, there is still no satisfactory means of ordering these sites to correspond with the direction and magnitude of the climatic change.

These considerations lead to the conclusion that information from additional sites, even sites dated to the Last Glacial Maximum, cannot be included with the Grubgraben data in an effort to enhance or otherwise strengthen the analysis. Because the success of a pattern recognition approach rests heavily on the quality of the controls that can be implemented, the introduction of other sites would seriously compromise most of the control conditions that Grubgraben provides. In particular, the timing and especially the direction of climatic change may not be maintained; the stability of site type cannot be assured unless the additional sites are residential in nature (and even demonstrably residential sites may not be equivalent or comparable); constancy of seasonality of occupation will be called into question; the geological data necessary for reconstructing the site-specific record of climatic change may not be available; and the consistency of field technique and data recovery cannot be assured. Furthermore, it cannot at this point be anticipated with any confidence exactly what classes and combinations of classes of material remains will prove most sensitive to the organizational responses to climatic change. A compelling advantage of the Grubgraben site is that data are available for classes of remains such as shell, quartz, cobbles, and bone tools in addition to the lithic information and the unparalleled faunal data set. Introducing additional, less well-reported sites can only reduce the number of artifact classes that can be explored for patterning.

3.0 How to Research the Problem

In the previous chapter the site of Grubgraben was introduced as a provocative archaeological test case characterized by a number of properties believed to be crucial to the study of local, organizational adaptations by past hunter-gatherer systems to climatic change during the Last Glacial Maximum. It was necessary to introduce the site and discuss its most significant properties before returning in this chapter to several of the points raised in chapter 1, and specifically to the issue of how to recognize the response of past systems to climatic change. In other words, now that the matter of where to look—Grubgraben—has been resolved, the issue of what to observe must be addressed. What observations are relevant for pursuing the stated research goal?

The task in this chapter is to consider the general problem of how to recognize the local organizational responses of past systems to climatic change and the onset of ice-age conditions. Are there contemporary situations that can be examined for ideas about what the past was like during the Last Glacial Maximum? Can prior knowledge of hunter-gatherer systems be used to postulate specific expectations for the archaeological variability that results from adaptation to climatic deterioration and an ice-age environment? What kinds of data are relevant for researching the problem? The issue to be resolved in this chapter is not that of selecting a particular analytical method, but of identifying an appropriate research strategy and of determining the observations to be made. The specific analytical approach dictated by the nature of the relevant data and observations will be discussed in the following chapter.

3.1 Expectations for Variability

A cornerstone of Binford's program for middle-range research in archaeology is the need to develop a corpus of sustainable uniformitarian assumptions that provide robust linkages from the present into the past, analogous to the uniformitarian principles upon which much of modern geology is founded (Binford 1977a, 1981:21–30, 1982c, 1987a, 1989a:267–281, 1989c; Watson et al. 1984; S.J. Gould 1977:150). It is only by means of such justifiable uniformitarian projections that our observations and knowledge of the present can be of use in accurately learning about the past.

Successful middle-range research in archaeology increases our knowledge of the causal relationships between dynamic processes and the static properties of the archaeological record that are conditioned by those processes (Binford 1977a, 1981, 1984b). An understanding of the relationships between process and product improves our ability to develop realistic expectations for the archaeological variability generated under known conditions and, conversely, to supply warranted processual interpretations for specific archaeological observations. Put another way, the archaeological patterning generated by a specific process cannot be identified without invoking a comparison, explicitly or otherwise, to a situation in which this process is controlled and understood. Successful middle-range research makes this comparative process explicit and available for scrutiny, evaluation, revision, and elaboration.

The assertion was made in chapter 1, however, that there is currently no completely satisfactory middle-range research context available in which to develop firm expectations and recognition criteria for the organizational changes in past systems conditioned by climatic changes characteristic of the Last Glacial Maximum. This assertion followed from the fact that there exist no contemporary or historically accessible situations involving traditional hunting societies that have experienced long-term climatic deterioration and the onset of ice-age conditions, and that can provide learning contexts for generating ideas about what the past was like during the events and conditions of the Last Glacial Maximum in central Europe. In other words, our "knowledge of the moment" (Binford 1984b:9–17) with respect to the archaeological products and patterns resulting from extended climatic processes is weak and uninformed by middle-range experiences.

3.1.1 Ethnographic Analogy

In an effort to develop a proxy middle-range research context, one might be inclined to accept modern arctic or subarctic hunter-gatherer peoples as ethnographic analogs for Late Glacial Pleistocene populations. There are at least two serious problems with this approach, however. First, there are no appropriate contemporary analogs for the full ice-age environmental conditions which obtained during the Last Glacial Maximum:

> ...the common practice of visualizing glacial environments by analogy with modern arctic or antarctic ones is flawed; the mid-latitude 'arctic' zones at 18 000 BP possessed the variations in daylight hours, insolation, and even temperature that fit their present latitude and not those of Greenland or Antarctica (van Andel 1990:33).

A second difficulty with appeals to ethnographic analogy in the present research is that nearly all modern hunter-gatherer groups have passed through an "aquatic transition" in their adaptation to cooler and drier latitudes:

> ...the vast majority of the historically documented hunter-gatherers compensate for the decreasing potential of plant resources in higher latitudes by increasing the exploitation of aquatic resources.
> .... This pattern has enormous importance for our use of historically documented hunter-gatherers as analogies to Pleistocene peoples, who, it is well known, favored terrestrial resources (Binford 1990:134).

It must also be considered that, although modern arctic or subarctic populations can provide relevant contexts for studying some aspects of hunter-gatherer organization, such as a subsistence strategy based primarily on the hunting of caribou (Binford 1978b:12; Spiess 1979; Enloe 1993), it is still the case that no direct observations relevant to the organizational responses of past systems to *long-term climatic deterioration* can be made using any human groups, past or present. There are simply no contemporary, directly observable, actualistic middle-range learning situations from which to seek insights regarding the nature of organizational responses by hunter-gatherer groups to the climatic dynamics associated with the Last Glacial Maximum and the manner in which these organizational responses will be manifested archaeologically.

3.1.2 Actualistic Archaeology and Ethnohistory

Actualistic archaeology and ethnohistory are two middle-range research contexts that are clearly inaccessible given the stated research goal. With regard to ethnohistory, there certainly exist no written accounts dealing with the responses of human populations to the Last Glacial Maximum. From an actualistic or experimental perspective, it is not realistic to initiate an ice age on the planet and observe the archaeological products generated by the responses of contemporary hunter-gatherer societies to the resulting (and presumably controlled) changes in climate and environment.

There is an intriguing possibility, however, that should be mentioned and that may prove worthy of future consideration. There have been a number of historical fluctuations in climate, most significantly the *Little Ice Age* from 1450 AD to about 1890 AD (Crowley and North 1991:92–109; COHMAP 1988; Wright et al. 1993). This event consisted of two cold stages, each of about 100 years duration, in the 17th and 19th centuries, and was a very widespread if not global climatic event. Alpine glaciers advanced in nearly all mountainous regions of the world, sea ice and snowcover on land expanded, lakes and rivers froze, average winter temperatures declined, phenological patterns were modified, and agricultural trends changed (Crowley and North 1991:94–96).

The Little Ice Age occurred recently enough that historical records could conceivably be used to study some of the settlement and subsistence changes that developed in response to the widespread cooling. Reports of climatically conditioned changes are available for developed countries such as Iceland and some areas of northern Europe (e.g., Dansgaard et al. 1975; Bergthórsson 1969). Ethnohistorical documentation may exist for traditional societies in the form of accounts of missionaries, traders, and explorers in regions such as New Guinea, New Zealand, and the South American cone where the climatic effects of the Little Ice Age were most pronounced (Crowley and North 1991:96). Obviously the detail of the reporting cannot be expected to be high, but ethnohistorical accounts could conceivably provide insights into how traditional settlement and subsistence systems responded to several centuries of climatic change.

3.1.3 Generalizations from Modern Hunter-Gatherers

A highly promising energetics-based frame of reference that can be used to generate expectations about the responses of past systems to climatic change is the emerging corpus of well-supported generalizations from contemporary hunter-gatherer groups. This frame of reference has been explored recently and most intensively by Binford using a worldwide sample of 198 historically known hunter-gatherer societies (Binford 1989a:278, 1989c, 1990, 1991a; Gamble 1991; see also Murdock 1967; Lee 1968; Oswalt 1973, 1976; Testart 1982; Whitelaw 1983, 1989, 1991; Kelly 1995). These comparative data on contemporary hunter-gatherer adaptations:

> ...serve as a provocative summary of the behavior of fully modern humans, a summary against which to play off our archaeological evidence from earlier time periods and differing environments (Binford 1990:122).

In other words, the worldwide patterns in contemporary hunter-gatherer societies are expected to provide a source of general principles which can be projected into the past to serve as interpretive tools. These generalizations are based on uniformitarian principles of energetics and ecology, using well understood environmental variables such as *effective temperature* and *net above-ground annual productivity*, and are not simply a modification or repackaging of old arguments from ethnographic analogy. The use of generalizations from modern hunter-gatherer groups is not completely without risk, however; as noted earlier, most modern hunter-gatherer groups have passed through the "aquatic transition" in their adaptation to cooler and drier latitudes, whereas Pleistocene groups are known to have intensified their exploitation of terrestrial rather than aquatic resources (Binford 1990:134).

Of particular relevance to the present research are several robust patterns that emerge when the world's hunter-gatherer populations are tabulated according to the environmental variable of *effective temperature*. The effective temperature of a region is a composite measure of temperature and length of growing season (Bailey 1960) and is strongly correlated with latitude. When the world's existing hunter-gatherer societies are studied using an environmental baseline, variation in hunter-gatherer housing, mobility patterns, storage practices, relative dependence on plant, aquatic, and terrestrial hunted resources, and type of weaponry used in hunting is found to be understandable in large measure in terms of basic ecological and energetic relationships (Binford 1989c, 1990, 1991a; Gamble 1991).

Given that robust synchronic patterning in response to effective temperature is exhibited by the variables of mobility, housing, and storage in contemporary hunter-gatherer societies, can similar patterning be expected in the diachronic responses of Pleistocene hunter-gatherers to the increasingly arid and cold conditions of the last ice age? In other words, can variation in effective temperature from temperate to arctic regions serve as a proxy for the increasing aridity and cooler temperatures created by the last advance of the ice sheets? If so, can the observed variability in contemporary systems with latitude and effective temperature provide surrogate expectations for climatically conditioned variability in past systems? Wobst (1990) appears to be thinking along these lines:

> Of course, a transect across hunter-gatherers in the ethnographic present, from equator to permafrost, would have very similar features at the periglacial margins as in the Upper Palaeolithic, 18 000 years ago. For example, in the ethnographic present and in the Palaeolithic, the northern margins of the population distribution have produced highly stylized and easily 'typed' material culture, high intensity of decorative art, curative

technology, and impressive facilities (for example, shrines and mammoth bone structures in the past and drive lines tens of miles long in the present) (Wobst 1990:334).

There are clearly some difficulties with drawing a parallel between change in effective temperature and change in climate, two of which have already been mentioned (van Andel 1990:33; Binford 1990:134). The frame of reference offered by modern hunter-gatherer generalizations is appealing, however, for its explicit attention to environmental variation. Can this frame of reference be implemented at Grubgraben to develop testable expectations for the archaeological variability generated in response to climatic change during the Last Glacial Maximum?

Assuming for the moment that variation with effective temperature in contemporary hunter-gatherer systems can be used as a frame of reference for recognizing and explaining some kinds of archaeological variability as a response to climatic change, then the relevant observations of the archaeological record should be ones which implicate patterns of mobility, housing, and storage (Binford 1990). Unfortunately, observation of these variables at Grubgraben presents special difficulties.

3.1.3.1 Housing: Evidence for housing at Grubgraben is difficult to evaluate. Although claims have been made for the existence of semicircular stone tent rings and other indications of dwelling structures, based on observations made during the excavations of the spatial patterns of various size classes of stones (Montet-White 1990c, 1991b), the evidence is in need of further study and remains unevaluated at the present time (see also comments by Binford 1978a:357). Even if the evidence for housing structures is accepted, however, it appears in any case to be restricted to the uppermost occupation levels (AL1 and AL2), so that changes in housing cannot be examined across all levels at the site. The small pit-like structures resembling post-molds in AL4 (chapter 2) may have been related to the use of dwelling structures, but this is purely conjectural. Given the variability in pit construction and content in AL4, and the evidence that some of these pits were used for boiling and processing purposes (West 1995), any above-ground structures in the excavated area of AL4 seem more likely to have been used in processing tasks instead of serving as domestic shelters.

3.1.3.2 Storage: Evidence for storage at Grubgraben is less equivocal, but still insufficient to evaluate the possibility of climatically conditioned changes in storage practices. Although a number of suggestive features were recovered that could have functioned as storage facilities [e.g., the "meat cache" in AL1 and the large, stone covered pits in AL3 and AL4 (Montet-White 1990c, 1991b; West 1995)], the identification of these features as storage-related is not secure. The pits in the lower levels (AL3 and AL4), for example, may have been involved in processing tasks rather than true storage tasks. Furthermore, although caches are a common mode of storage at residential sites in low effective temperature environments, above-ground structures such as racks are most commonly used (Binford 1983a, 1990:144, 1993) and may be difficult if not impossible to recognize archaeologically at Grubgraben.

3.1.3.3 Mobility: If diachronic data on housing and storage at Grubgraben are currently absent or inadequate, information on mobility patterns is more accessible. The use of raw material economies to reconstruct mobility and settlement patterns is well established in Paleolithic archaeology (Malina 1970; Hayden 1982; Svoboda 1983; Hahn 1987; Weniger 1987a,b, 1989, 1990, 1991; Montet-White 1988a, 1991c, 1994; Montet-White and Holen 1991; Otte 1981; Kozlowski 1972–73, 1986, 1990, 1991b; Bíró 1987, 1988; Bíró et al. 1986; Valoch 1987) and studies of the lithic raw materials and raw material economy at Grubgraben are available (Pawlikowski 1990b; West and Montet-White 1990; Montet-White 1991b). Unlike conventional typological summaries of lithic assemblages, which are ambiguous and monitor unknown or varying properties of cultural systems and cannot be expected to necessarily monitor general system changes (Vierra 1975; Binford 1978b, 1982a), raw material economies are more directly understandable in terms of system properties and changes. Comparisons of the distributions of raw material procurement distances during the Upper Paleolithic, for example, have demonstrated that larger procurement and exchange networks were in place during the Gravettian than during either the Aurignacian or the Magdalenian (Weniger 1990, 1991; Hahn 1987; Spieksma 1989; Rensink et al. 1991; Kozlowski 1991b; Montet-White 1994).

Varieties of flint and radiolarite contribute the majority of the raw material used as tool stone at Grubgraben. Three major raw material types appear to be positively sourced: a bluish northern (Baltic) flint from glacial moraines along the Upper Oder basin (approximately 200 km from Grubgraben); a grayish-white flint from outcrops at Stránksá skála in Moravia (100–120 km); and a type of radiolarite found locally in Kamp and Danube river gravels and also available from outcrops along the Vah valley to the east (150–180 km) (Montet-White 1991b, 1994; Pawlikowski 1990b).

Analysis of the lithics recovered during the 1986–1987 excavations at Grubgraben clearly shows several major trends in raw material exploitation that are suggestive of changes in mobility patterns (West and Montet-White 1990; Montet-White 1991b, 1994): (1) flint from Upper Silesia declines markedly (by weight, for both tools and waste) from the lower to the upper levels at Grubgraben; (2) Stránská skála flint is present in approximately constant amounts throughout the four occupations; (3) use of radiolarites from the Vah valley increases steadily from AL4 to AL1. Thus it appears that as the climate in central Europe became increasingly severe during the Last Glacial Maximum, access to the far northern flints (Upper Oder basin) was greatly reduced, and exploitation of the Vah radiolarites to the east was intensified (Montet-White 1991b, 1994). (Alternatively, the decline in Upper Silesian flints and the increase in Vah valley radiolarites throughout the sequence of occupations at Grubgraben may only reflect shifting reindeer migration patterns—that were not climatically induced—and the embedded nature of lithic raw material procurement). There is, therefore, convincing evidence for changes in the *direction* of raw material procurement as the climate became progressively less hospitable, but because all of the presently identified sources are essentially long-distance sources (100–200 km), it is not at present possible to recognize changes in the distribution of procurement *distances* that have been suggested as responses to climatic deterioration during the Last Glacial Maximum (Weniger 1990:190).

In summary, a promising frame of reference for recognizing the organizational responses of past systems to climatic change is provided by ecologically and environmentally informed generalizations based on variation among the world's contemporary hunter-gatherer societies. These generalizations have been developed most fully for aspects of hunter-gatherer society such as mobility, housing, and some kinds of subsistence technology such as storage and weaponry. However, the observations of mobility, housing, and storage needed to test ideas about climatically conditioned organizational changes are presently inaccessible or unavailable at Grubgraben, although directed analyses of the existing data or additional excavations could improve this situation considerably.

3.2 A Pattern Recognition Approach

The conclusion that contemporary middle-range research cannot provide a fully relevant learning context for the present research goal is not unexpected, nor is it particularly discouraging. The process and product to be investigated—local organizational changes by hunter-gatherer systems in response to long-term climatic deterioration and severe ice-age conditions—are sufficiently removed from contemporary human experience that relevant controls are difficult to recognize and implement in the present. In fact, the attempt to recognize and characterize climatically conditioned organizational changes at Grubgraben can be expected to contribute ideas for investigation and further evaluation as appropriate sites and techniques become available. At some point it may also be possible to accept specific archaeological cases such as Grubgraben as well-understood examples of the patterns that result from the processes now being investigated at more elementary levels of understanding (Binford 1982c, 1983c:394).

In the absence of a body of relevant middle-range knowledge to generate ideas and testable expectations about what the past was like, a more responsible and productive alternative is to engage in pattern recognition work (Binford 1987a, 1989a:27–40). With a pattern recognition approach one is essentially acknowledging an ignorance or uncertainty of the expected relationships in the data and is endeavoring to derive a framework of meaning from the data rather than impose upon them an *a priori* model (P. Gould 1981:173; Carr 1985, 1991; Tukey and Wilk 1970). The basic strategy of pattern recognition work is to explore the interaction (i.e., patterning) between our basic observational data and then seek to gain some understanding of what the interaction implies about the past. Directed pattern recognition work does not assume that data are inherently meaningful ["letting the data speak for themselves" (P. Gould 1981)], and does not constitute "shotgun empiricism" (Raab and Goodyear 1984:256), but is more appropriately described as a strategy for allowing the archaeological record to "talk back" (Binford 1987a:493, 1989a:34–39).

In contrast, an ineffective strategy for learning about the past would be to impose a "model" of expected organizational changes in response to the Last Glacial Maximum and then attempt to assess the "goodness-of-fit" of the model to the data. This approach deflects attention from the real issue—interpreting the archaeological record and understanding the past in its own terms (Binford 1989a:10)—and involves archaeologists in unproductive arguments of relevance, i.e., arguments about the applicability of a model in a given context or to a given set of data (Binford 1972:244–294, 1982d, 1983c:157–167, 1983c:389–394, 1984b; see also P. Gould 1981; Whallon 1982, 1984; Carr 1985, 1991). The intellectual straitjacket imposed by model-bound approaches is by no means unique to archaeology; recently it has been strongly criticized with respect to all sciences:

> ...the current paradigm virtually implies that to inquire in an acceptable manner the inquirer must postulate a "model," an a priori structure put forward before the research is actually begun. It matters little how simplistic such a model is, or how unexamined its assumptions are; postulation can always be followed by refutation, providing accepted procedures are followed. One wonders if research proposals to describe the structure of DNA would ever have received approval under such conditions. Fortunately, Rosalind Franklin was allowed to look at X-ray photographs, and think about them for seven years (P. Gould 1981:166).

With respect to the present research, postulation of a model of climatically conditioned organizational changes in past systems would require that one make guesses (intelligent and believable ones perhaps, but guesses nevertheless and not true deductions) about how one expects the past to have been under the conditions of the model. Confirmation or refutation of the model would only evaluate one's skill at guessing, and initiate an argument as to whether the model was relevant or not to the given archaeological test case (Binford 1982d, 1983c:390). Because these arguments of relevance are "tested" by evaluating the "goodness-of-fit" between an imagined past and the empirical archaeological present (Binford 1983c:67), the past itself is not implicated by the results of the test and the process of learning about the past is aborted.

It is not necessary to engage in arguments of relevance, however. A more responsible and productive method of inquiry is to explore the patterning and variability in archaeological data and seek to interpret the observations using the available knowledge of process and product in behavioral and physical systems. Such "knowledge of the moment" is of course highly variable in quality and always subject to the criticism that it is wrong or inadequate (Binford 1984b:9–17). Irrespective of its quality, however, making use of available knowledge can reveal deficiencies in our understanding and identify areas in need of further study:

> ...I do not assume I know what the past was like and use such assumptions to guide my analysis. On the contrary, I assume that it is the *patterning* that is the source of information about the past, and the knowledge available to me for understanding patterning is the ultimate justification of any subsequent interpretations. In short, it is the middle-range knowledge of process and pattern that makes interpretation possible (Binford 1987b:64, original emphasis).

The implication is clearly that our ability to learn about the past can improve only as our knowledge of process and pattern increases, because it is knowledge of the links between process and pattern that enables model-bound guesswork to be replaced with the formulation of robust inferences and the testing of hypotheses (Platt 1964). Middle-range research and pattern recognition studies are two productive means of increasing our knowledge of process-pattern relationships, but arguments of relevance simply cannot contribute (Binford 1977a, 1983c:14–17, 1983c:389–394, 1989a:267–281).

3.2.1 Residential Interassemblage Variability

In the present situation, where satisfactory middle-range contexts are unavailable for study, a pattern recognition strategy is called for as the best means currently available for learning about the organizational responses of past systems to long-term climatic change. Accordingly, a pattern recognition strategy is used to investigate the structure of interassemblage variability between the four occupation levels at Grubgraben. The goals in this endeavor are to identify some of the multiple agents that contribute to the variation in assemblage composition between levels, and to examine the interaction between these dimensions of variability and other characteristics of the deposits such as their temporal sequence, feature content, and climatic indicators (Binford 1987b, 1989b:440). The recognition of patterning in archaeological data is an initial step toward gaining some perspective on the agents that were operative in structuring the archaeological record, and ultimately in addressing the broader issues of past dynamics and the organization of past cultural systems (Binford 1981:283, 1983a, 1987a, 1989a).

There are several reasons for expecting facts of interassemblage variability to be informative of organizational changes arising from long-term processes such as climatic change. The main reason concerns the time scale involved: because climatic processes typically operate on a time scale much longer than is represented by any single episode of occupation at a site, it is unproductive to investigate organizational responses to climatic change by examining a single archaeological assemblage or palimpsest deposited during a period of relative climatic constancy. An investigation using multiple assemblages will be required to achieve the necessary chronological perspective on climatic change.

The assemblages chosen for study must furthermore stand in a known climatological relationship to one another if climatically conditioned variability is to be recognized (Wobst 1990; Gamble and Soffer 1990b). For reasons discussed in the previous chapter, a relevant sequence of assemblages is unlikely to be assembled from multiple sites but must come from a single site at which the dynamics of climatic change are independently understood through geological, palynological, malacological, or other studies.

Just as the nature of the anticipated causal process (climatic change) points to interassemblage variability as the relevant observational context, the nature of the anticipated response (organizational changes in past systems) suggests that these assemblages should derive from residential sites instead of special-purpose sites such as lithic extraction sites, kill sites, or hunting stands. Ethnoarchaeological research on contemporary hunter-gatherer systems has indicated that residential assemblages are generally informative of overall system adaptations, whereas special-purpose locations primarily monitor particular strategies (Yellen 1977; Binford 1978b, 1980; Whitelaw 1991; Kelly 1992, 1995; Chatters 1987; Gamble and Boismier 1991; O'Connell 1987):

> The accumulated debris at such a base or hub of operations [i.e., a residential location] reflects the execution and relative success of all the separate strategies executed during the occupation. It is, in many ways, an accumulated sample of the adaptive system, composed of numerous strategies and different activities with very different goals—clothing production versus food procurement, and so on. *Residential assemblages from hunting and gathering societies are close to being conditioned in their content by the total form of the adaptation effected during the course of the occupation.* Assemblages from special-purpose locations at best reflect the accumulated consequences of various strategies, the use of various resources, and their storage and transport (Binford 1978b:487, emphasis added).

In other words, because of the specialized nature and restricted number of activities performed at special-purpose locations such as kill sites or hunting stands, the archaeological record at these sites becomes primarily informative of particular system strategies. Residential locations, however, at which many activities and strategies are represented, are in general informative of overall system adaptations (Binford 1978b:487). (Some archaeologists may view the varying sensitivity of different kinds of sites to the properties of a cultural system as a reflection of current methodological approaches in archaeology rather than of any inherent ontological limitations of the archaeological record. In other words, it might be argued that as archaeological method and theory become increasingly sophisticated, special-purpose sites will ultimately prove to be as informative of overall system states as are residential sites. What is important, however, is only that a type of site can be recognized that, in principle, is "conditioned in [its] content by the total form of the adaptation"; whether future archaeological methodology eventually reveals several types of site as having this property is beside the point).

These considerations of observation and analysis serve to highlight two of the more significant advantages afforded by Grubgraben as a test site (chapter 2): the deposits at Grubgraben are arguably residential assemblages or palimpsests (Montet-White 1990c, 1991a,b; Montet-White et al. 1990), and these assemblages were deposited during a period of essentially monotonic climatic change, in the direction of increasing aridity and cooler temperatures (Haesaerts 1985a, 1990b; Pawlikowski 1990a; Montet-White et al. 1990). Consequently, observations of the structure of interassemblage variability and of the organizational properties of the archaeological record at Grubgraben should be informative of the overall system adaptations by hunter-gatherer groups in response to the long-term climatic change experienced during the Last Glacial Maximum.

3.2.2 The Structure of Variability

With the potential for residential sites to monitor the overall state of a cultural system, then the patterns defined by multiple residential assemblages are precisely what is needed to investigate the organizational responses of past systems to a long-term process such as climatic change. In other words, if each archaeological assemblage from a residential site can be considered informative of the overall system adaptation during the time the assemblage was deposited, then the patterns defined by multiple assemblages should be informative of how the overall system adaptation changed over the course of time represented by the sequence of assemblages. Relationships can then be sought between the patterns of interassemblage variability and the pattern of climatic variability.

Any given archaeological assemblage is most realistically regarded as the product of multiple sources of variation combining and interacting in various ways. The task in interassemblage analysis, therefore, must be to look beyond the aggregate form of the assemblages and evaluate the nature of and degree to which multiple sources of variation have contributed to the final form of the observations (Binford 1984a:166). In other words, analysis should be directed toward describing the structure of interassemblage variability by making "second- and third-order observations" of the archaeological record (Spaulding 1954; Binford 1989a:35–36, 276–278).

The term "structure of variability" as used here refers to the manner in which interassemblage variability—the variability in assemblage composition between archaeological levels at a site—is organized (Binford and Binford 1966; Binford 1987b, 1989a:267–268, 1989b). Specifically, what are the patterns of covariation between different classes of artifacts and remains, and what implications do these patterns carry for the multiple agents that contributed to the composite structure of the assemblages? For example, what classes of lithic remains covary between archaeological levels? How are events involving lithic tools and lithic waste related? What covariant relationships are observed between classes of faunal remains? What relationships are observed between different classes of remains, such as between lithics and various animal species or between stone tools and specific anatomical elements of the primary subsistence species?

These relationships between different kinds of materials and behaviors are collectively referred to as organizational properties (chapter 1), and it is in terms of organizational properties that the archaeological record must be understood:

> One could document the use of stone pebbles to smooth pottery, shells to scrape it, wood to support a vessel being built, even stone tools or antler tools used in procuring clay and decorating pots. *The archaeological record was produced in the context of many variable ways of organizing natural materials,* including the organization of human labor itself. *It could therefore be profitably explored for patterning in terms of relationships among different things* for the purpose of understanding how the past was organized (Binford 1989a:270, emphasis added).

3.3 Conclusions

The primary conclusion developed in this chapter is that contemporary middle-range research has not yet provided robust and accurate knowledge of the interaction between long-term climatic change, the onset of ice-age conditions, and the organizational properties of cultural systems. Actualistic studies of the adaptations by human groups to an increasingly arid and cool climate are impractical. Accounts of historical changes in climate such as the Little Ice Age, the Dust Bowl in the American Midwest, and the extended drought in the African Sahara, may eventually prove to be relevant sources of "delayed" actualistic information on the effects of climatic change on the organization of human groups, but these events are not reviewed here. Generalizations drawn from the variation in modern hunter-gatherer societies with effective temperature suggest several potentially testable expectations for the archaeological variability conditioned by organizational changes in past systems in response to climatic change, but the observations mandated by these arguments cannot at present be made in sufficient quantity or detail at Grubgraben.

In summary, the position argued here is that although we may *imagine* a number of adaptive responses by past systems to a climate that became steadily cooler and drier, and although we may *guess* at the archaeological consequences of these cultural adaptations, the contemporary world does not offer observable situations that are completely satisfactory for learning about the effects of such climatic change on the organization of human groups, and from which to develop relevant controls and recognition criteria (Binford 1984b:15, 1983c:390). Consequently the investigation of climatically conditioned archaeological variability during the Last Glacial Maximum cannot take the form of "asserting hypotheses" and "deducing test implications".

In the absence of relevant or accessible middle-range experiences a pattern recognition strategy was indicated as the most productive means of pursing the research goal. A consideration of the archaeological variability that can be expected at residential sites versus special-purpose sites suggested that the relevant observations in a pattern recognition approach should be those of the structure of interassemblage variability at a multi-component residential site such as Grubgraben at which the dynamics of local climatic change are independently understood.

Finally, it should be pointed out that the use of ethnographic analogs, ethnoarchaeological data, site comparisons, or any other relevant body of knowledge, has not been rejected. These are all forms of the "knowledge of the moment" (Binford 1984b:9–17) that must be appealed to in the interpretation of archaeological patterning when such patterning is not otherwise understood as the result of known processes. In this chapter it has been argued only that *there is no contemporary context in which to observe the effects of an increasingly cool and arid ice-age climate on the organization of hunter-gatherer groups and develop recognition criteria for the archaeological variability that results.*

In retrospect, the requirements of a multi-component residential site and an independently reconstructed pattern of climatic change can be seen as kinds of "prior knowledge" that guided the choice of Grubgraben as an archaeological test case from which to learn about the responses of hunter-gatherer systems to a changing environment. The decisions to adopt a pattern recognition strategy, examine the structure of residential interassemblage variability, and elicit the organizational properties of the archaeological record, now point to a specific analytical approach.

4.0 Quantitative Procedure

The arguments of the last chapter established that the relevant data for elucidating diachronic change in the overall adaptation of a hunter-gatherer system are found in the structure of interassemblage variability at a multi-component residential site. This conclusion has direct implications for the analytical strategies needed to "observe" interassemblage variability and its organizational properties, and suggests the use of a specific quantitative method.

4.1 Structural versus Classificatory Analysis

Fundamental to the study of interassemblage variability is the acceptance of the archaeological record as a complex mix of materials resulting from a variety of activities and processes which, in turn, are conditioned by a variety of cultural and natural factors (Binford 1978a:357). Minimally, variability in the location, assemblage content, and internal organization of a site is expected to be conditioned by the activities performed at the site. These activities themselves may be responsive to many different factors, such as seasonal variables (e.g., spring versus winter occupations), the character of the tasks performed (e.g., extractive versus maintenance tasks), and the function of the site within the larger subsistence-settlement system (e.g., residential versus special-purpose sites). The function of a site can also be expected to change as the "economic zonation" (Binford 1983b) of the landscape is modified in response to organizational changes in the overall settlement-subsistence systems, or in response to the repositioning of these systems without significant internal restructuring (Binford and Binford 1966; Cowgill 1968; Jochim 1976, 1981, 1991; Albrecht et al. 1976; Binford 1978a,b, 1980, 1983a,c, 1989a; Whallon 1984; Read 1985; White 1987; Chatters 1987; Kelly 1992, 1995).

This view of the archaeological record as a complex product of many processes, acting both independently and in combination, has significant implications for the methods needed to investigate its structure. Most archaeologists would probably agree that it is naïve to expect customarily collected data, such as frequencies in some set of lithic and faunal categories, to be singly and directly informative of the complex processes structuring a particular archaeological deposit. Perhaps the main reason for this lack of correspondence is that the taxonomies used to organize and standardize archaeological data collection [e.g., the Upper Paleolithic type list (de Sonneville Bordes and Perrot (1954–56)] are instruments for measurement with ambiguous meanings (Binford 1973:234–235, 1973:249, 1989a:277; Schiffer 1975; Dewez 1982; Binford and Sabloff 1982; Read 1985).

A more realistic expectation is that the variables measured and the attributes recorded by archaeologists are in some ways independent of one another, monitoring events and processes that operated independently in the past, and are in other ways dependent, monitoring quantities that were organized in some common context of use in the past (e.g., were treated similarly, or were consistently used together) (Binford 1965, 1972, 1973, 1983a,c, 1989a; Binford and Binford 1966; Cowgill 1968:371; Schiffer 1975; Whallon 1984):

Since a summary description of a given assemblage represents a blending of activity units and their determinants, it becomes essential to partition assemblages of artifacts into groups of artifacts that vary together, reflecting activities (Binford and Binford 1966:241).

The above argument may benefit from a non-archaeological illustration. Manly (1986, chapter 5) demonstrates how a set of five metrical variables, each measuring a different anatomical dimension in a sample of sparrows, are reduced by principle components analysis to a single composite variable that is convincingly interpreted as "body size". The composite variable "body size" accounts for more than 70% of the variation in the original five metrical variables. Clearly "body size" is an empirical quantity that is in principle quantifiable, but may not be easily or effectively measured in practice. Essentially equivalent information is obtained, however, from a linear combination of five separate and more easily measured metrical variables.

The situation with archaeological data is believed to be similar. We expect that there are certain variables that, if they could be measured in practice, would be directly informative of the character of the processes and organizational principles that structure a given assemblage. The variables we are able to measure, however, are typically ones such as frequencies or weights for specified classes of remains, values for metrical properties of artifacts, artifact attributes, and so on. We may suspect that each of these directly measurable quantities is in a sense "measuring around" a smaller number of organizationally informative composite variables, in the same way that a series of linear body dimensions are "measuring around" the anatomically informative dimension of "body size". Provided the organizationally informative composite variables can be constructed as *linear* combinations of the original variables, then a technique such as principle components analysis or factor analysis should be successful in identifying them. Of course, if the important relationships in the data are non-linear in nature, then techniques that are based on linear models of variation (such as principle components analysis and factor analysis) will not detect them (Christensen 1991:125). In cases where the form of the underlying relationships is *a priori* known or suspected, a suitable transformation of the original data may linearize the relationships and so enable their detection (Kendall 1980:28). For example, Binford (1981:263, 1987a:481–482) attempts to linearize the suspected curvilinear relationships in a set of faunal data by applying a logarithmic transformation to the data before conducting a factor analysis. Based on substantial prior experience the underlying relationships in the data were strongly suspected to be curvilinear, yet factor analysis is based on a model of linear variation. Binford's use of a logarithmic transformation represents an effort to bring the data into line with the assumptions of the statistical method, and is a good example of using prior knowledge of the structure of the data to select appropriate methods and conduct appropriate analyses (Christenson and Reed 1977; Carr 1984, 1985).

To effectively address processual questions with conventionally reported archaeological data, analytical techniques are needed that are capable of isolating independent dimensions of variability in the data. Methods must be sought that construct new "views" into a data set using weighted combinations of the variables originally observed by the archaeologist (Binford 1965, 1972:264–266, 1973; 1978a:336–338, 1983:148; Binford and Binford 1966; Doran and Hodson 1975; Cowgill 1986; Read 1985; Harpending and Rogers 1985). Multivariate approaches that provide structural simplification of complex data sets and are therefore best suited to the study of interassemblage variability include: factor analysis (e.g., Binford and Binford 1966; Vierra 1975; Schiffer 1975; Doran and Hodson 1975:197–205; Freeman 1978; Binford 1987a; many additional references are given in Vierra and Carlson 1981); principle components analysis (e.g., White and Thomas 1972; Doran and Hodson 1975:190–197; Thomas 1978; Montet-White and Johnson 1976; Whallon 1984; Harpending and Rogers 1985:66–73; Binford 1987b, 1989b); and multidimensional scaling (Cowgill 1968:373–374; Doran and Hodson 1975:213–217; Harpending and Rogers 1985:73–82). These methods are broadly similar in that they are designed to achieve structural simplification of a complex data set by analyzing the linear dependencies between the original variables and partitioning the total variability in the data into multiple, independently operating sources of variation. If there are no linear dependencies among the variables (i.e., if the original variables are totally uncorrelated with one another), then composite variables cannot be defined (Doran and Hodson 1975:187–217; Kendall 1980; Manly 1986; Christensen 1991).

In contrast, the challenge of recognizing and interpreting processual variability and structure in archaeological data cannot be productively treated as a problem in classification. Consequently, multivariate classificatory techniques such as numerical taxonomy, cluster analysis, or discriminant function analysis are completely unsuited to the recognition of the multiple and independently operating processes structuring a set of data. Classificatory or taxonomic methods can only assign cases to groups based on similarity criteria imposed by the investigator and cannot elucidate independently operating sources of variation:

> Any taxonomy is an instrument for measurement, and unless we know what it is we are measuring any statements concerning the meaning of the various groupings of empirical data produced by the taxonomy remains [sic] sheer guesswork. Arranging archaeological data according to a taxonomy can contribute nothing to our knowledge of the past (Binford 1969:299).

Successful taxonomies may bring forth apparent order from disorder, yet it is precisely the resulting order which is presumably a product of cultural and natural processes and in need of explanation by reference to processual factors if the past is to be implicated (Spaulding 1960, 1977; Binford 1965, 1973; Christenson and Read 1977; Aldenderfer and Blashfield 1978; Whallon 1982, 1984).

Some archaeologists may object that all studies are ultimately taxonomic in nature because at some level they must rest on the classificatory foundation used as an observational language. For example, the lithic category of "scraper" is an observational taxon that subsumes those lithic items exhibiting a widely agreed-upon suite of attributes and range of variable values (e.g., shape of working edge, angle of working edge, type of retouch). Thus any study involving the item "scraper" must be ultimately taxonomic in nature.

This objection fails to recognize, however, that the inappropriateness of classificatory approaches for the study of archaeological process is directed at *the form of the analytical manipulation of the observational categories,* and not at the fact that a classificatory observational language is used to define and organize the data. In other words, the continued classification alone of observational categories by whatever means (e.g., cluster analysis, discriminant function analysis, numerical taxonomy) remains an exercise in the grouping of observations according to formal similarity criteria, and so cannot recognize or report the interaction of "dissimilar" categories. To address issues of process and processual variability the structure and interaction between the observational categories must be investigated, using multivariate methods of structural analysis and simplification to learn, for example, how a taxon such as "scraper" participates with other observational taxa.

One of the conclusions reached in chapter 3 was that a pattern recognition strategy would be the most productive approach for investigating interassemblage variability in the absence of relevant middle-range experiences regarding the effects of long-term climatic change on the organizational properties of hunter-gatherer societies. There are then two principles that any pattern recognition approach is well advised to follow.

First, there is much to recommend the view that pattern recognition studies in general will be most effective when analytical techniques are held constant and various representations of the data are submitted for analysis (Binford 1987a:478–479). By adopting a uniform, descriptive, structure-oriented, and well understood methodology, a potentially confusing or misleading source of variation in the results of the analyses is eliminated. By varying the classificatory language used to summarize and describe the data, the effectiveness of the pattern recognition strategy is maximized and the ability to recognize robust structure in the data is increased.

Furthermore, because knowledge of the past is something we seek to acquire rather than assume, it is most productive to adopt an exploratory and descriptive approach to data analysis rather than a formal hypothesis testing strategy (Binford 1987a; Carr 1984, 1985, 1991; Tukey 1977; Tukey and Wilk 1970; P. Gould 1970, 1981). This attitude runs counter to the conventional wisdom of hypothesis testing in which analytical methods are matched to expectations (e.g., Carr 1984; cf. Carr 1985, 1991) but is a more reasonable posture for archaeologists given that the challenge in pattern recognition work is one of interpretation and inductive inference rather than identification (Binford 1977a, 1987a:465–466, 1987b:64). Not all archaeological analysis is necessarily pattern recognitive, but formal hypothesis testing cannot proceed without knowledge of the causal relationships between process and product—knowledge from which binding expectations under the stated hypothesis can be deduced. This kind of knowledge is exceptional in current archaeology. In the absence of robust knowledge of cultural and non-cultural processes and their archaeological patterning, any expectations that are "deduced" from a hypothesis can be nothing more than guesses about the form of the archaeological record. Thus much of what is offered as "hypothesis testing" in archaeology involves only arguments of relevance, debates over criteria for identification, and tests of the "goodness-of-fit" between an imagined past and the empirical archaeological present (Binford 1977a, 1983c:67, 1983c:391–392).

For these reasons the quantitative manipulation of the data on interassemblage variability is kept simple and descriptive, and a single multivariate procedure similar to ordinary principle components analysis is used. The principle components approach is chosen over factor analysis and multidimensional scaling because it is one of the simplest multivariate methods; it is not based on any particular statistical model as is factor analysis; it provides results in a more convenient form than does multidimensional scaling; and it constructs composite variables, or dimensions, which are less objectionable from statistical theoretical and interpretive standpoints than the common factors resulting from a factor analysis (Manly 1986:84; Kendall 1980:59; Christensen 1991:107–143; Krzanowski 1988:481–483; Harpending and Rogers 1985:71). Unfortunately these distinctions are not always recognized or appreciated, and principle components analysis has often been dismissed in the same breath with factor analysis (e.g., Vierra and Carlson 1981; Whallon 1984).

4.2 The Harpending-Rogers Method

The quantitative approach to the analysis of interassemblage variability used here is a multivariate descriptive procedure suggested by Harpending and Rogers (1985). The procedure is similar to ordinary principle components analysis, and is accurately described as a scaled principle components analysis of normalized frequency data.

A similar technique, known as R-matrix analysis, was introduced into population genetics studies by Harpending in 1973 (Harpending and Jenkins 1973) and differs from the present method only in the normalization of the raw data. The R-matrix approach (and the method used here) has a number of advantages over ordinary principle components analysis (Harpending and Jenkins 1973), and has since been widely and very successfully applied in population genetics studies.

Previous archaeological applications and discussions of the Harpending-Rogers method include: an analysis of interassemblage variability at Olorgesailie (Harpending and Rogers 1985) and at Torralba (Binford 1987b); clarification of faunal-stratigraphic relationships at Klasies River Mouth (Binford 1986b); and a study of the changing organization of stone tool technology between the Bed I and Bed II deposits at Olduvai Gorge (Binford 1989b). Additional examples of the normalization procedure used in the Harpending-Rogers method to prepare raw frequency data for multivariate analysis are found in Binford (1986a), Binford and Stone (1986), and Todd (1987).

It should be pointed out that Binford (1986b, 1987b, 1989b) repeatedly refers to the Harpending-Rogers method as the "singular-value decomposition of chi-squares". This nomenclature is unfortunate, however, because "chi-squares" in the strict sense are not required at any point in the analysis, and "singular-value decomposition" (Horn and Johnson 1985; Press et al. 1989) is not a statistical procedure, but a matrix decomposition technique having many applications. The method is referred to here simply as a "principle components analysis of normalized frequency data", or as the "Harpending-Rogers" method.

4.2.1 Conducting an Analysis

The programs required for conducting a Harpending-Rogers analysis are available as part of the ANTANA (ANThropological ANAlysis) exploratory statistical package developed and distributed by Henry Harpending and Alan Rogers (Harpending and Rogers 1985). A complete analysis is conducted using two procedures, CHISC and SVD, from the ANTANA library: CHISC (CHI-SCore) is invoked to transform the raw frequency data, then SVD (Singular-Value Decomposition) is invoked to extract and scale the principle components. Harpending and Rogers (1985:66–82) provide a complete tutorial demonstration of the procedure using data on interassemblage variability at Olorgesailie. Applications by Binford (1986b, 1987b, 1989b) are additional sources of raw data, results, and interpretation. The procedures described by these authors were followed after confirming the operations of data transformation and analysis using published data and results.

4.2.2 Data Normalization

An elegant and powerful feature of the Harpending-Rogers approach is the initial transformation of the data (using the CHISC procedure in ANTANA) from an array of raw artifact frequencies to an array of *chi-scores* before principle components are extracted using the SVD procedure. [Note that Binford and Stone (1986), Binford (1986b, 1987b, 1989b), and Todd (1987:254) erroneously refer to these normalized frequencies as *chi-squares*, but they are actually the positive square roots of the more familiar chi-square values. Their computation is correctly described, however, by Harpending and Rogers (1985:36–37) and Binford and Stone (1986:456)]. A chi-score can be thought of as the equivalent for frequency data of the z-score (standard score) used for standardizing continuous data. The transformation of raw frequencies to their chi-scores prior to constructing principle components accomplishes two important things.

As with continuous data and their z-scores, the transformation of frequency data to chi-scores ensures that any scale effects among the variables are removed prior to the construction of principle components. This form of data normalization is loosely referred to as controlling for "sample-size effects" (e.g., Binford 1987b, 1989b), but is better described as removing the variance in the data that is contributed by variability in the scale of measurement among the variables. Principle components analysis is *not* invariant under a change of scale of the variables, and the problem of scale becomes especially critical if the components are to be eventually interpreted and assigned meanings (Kendall 1980:19–23; Manly 1986:63). Following the transformation of raw frequencies to chi-scores, however, all variables are on equal footing with respect to scale of measurement and receive equal weight in the construction of the principle components.

In the Grubgraben data, for example, counts of reindeer remains are typically many times larger than counts for any other quantity, consequently the variance in counts of reindeer remains is much larger than the variance of any other variable. This is a scale effect, and it should be removed prior to analysis:

> This variance may arise from numerous conditions that do not interest archaeologists at this stage of pattern recognition study. Some units may be small in terms of size of excavation, or variable in size as a result of differential placement of past occupations relative to the particular "grid squares" excavated through a stratified deposit. Such variance may well be a function of excavation strategy, and we do not want to confuse this patterning with patterning that might result from organized dynamics in the past (Binford 1987b:63).

The transformation to chi-scores ensures that variables with consistently large counts (e.g., reindeer remains) do not overwhelm variables with consistently small counts (e.g., small mammal remains) and unduly influence the construction of principle components. Without some form of transformation, the variance contributed by scale effects among the variables can overwhelm the more meaningful variance in the data that is presumably referable to processes of archaeological interest (cf. Plog and Hegmon 1993).

The second important advantage gained by the transformation of the raw frequency data to their chi-scores is appreciated by interpreting the raw data array as a contingency table between archaeological assemblages and variables. Each chi-score in the transformed data array represents the weighted deviation of an original frequency from the count that would be expected under the null hypothesis of independence between cases and variables. Archaeologically interpreted, independence between cases and variables implies that variation in the variables (e.g., lithic classes) is not a useful predictor of variation in cases (e.g., assemblages). In other words, the hypothesis of independence between cases and variables amounts to a statement that all cases are identical with respect to the variables and vary only in size (Binford 1989b:441). The chi-score used in the Harpending-Rogers method is thus a measure of the variability that is referable to the lack of independence between variables and cases, and this is information that should be of direct processual significance.

4.3 Interpretation of Results

The result of applying the Harpending-Rogers method to a data set organized as values of variables across a series of cases is a set of principle components, or composite variables [also referred to as "pseudo-variables" (Harpending and Rogers 1985:69), "dimensional scores for variables" (Binford 1989b:441), or "dimensions of variability"]. These composite variables are the linearly weighted combinations of the original variables that are most efficient in explaining the variance in the data set. The weights of the original variables on the composite variables [these weights would be called "loadings" in the jargon of factor analysis (Kendall 1980:49)] are essentially covariances between the composite variables and the original variables (Doran and Hodson 1975:197; Krzanowski 1988:63).

To infer the meaning of a composite variable, its structure must be examined and interpreted by the archaeologist. The interpretation of a composite variable is guided by the expectation that those original variables which covary directly (i.e., are similarly weighted, positively or negatively) on a given component are likely to have been treated in similar ways in the past (Cowgill 1968:371; Schiffer 1975; Binford 1987a:479). That is, quantities which covary strongly are expected to be related in some way; we certainly do not interpret covariant variables as independent and unrelated. For example, if burins and backed bladelets exhibit similarly large weights (either positive or negative, but of the same sign) on a given principle component, then they are expected to have been similarly organized in whatever past process or events led to their deposition; it makes no sense to argue that burins and backed bladelets were totally unrelated or were organized in independent contexts. If this guiding principle leads to inaccurate or misleading conclusions, it is a shortcoming of our pattern-recognitive and -interpretive skills and of the "knowledge of the moment" (Binford 1984b:9–17, 1987b:64) that is appealed to in the development of interpretations and the assignment of meaning.

These concerns have been addressed before with regard to factor analysis of interassemblage variability:

> One hopes that it makes sense to regard those variables which share a high loading on the same factor as being measures of some single underlying entity, or, at any rate, as being somehow closely associated with one another (Cowgill 1968:371).

> Our analysis does not provide information as to the particular activity represented by a factor; it simply allows us to identify a regular relationship between a number of artifact types. Our identification of the function of a factor depends on analogy with the tools of living peoples, tool wear, and associations with refuse. Whether or not our interpretation of a factor in terms of function is correct, this does not affect the demonstrable relationship between the variables analyzed (Binford and Binford 1966:243).

Binford and Binford (1966) explicitly separate the task of recognizing patterns from the task of interpreting patterns: patterned relationships are recognized and investigated through the use of quantitative methods, but the meanings of the patterns must come from the archaeologist and are necessarily based on theoretical arguments, analogies, actualistic knowledge, associations with other artifacts, features, and patterns, and so on. As discussed in chapter 3, these are all aspects of the "knowledge of the moment" (Binford 1984b:9–17) that is appealed to in pattern recognition studies.

A distinction that often will be necessary in the discussion and interpretation of the dimensions of interassemblage variability is that between the "importance" and the "information" of the variables chosen for analysis. The former is a cultural valuation, the latter is a statistical measure, and the two are not necessarily congruent.

For example, classes of remains such as "bone tools" or "reindeer mandibles" may have been of great importance in the adaptation of hunter-gatherer groups at Grubgraben, yet these same variables may be relatively uninformative for describing the variation observed between assemblages, i.e., of little use in distinguishing one archaeological level from another. All other things being equal, we might even expect that many "culturally important" classes of remains may prove to be statistically uninformative for distinguishing assemblages exactly because they are "important" and are represented in relatively constant frequencies in each level.

On the other hand, a variable such as "isolated reindeer teeth" may *prima facie* seem unimportant for understanding the organizational properties of a hunter-gatherer system, yet prove to be highly informative for describing the variation between assemblages.

The distinction between cultural importance and statistical information is important because the quantitative method used here identifies those suites of variables which are most informative in a statistical sense for describing interassemblage variation. There is, however, no necessary relation between variables that are most informative and those that are most "important" in the past cultural system. Keeping in mind this caveat often resolves apparently ambiguous or contradictory structure in the principle component solutions.

4.4 Robusticity of the Solutions

Experimentation with the Harpending-Rogers method, using a variety of data sets with widely differing numbers of cases and variables, has repeatedly indicated that the patterning disclosed by the procedure is remarkably robust not only to variations in the number and definition of the variables but also to the inclusion or exclusion of variables with minor numerical representation. In the analyses reported here, therefore, variables with very small or zero numerical representation in all archaeological levels were either combined with related variables or were simply omitted from the analysis.

As a means of estimating the amount of interassemblage variability that might be referable to recovery bias between the 1986–1987 and 1989–1990 excavation campaigns, reduced data sets comprising only the artifact frequencies for trenches K, L, M, and N (Haesaerts 1990b: Figure III-7; Brandtner 1989: Figure 2) were analyzed and compared to the results obtained using data from all seasons of excavation. The definition of the principle components for the reduced and full data sets were remarkably similar, however, and all subsequent analyses were therefore conducted using data from all four seasons of excavation.

4.5 Surrogate Scale/Sample Size Effects

Although transformation of the original frequency data to chi-scores eliminates the variance in the data contributed by differences in the scale of measurement of the variables (or, loosely speaking, removes "sample size effects"), Binford (1986b, 1989b) has argued that it may not remove the variance contributed by other properties of the data that also scale with sample size. One such source of a secondary sample size effect is termed an "autocorrelation with diversity" (Binford 1986b, 1989b:445). The nature of this effect is for variation in assemblage diversity (Pielou 1975, 1977; Kintigh 1984; Rhode 1988) to behave as a surrogate for variation in sample size, thereby introducing a scale effect even when data have been properly transformed to their chi-scores.

Surrogate covariation with sample size may also be introduced by the variation in the temporal span, or "collection time", represented by the assemblages, even if the sample size taken from each assemblage is held constant (Binford 1986b:512; Grayson 1984). Consequently, properly transformed data from assemblages that accumulated over different intervals of time may continue to exhibit variation with sample size because of the differences in assemblage diversity created by the varying collection times.

These relationships between diversity and sample size, and diversity and sampling time, are well understood in ecology and are actually of utility in designing field collection programs (Odum 1971; Cox 1980). In archaeology, however, although the concept and measurement of diversity has received much attention recently (Conkey 1980; Kintigh 1984; Shott 1989; Leonard and Jones 1989), the cultural and environmental factors conditioning diversity in archaeological assemblages are not well understood (Binford 1982b:179, 1983c:393, 1986b:512; Rindos 1989:18; Dunnell 1989; Cowgill 1989). Consequently, any variance in the data that is diversity-mediated and is not removed by the transformation to chi-scores may be difficult to interpret.

It is a simple matter to determine whether secondary sample size effects are present in a principle components solution by plotting the principle component weights against the respective case sample sizes. If the weights on a given principle component are found to scale with sample size, then other properties of the data, such as diversity, *may* be acting as proxies for sample size, and it *may* be nonsensical to attempt an interpretation of the component in organizational terms. Ecological, taphonomic, or other processes could instead be responsible for the observed structure of the principle component.

In his multivariate analysis of the Klasies River Mouth data, for example, Binford (1986b:512–513) argues that the first principle component actually represents an "autocorrelation with diversity" effect, and therefore cannot be interpreted in terms of organizational changes. His Figure 1, however, which is presented as evidence for the dependence on sample size of the first principle component scores, is unconvincing. The figure in fact indicates a complete lack of dependence of the principle component scores on sample size (Spearman's rho = 0.0245, $p = 0.9397$, $n = 12$; Kendall's tau = 0.0458, $p = 0.8358$, $n = 12$), and the first principle component reported by Binford

(1986b:513, Table 2) is clearly separating grassland and cover-loving fauna.

Nevertheless, the interpretation Binford provides for his first principle component appears to be fully justified: the first principle component reveals "not a structural relationship extant in the past but a relationship referable to the nature of the samples remaining from the past" (Binford 1986b:514). In other words, the first principle component in Binford's analysis is more informative of relationships of animal ecology rather than of organizational relationships between hominids and animals. This is obvious, however, by inspecting the structure of the component.

Binford's concern regarding the ability of other properties of the data to behave as proxies for measurement scale or sample size is well taken, however, and each dimension of variation extracted by the principle components analysis should be examined for variation with sample size. This is quickly and effectively accomplished by plotting the principle component weights for each case against the respective case totals, or against one of the conventional measures of collection diversity (Pielou 1975, 1977). If a patterned relationship is detected, the given principle component may primarily be summarizing the variance due to differences in assemblage diversity or to differences in some other assemblage property that also scales with sample size. In these cases the principle component should *not* be discarded out-of-hand, because it may well be reporting information of interest. Its interpretation should proceed, however, with an awareness of potential sample-size- or diversity-mediated effects (Plog and Hegmon 1993).

In the analysis of interassemblage variability at Grubgraben the strength of any surrogate (e.g., diversity-mediated) relationship between principle component scores and sample size is assessed by computing correlation coefficients. Two non-parametric rank-order measures of correlation are used: Spearman's rho and Kendall's tau (Snedecor and Cochran 1980:191–193; Press et al. 1989:532–543). These statistics have two major advantages over parametric measures such as Pearson's product-moment correlation coefficient r. First, the statistical significance of these coefficients can be accurately determined even though the distributions of sample sizes in the data on assemblage composition are generally markedly right-skewed. Second, because the relationship between diversity and sample size or between diversity and sampling time is usually exponential or logarithmic in nature (Pielou 1977; Jones et al. 1983; Leonard and Jones 1989), it is arguable as to whether correlations should be determined (or plots prepared) using raw sample sizes or the logarithms of sample size. The use of rank-order statistics renders this concern moot, because such measures are invariant under monotonic transformations of the data. Thus the same value for the statistic is obtained whether raw sample sizes or the logarithms of sample size are correlated with the principle component scores.

5.0 INTERASSEMBLAGE VARIABILITY AT GRUBGRABEN

In this and the following two chapters a multivariate quantitative analysis of interassemblage variability at Grubgraben is presented. The analysis is performed using the Harpending-Rogers method (Harpending and Rogers 1985) discussed in chapter 4 for the structural simplification of multivariate frequency data.

Two separate analytical tasks are involved in the recognition of the variability between archaeological assemblages that is conditioned by the local and organizational responses of hunter-gatherer systems to climatic change during the Last Glacial Maximum. The first task, and the subject of this chapter, is the analysis of interassemblage variability to elucidate organizational relations between different classes of remains. The result of this part of the analysis will be the recognition and interpretation of various organizational properties that structure the assemblages.

The second analytical task, and the subject of chapters 6 and 7, is the inspection of these organizational properties for patterned diachronic change. In other words, how do the assemblages from the four episodes of occupation at Grubgraben differ when they are "measured" on the organizational relations recognized in the first part of the analysis? It is diachronic change in the organizational structure of the assemblages from the site that is ultimately expected to be conditioned by local and extra-assemblage factors such as climatic change or intra-site functional variability.

The remainder of this chapter is devoted to the first aspect of the study: the analysis of interassemblage variability and the recognition and interpretation of the organizational relations that structure assemblage composition. Following Binford (1987a,b, 1989b) the analysis is conducted in several stages, and new variables (classes of remains) or combinations of variables are introduced at each stage. The variables used in any given stage of analysis represent a specific way of conceptualizing and describing the assemblage inventories. By varying the classificatory language used to summarize assemblage content, yet maintaining a uniform descriptive analytical procedure, the analysis is able to implicate the properties selected for manipulation and the strength of the pattern recognition strategy is increased (Binford 1987a:465–466, 478–482, 493).

Obviously the specific classificatory schemes used in the analysis can be debated *ad nauseam;* the important point is that patterning in the data be examined using a variety of observational languages:

> It is almost trivial to comment that any item or entity can be considered to have a potential infinity of attributes in terms of which it might be classified. Basic to archaeology is the stage of research when we *decide* which attributes to use and how they are to be arranged for use in classificatory schemes. .... In this situation, the archaeologist uses judgment, based on his/her current knowledge of how the world works, as a guide for selecting the properties of "things" to be used in generating classifications. Always we must face uncertainty, is our knowledge adequate and relevant to the actual processes of the concrete world that we seek to know and measure? (Binford 1987a:478–479, original emphasis).

The analysis of interassemblage variability therefore uses varying but conventionally defined lithic and faunal categories as well as additional classes of remains that exhibit variation among the archaeological deposits. However, many kinds of data are not included: for example, worked and unworked dentalia are not distinguished; some faunal species represented at the site are not included; first, second, and third phalanges are not separately tabulated; bone and antler tools at Grubgraben are not examined with reference to other sites and established typologies; and spatial distributions of the artifacts and features are not investigated in detail. That such decisions must be made is hardly a weakness of the study; choices of data and method are necessary in any quantitative analysis.

In the first stage of analysis the data on assemblage composition are examined using a small number of general classes of remains to obtain an initial impression of the patterned variability between assemblages. Because this stage of analysis also serves to introduce the procedures for interpretation of the principle components, greater attention is given to certain methodological details in the discussion of the results of the first stage than will be necessary with subsequent stages.

The structure of interassemblage variability in the lithic inventories is examined next, using a data set comprising frequencies in various classes of tools and waste for each archaeological level. Patterns of covariation elicited at this stage are informative of the organized use of different tool classes, and of the organization of tools and non-tool items such as cores and classes of debitage.

A third analysis is conducted of the variability in anatomical part frequencies for the two focal subsistence species at the site, reindeer and horse. Patterns of covariation in classes of faunal elements from horse and reindeer are informative of the ways in which different anatomical elements of these animals were organized, and of the differential treatment of these species from assemblage to assemblage.

In the fourth and final stage of analysis the lithic and faunal data sets of stages 2 and 3, respectively, are combined and the structure of interassemblage lithic-faunal variability is investigated. Having previously examined in separate analyses the variability in lithic and faunal remains, the study and interpretation of their joint covariant patterning becomes more meaningful and informed.

It is convenient to present all four stages of the analysis of interassemblage variability (chapter 5) before moving to the second part of the study and examining the organizational relations from any specific stage for patterned variation in response to climatic change (chapters 6 and 7). The reason for this is that the organizational patterns recognized in one stage of analysis are often found to refine or clarify the interpretation of the patterns elicited in other stages of analysis. Once all the organizational relations from the four stages of analysis of interassemblage variability have been discussed, they are reviewed and examined for diachronic change in chapters 6 and 7.

5.1 Analysis Stage 1: General Classes of Remains

The first stage of analysis is introductory and intended to provide an overview of the major organizational relations that structure interassemblage variability. The archaeological deposits are summarized in terms of a small number of broadly defined classes of remains and several composite variables, or dimensions of variation, are elicited. Subsequent stages of analysis will explore in greater detail the patterns of covariation in separate and combined lithic and faunal inventories. The patterns elicited in these later stages, however, are often found to complement or contribute details to a fundamentally small number of broad organizational relations between the assemblages. In this respect the introductory analysis is the most important stage, providing both an initial assessment of interassemblage variability and supplying a backdrop for interpreting the results of subsequent stages of analysis.

5.1.1 Description of the Data

Frequencies were tabulated for the following classes of artifacts and remains in each archaeological level: bone tools (implements of bone, antler, and ivory); shell; quartz objects; lithic tools; lithic waste; cobbles and hammerstones; reindeer (Rangifer and cf. Rangifer remains); horse (Equus and cf. Equus remains); small mammals (Alopex, Lepus, and cf. Lepus remains); mammoth; nondiagnostic faunal specimens. NISP values (number of identifiable specimens) were tabulated in the faunal categories for reasons discussed below; simple counts were used for the remaining classes. The resulting array of frequencies, comprising 11 variables and 4 cases (archaeological levels AL1–AL4), is given in Table 5.1.1.

The class of lithic tools comprises tool types 1 to 92 in the list of de Sonneville-Bordes and Perrot (1954–56); all other lithic items are combined in the category of lithic waste. The quartz artifacts are mostly large cortical flakes, shatter, and small retouched flakes (Hill 1993), but include a few quartz tools as well (Montet-White 1990d:133–136).

Frequencies in the faunal classes were tabulated from data made available by West (1995) and Logan (1990a,b). Reindeer bones overwhelmingly predominate in every level at Grubgraben, reaching their greatest abundance in AL3. A lesser but nevertheless substantial amount of faunal material in each level is contributed by the class of nondiagnostic remains. This class comprises highly fragmented bones that are difficult to identify as to taxon or skeletal element, although based on the thickness of the specimens most of the nondiagnostic material is believed to be smashed reindeer bones (West, personal communication 1994; West 1995).

Following reindeer and nondiagnostic faunal material in frequency is the class of horse remains; these are most numerous in levels AL3 and AL4, but are an important component of the faunal assemblage in the other levels as well. The smaller, fur-bearing animals such as Alopex and Lepus are also present in all levels: Alopex is represented exclusively by isolated teeth except for five specimens from AL3 that are mandibular or postcranial fragments; Lepus remains are more numerous and varied. Mammoth remains are present in all levels at Grubgraben but only as fragments of ivory, and the status of mammoth as an economically important species is doubtful (Logan 1990a; West 1995).

Of the 44,079 specimens of bone recorded in the databases provided by West (1995) and Logan (1990a,b), 41,850 are represented by the frequencies in Table 5.1.1. The only faunal species identified at Grubgraben by West (1995) that are not included in Table 5.1.1 are those with very minor representation [Canis, Ursus, Ibex, unspecified large mammals (cf. Bos/Equus), and unspecified bovids]. Ursus and Canis are quite rare, represented only by an incisor for the former and a calcaneus and long bone fragment for the latter. The NISP values for ibex, bovids, and large mammals are small and do not contribute significantly to the structure of interassemblage variability.

Table 5.1.1. Analysis Stage 1: Frequencies in General Classes of Remains.

Level	Bone tools	Shell	Quartz	Lithic tools	Lithic waste	Reindeer
AL1	5	109	82	207	1505	1697
AL2	6	53	101	116	866	3547
AL3	21	115	204	186	1578	16009
AL4	16	18	462	235	2374	9243

Level	Horse	Nondiagnostic bones	Small mammals	Mammoth	Cobbles
AL1	126	1174	76	3	16
AL2	89	2241	7	12	32
AL3	328	5377	36	34	48
AL4	431	1310	5	57	30

Numbers of identifiable specimens (NISP) have been used to summarize the Grubgraben archaeofauna rather than minimum numbers of individuals (MNI), minimum animal units (MAU), minimum number of elements (MNE), or some other index of faunal representation. The relative merits and demerits of these and other indices of faunal abundance and faunal assemblage composition have been discussed at length (Binford 1978b:69–72, 1978b:478–479, 1981, 1982b, 1984b:48–51; Klein and Cruz-Uribe 1984; Grayson 1984; Ringrose 1993), and it is recognized that different indices may yield conflicting results. The choice of NISP for the present analysis is motivated by several considerations: its ease of collection; its utility as a gross indicator of species abundance; and the observations of Logan (1990a:71) and Whitney (1992:54) that MNI and NISP yielded comparable patterning for their studies of the faunal assemblages from Grubgraben.

5.1.2 Dimensions of Variability

The frequencies in Table 5.1.1 were first transformed to chi-scores to eliminate the variance in the data referable to scale (sample-size) effects (chapter 4). The matrix of transformed frequencies was then subjected to a principle components analysis and, following the recommendation of Harpending and Jenkins (1973), the principle components were scaled by their standard deviations to yield geometrically accurate representations of the dimensions of variability.

Table 5.1.2 details the numerical construction of each scaled principle component; the numbers may be described as the weights of the original variables on the principle component axes, and actually represent measures of covariation (Doran and Hodson 1975:197; Krzanowski 1988:63). The singular value (proportional to the standard deviation of the principle component), variance (proportional to the square of the singular value), and percentage of total and cumulative explained variance are also reported for each dimension. The first two dimensions account for 96.77% of the total variance between assemblages in the chosen variables; the third dimension is minor and explains the remaining 3.23% of the total variance.

In all of the analyses reported here the proportion of explained variation is determined using the square of the singular value (which is proportional to the variance along a given dimension) and not, as Binford (1987b, 1989b) does, using the singular value itself (which is proportional to the standard deviation along the dimension). Thus, the proportion of explained variation for any given dimension is obtained by dividing the square of the singular value for that dimension by the sum of the squared singular values for all dimensions (Good 1969:827–828; Krzanowski 1988:27). This procedure yields figures of merit for each dimension that are analogous to the proportions of explained variation reported by a conventional analysis of variance procedure.

Table 5.1.3 shows the rank-order correlation of the scores on each principle component (Table 5.1.2) with sample sizes (variable totals summed across cases; Table 5.1.1). All probabilities are nonsignificant at the 0.10 level, indicating that the principle component scores are not correlated with sample sizes through some intermediate variable such as diversity or sampling time (see chapter 4).

The structure of Dimension 1, which explains 60.27% of the total variation between assemblages, is highly distinctive (Table 5.1.2): reindeer and nondiagnostic faunal remains are grouped on the positive aspect and all other variables are grouped on the negative aspect. Because the nondiagnostic faunal material at Grubgraben consists primarily of splintered and smashed reindeer bones, the strong covariation on the first principle component of the nondiagnostic material with the larger, more easily identified reindeer specimens is not unusual. Dimension 1 indicates that the single greatest contribution to the variation between the assemblages at Grubgraben, when these assemblages are conceptualized in terms of general classes of

Table 5.1.2. Analysis Stage 1: Scaled Principle Components for General Classes of Remains.

Dimension 1		Dimension 2		Dimension 3	
Reindeer	25.90	Reindeer	15.18	Small mammals	8.50
Nondiagnostic bones	4.02	Quartz	14.48	Shell	4.75
Mammoth	–0.13	Horse	10.04	Reindeer	3.77
Bone tools	–0.39	Lithic waste	7.35	Lithic tools	0.46
Cobbles	–1.60	Mammoth	5.46	Bone tools	–0.06
Horse	–7.25	Bone tools	0.73	Horse	–0.70
Quartz	–7.46	Lithic tools	–1.56	Lithic waste	–1.36
Shell	–12.16	Cobbles	–2.35	Mammoth	–2.46
Small mammals	–15.64	Small mammals	–7.22	Cobbles	–2.76
Lithic tools	–17.89	Shell	–10.21	Nondiagnostic bones	–4.67
Lithic waste	–45.15	Nondiagnostic bones	–36.89	Quartz	–6.56
Singular value	59.58		46.37		13.78
Variance	3549.55		2150.05		189.97
% Variance	60.27%		36.51%		3.23%
Cumulative %	60.27%		96.77%		100.00%

Table 5.1.3. Analysis Stage 1: Correlation Coefficients between Principle Component Scores and Sample Sizes.

Principle Component	n	Spearman's Rho	Probability	Kendall's Tau	Probability
1	11	0.1091	0.7495	0.0545	0.8153
2	11	0.3091	0.3550	0.2000	0.3918
3	11	−0.1727	0.6115	−0.1636	0.4835

Probability values are two-tailed.

remains, comes from the opposition between reindeer remains and all other classes of material.

Covarying oppositely to the classes of reindeer remains and nondiagnostic faunal material is a suite of classes comprising lithic waste, stone tools, small mammals, shell, quartz artifacts, and horse. The classes of cobbles, bone tools, and mammoth remains have very small weights on the negative aspect and do not contribute importantly to the structure of Dimension 1. However, the weights of the remaining classes on the negative aspect suggest three distinct and closely covariant subgroups: the first group contains only lithic waste, which is weighted very strongly; the second grouping comprises the classes of tools, small mammals, and shell, which have large and comparable weights; and the third subgroup is defined by horse remains and quartz artifacts, which are also similarly weighted.

These well defined covariant groups of classes of remains give evidence of three organizational relations. The first is the importance of lithic waste in distinguishing the archaeological assemblages. Most interesting is the fact that lithic waste does not covary closely (either positively or negatively) with any other class of remains. Obviously, lithic waste is a byproduct of lithic reduction and tool manufacture, and lithic waste and tools do covary as one would expect (they are grouped on the same aspect of the dimension). However, the disparity in the weights for tools and waste indicates that lithic waste did not enter the archaeological record in amounts that were closely related to the deposition of tools. This disparity is potentially an indicator of the curation (Binford 1979) of stone tools; one might expect that if tools were abandoned immediately after manufacture then the covariation between tools and waste would be stronger, whereas the curation of tools would act to depress the observed covariance between tools and waste. In any event, the amount of lithic waste in each assemblage is highly informative for distinguishing the assemblages, and is not strongly related to any of the other classes of remains.

The close covariance of shell items, small mammal remains, and tools is most satisfying; these items were most likely organized in the context of clothing manufacture, repair, and decoration (the organization of these items is discussed further in the context of Dimension 2, where the covariance of shell and small mammal remains reappears). The covariance of tools with the shell and small mammal remains indicates that some component of the lithic technology was organized with clothing production; thus small mammals must be skinned, pelts are scraped and cleaned, shell is cut and worked, fox teeth are drilled and perforated, and so forth (Soffer 1985:310–323).

Most interesting, however, is the indication that events involving lithic *tools* covary most closely with events such as clothing and outfitting tasks, and not with events related to subsistence animal exploitation. In other words, the tools covary primarily with craft-related events rather than with the subsistence animals, presumably because animal butchery does not require a sophisticated tool kit (Binford 1978b:62–63, 1981, 1984b).

The similar and moderately large weights on the negative aspect for horse and quartz are provocative, suggesting that the deposition of horse remains covaried closely with the quartz component of the lithic technology in each assemblage. In other words, the negative aspect of Dimension 1 provides evidence that events involving horse remains at Grubgraben were organized most directly with events involving elements of the stone tool technology. This relationship is supported by the presence of cut marks on the horse remains (West, personal communication 1995), and examination of the cut marks themselves could shed additional light on the nature of the tools employed and further support the ostensible organization of horse exploitation and quartz technology.

It would be mistaken, however, to interpret the structure of Dimension 1 as an indication that horse exploitation was tool-assisted, but that reindeer exploitation was not, simply because reindeer does not covary with technological classes on this dimension. Exploitation of all animal species was certainly tool-assisted in some way (see further discussion below in the context of Dimension 2). Dimension 1 is only one of several independent dimensions of variability defined by the assemblages, and its structure is determined solely by the requirement that it, as the first principle component, explain a greater amount of the between-assemblage variance than does any single subsequent component. The structure of the multivariate data set in Table 5.1.1 is such that the principle component summarizing the greatest amount of variance involves an opposition between reindeer and all other classes of remains, with strong covariation between horse and the quartz technology.

The second principle component (Dimension 2 in Table 5.1.2) explains 36.51% of the total variation between assemblages, or slightly more than half of the variance explained by Dimension 1. The positive aspect of Dimension 2 is dominated by the covariation between reindeer, quartz, and horse. Weighted strongly on the negative aspect of Dimension 2 are nondiagnostic faunal remains, followed by the classes of shell and small mammal remains with smaller but comparable weights. These suites of covariantly related artifact classes were initially suggested by the structure of the negative aspect of Dimension 1, and are indicative of several organized relationships between technology, animal exploitation, and human behavior.

The positive aspect of Dimension 2 groups reindeer, horse, and quartz artifacts with similar weights. Some of the covariation between horse and quartz was reported by the negative aspect of Dimension 1, which may account for the slightly smaller weight for horse on this aspect. The close covariation of quartz artifacts with the subsistence species is clearly indicating the organization of quartz tools and flakes in the context of processing reindeer and horse.

Quartz artifacts are found in all levels at Grubgraben and contribute about 3–10% of the chipped-stone inventory from the 1986–1987 excavations (Montet-White 1990d:133–136). The quartz raw material was locally available from the Kamp river terraces and from the gravel beds of nearby, smaller streams. Quartz cobbles were used as percussors (Beck 1993), and quartz flakes were worked into crude but serviceable denticulates, side scrapers, and other flake tools. A single specimen of a quartz core was recovered, although many smaller quartz cobbles are present. The majority of the quartz assemblage consists of large cortical flakes, shatter, and small retouched and unretouched flakes (Montet-White 1990d:133–136, 1991b:209; Hill 1993).

The mechanical properties of quartz make it an efficient choice of material for use in the butchering and disarticulation of animals with thick or large hides, and this activity has been suggested as the main context of quartz use at Grubgraben (Hill 1993). The working edges on tools made of quartz are not as sharp as edges on tools made of finer-grained cherts and radiolarites, but quartz tools are durable and well suited to heavier-duty cutting, hacking, and scraping tasks (Frison and Todd 1986:129; Hahn 1993:20; Bradley 1995).

Hill (1993) examined 449 quartz artifacts, or about one-half of the available quartz assemblage from Grubgraben, from a "multiaspectual" or "dynamic technological" perspective (Schild 1980). Hill concluded that quartz usage at Grubgraben was most likely organized with animal butchering and disarticulation rather than with activities such as cooking or stone boiling. If complete information were available on the frequencies of specific types of quartz implements (e.g., flakes, scrapers, resharpening chips, denticulates), the context of organization of quartz with the animal remains could be investigated in greater detail. It is also interesting to note the proximity of lithic waste to the main grouping of reindeer, quartz, and horse. This covariation may be contributed mainly by the larger, utilized flakes in the waste category; a more detailed subdivision of the lithic waste is needed to determine which kinds of waste are most directly organized with quartz artifacts and the subsistence species.

The covariant association on the negative aspect of Dimension 2 between shell and small mammal remains was initially observed on the negative aspect of Dimension 1. The covariance of these classes of remains makes a great deal of sense; these items were probably organized within the context of the manufacture, repair, and decoration of clothing. The use of shell in the Upper Paleolithic is well documented, and worked mollusc shells are a common class of artifact at archaeological sites and burials (e.g., Soffer 1985:440–442; May 1986:171–192; Binant 1991:87–100; Taborin 1993; Nuytten 1993). Shell items are generally regarded as elements of body ornamentation such as necklaces, pendants, and bracelets, although the spatial distributions of shells and beads in burial contexts provide evidence that they were also affixed to clothing (Gamble 1986:188; May 1986; Binant 1991).

Evidence for the use of shell is not regularly seen before the Aurignacian, at which time the favored species are helical forms such as periwinkle, turret shells, and moon snails (Taborin 1990). The shell material at Grubgraben is mostly Dentalia, however, although shells of other species of mollusc are present as well, several of which are perforated, cut, or otherwise modified (Montet-White 1990d:152). The use of Dentalia does not become common until after the last glacial advance, and the abundance of Dentalia at Grubgraben during the Last Glacial Maximum corresponds well with patterns of use seen elsewhere at this time. In western Europe, for example, the use of Dentalia does not become common until the Solutrean (Taborin 1990:217), and Soffer (1985:444) has noted that "evidence for specialized procurement of fur bearers, marine shells, and amber" appears on the central Russian plain only after the Valdai Maximum at 20–18,000 BP.

Unfortunately, the Dentalia from archaeological contexts, although generally reported, receive little systematic attention or analysis, and Dentalia and other marine shells are often excluded from surveys of "body ornaments" (e.g., White 1993). Cook (1993), however, examined the available Dentalia from Grubgraben and noted that many are cut, nested, or otherwise fashioned and modified. Abraded and polished exterior surfaces are common, and the interior surfaces at the edges of the shells are often worn and thinned. Cook (1993) argued that these features suggest the use of Dentalia in the decoration of clothing, where they would be subject to continual rubbing against other materials and develop worn and polished inner and outer surfaces.

Covarying with the items of shell on Dimension 2 is the class of small mammal remains, indicating that events involving shell covaried with events involving small mammals and implicating the organized use of both classes of remains in the context of clothing production. Because of their small size, the pelts from small mammals are unlikely to have provided material for entire garments, but probably were used for ornamental trim or for manufacturing gloves and other accessory items of clothing. The fur from mammals such as wolf, fox, otter, hare, and wolverine is especially valued for creating fur ruffs for parkas because the fur of these animals does not collect the ice formed by exhaled breath as will the fur of other animals (West, personal communication 1994; Oakes 1991:122–125). Perforated teeth from small mammals (mostly fox, but also bear) were also recovered at Grubgraben and may have been used in the decoration of clothing (Logan 1990a:71, 90; Montet-White 1990d:152) or as items of personal adornment. The long bones of small mammals are also favored for making certain kinds of bone tools such as bone needles and awls for sewing and hide work (Soffer 1985:312–313).

Also present on the negative aspect of Dimension 2 is the class of nondiagnostic faunal remains, comprising highly fragmented reindeer bones (West 1995). The covariation of the nondiagnostic material with reindeer remains was reported by the positive aspect of Dimension 1, and the negative aspect of Dimension 2 is now reporting another organizational context for the fragmented bones. However, the weight for this class is considerably greater than for any other class on the negative aspect, indicating that the nondiagnostic faunal material covaries only weakly with other classes of remains. (A similar situation was seen with lithic waste on the negative aspect of Dimension 1). Thus, the events involving fragmented reindeer bones that are monitored by Dimension 2 are not closely organized either with events involving the suite of shell and small mammal remains, or with events involving the suite of reindeer, horse, and quartz artifacts. Instead, events related to nondiagnostic faunal material exhibit a tendency to occur independently of other classes of remains, suggesting that the extreme negative aspect of Dimension 2 monitors a background accumulation of fragmented reindeer bones that is approximately independent of the deposition of other items.

The weak covariant relationship between nondiagnostic faunal material and the other negatively weighted classes of remains is unlikely to have a "functional" interpretation, and is probably a spurious correlation produced by the disposal of unrelated items (Whallon 1973b:118). In other words, events involving highly fragmented reindeer bones and events involving shell, small mammals, cobbles, and tools may appear "organized" by virtue of their separate covariation with some common third factor. A likely candidate for such a factor is the common spatial arena in which these events took place. We may imagine, for example, that clothing-related operations involving shell, small mammals, and tools were preferentially conducted in domestic spaces (near a hearth, for example) where events related to eating also transpired and generated accumulations of small bone fragments and splinters [the "dropped" component of food consumption (Binford 1978a, 1983a)]. The shared spatial organization of these otherwise independent activities produces a depositional covariation between their byproducts, but without the activities or items being organized in any direct, functional sense.

The third dimension of variability in Table 5.1.2 explains very little (3.23%) of the total variation between assemblages, and represents to some degree a "noise" component with no organizationally relevant structure. A noise component must be expected in any statistical analysis involving structural simplification of a complex data set, and it will ordinarily appear on the low-variance components after the (much larger) variance due to the patterned "signal" in the data has been accounted for. This purely statistical interpretation of a low-variance component is not necessarily complete or exclusive, however (Binford 1987b:493). Although many of the weights on Dimension 3 are small, several classes of remains are weighted much more strongly than others, forming well-defined positive and negative aspects and suggesting that a meaningful organizational property of the assemblages has in fact been isolated.

The positive aspect of Dimension 3 most strongly groups reindeer with small mammals and shell. Lithic tools follow with a substantially smaller but still positive weight. This suite of items can be seen as introducing reindeer into the contexts of hide-tailoring, clothing manufacture, and general outfitting tasks. The presence of stone tools on this aspect, although with a small weight, is consistent with this interpretation. One might have expected bone tools (e.g., eyed needles, awls) to appear on this aspect as well; these appear instead on the negative aspect, but with such a small weight that their assignment to this aspect cannot be accepted as conclusive.

It is interesting that reindeer remains are not grouped with the small mammals and shell until Dimension 3, yet all these items must certainly have been organized in the context of meeting general outfitting requirements. (Of course, the processing and working of hides may have little to do with the deposition of bone material). Reindeer pelage is extremely warm due to the presence of air-filled guard hairs (Spiess 1979:29–30), and probably provided the base material for most outfitting needs. The greater thickness of horse hide may have made it better suited for items such as shoes, or tents, blankets, and other non-wearable items where high durability is desirable (West, personal communication 1994).

Previous indications that tailoring events form an important dimension of assemblage variability appeared on the negative aspects of both Dimension 1 and Dimension 2 (Table 5.1.2). These dimensions did not clearly isolate, however, the contribution that reindeer (and to a lesser extent horse) must have made to general clothing and outfitting needs. Instead, aspects of the organization of subsistence and technology (horse and quartz on negative Dimension 1; reindeer, quartz, and horse on positive Dimension 2) explained the greater amount of variance. With the positive aspect of Dimension 3, however, the organization of reindeer with the small mammals, shell, and stone tools is finally revealed.

The negative aspect of Dimension 3 is defined primarily by the strong grouping of nondiagnostic faunal remains with quartz artifacts and cobbles. This aspect gives the first convincing indication of an organizational context for cobbles [which had very small weights on Dimensions 2 and 3 (Table 5.1.2)], and the covariant relationship of these items suggests their organization in a processing context, such as the cracking of long bones for marrow extraction, or the smashing of articular ends for boiling and bone grease production. Many of the smaller cobbles display evidence of having been used as percussors and anvils, and several were observed to have bits of bone debris adhering to their surfaces (Beck 1993); Kießling (1918:239) also remarks that small bone splinters were found adhering to the larger stones. Although suggestive, the significance of these observations for inferring the use of the stones is uncertain; it is possible that organic debris adhered naturally to the stones, or became sintered onto the surface of the stones during their long interment in the loessic matrix.

A new aspect of interassemblage variability involving quartz items is also isolated by the negative aspect of Dimension 3. Whereas Dimension 2 revealed the organization of quartz with reindeer and horse in the context of initial butchering and carcass reduction, the covariance on Dimension 3 of quartz with cobbles and with nondiagnostic faunal material indicates that quartz was also organized with other stages of animal exploitation and processing. As with cobbles, blocks of quartz may have found expedient use as hammerstones for breaking long bones and smashing articular ends, thereby generating the large amounts of quartz breakage observed in the assemblages. The durability of quartz flakes may have been a factor favoring their use for scraping and cutting needs during processing operations, e.g., for removal of the periosteum prior to marrow cracking to better control bone breakage (Binford 1978b:153, 1981:134). Very likely there were several processing-related contexts of use for quartz cobbles and flakes.

Another possibility suggested by the covariance of quartz and the nondiagnostic faunal material is that the quartz pieces represent the fractured remains of cobbles that were introduced to the site as boiling stones for use in the preparation of bone grease. Certainly the quantities of quartz shatter and large cortical flakes suggest a great deal of simple fracturing rather than intensive working of quartz cobbles. The study by Hill (1993), however, indicated that surprisingly few cobbles (perhaps 2–10 per level) were represented by the weight of quartz material recovered. If ethnographic accounts of stone boiling are accepted as a baseline for comparison, then far too few cobbles are present for the extraction of even small amounts of bone grease. Binford (1978b:159) has observed, for example, the use of 32 stones weighing 60.9 lb in the production of only 7 oz of bone grease. Of course, boiling stones were not necessarily exclusively of quartz, and many of the as-yet-unstudied non-quartz stones from Grubgraben may have been used in this capacity.

The interpretation of the negative aspect of Dimension 3 as indicative of processing activities is reasonable; in fact, it is precisely the nondiagnostic bone splinters which would be expected to covary strongly with cobbles (bone percussors) and quartz pieces. It may seem peculiar, however, that an important activity at Grubgraben—marrow extraction and bone grease production—is not recognized until the third dimension of variability is considered. Assuming for the moment that this interpretation of the third principle component in Table 5.1.2 is correct, one might draw the conclusion that marrow extraction and bone grease production were minor activities at Grubgraben. This conclusion seems unlikely, however, in view of the vast quantities of smashed and pulverized bone, and the numerous features in levels AL3 and AL4 suggestive of boiling and processing pits [chapter 2; see also West (1995)]. Instead, the proper interpretation is simply that the activities of marrow extraction and bone grease production contribute relatively little to interassemblage variability when the assemblages are summarized as shown in Table 5.1.1. Conceiving the assemblages in different terms could change the proportional variance explained by the organization of materials involved in marrow extraction and bone grease production. More importantly, if these activities and materials are represented in each assemblage to a relatively constant degree, they will contribute little to the explanation of interassemblage *variability* and would be expected to appear on a low-variance principle component (chapter 4).

5.1.3 Case/Variable Relations

The dimensions of interassemblage variability in general classes of remains, and the contributions of these dimensions to the structure of individual archaeological levels, are displayed graphically in Figure 5.1. Although all three dimensions of variability are informative of organizational properties, only the first and second principle component axes have been used to construct Figure 5.1. The first two axes summarize 96.77% of the total interassemblage variation in artifact classes (Table 5.1.2);

Figure 5.1. Analysis Stage 1: General Classes of Remains.

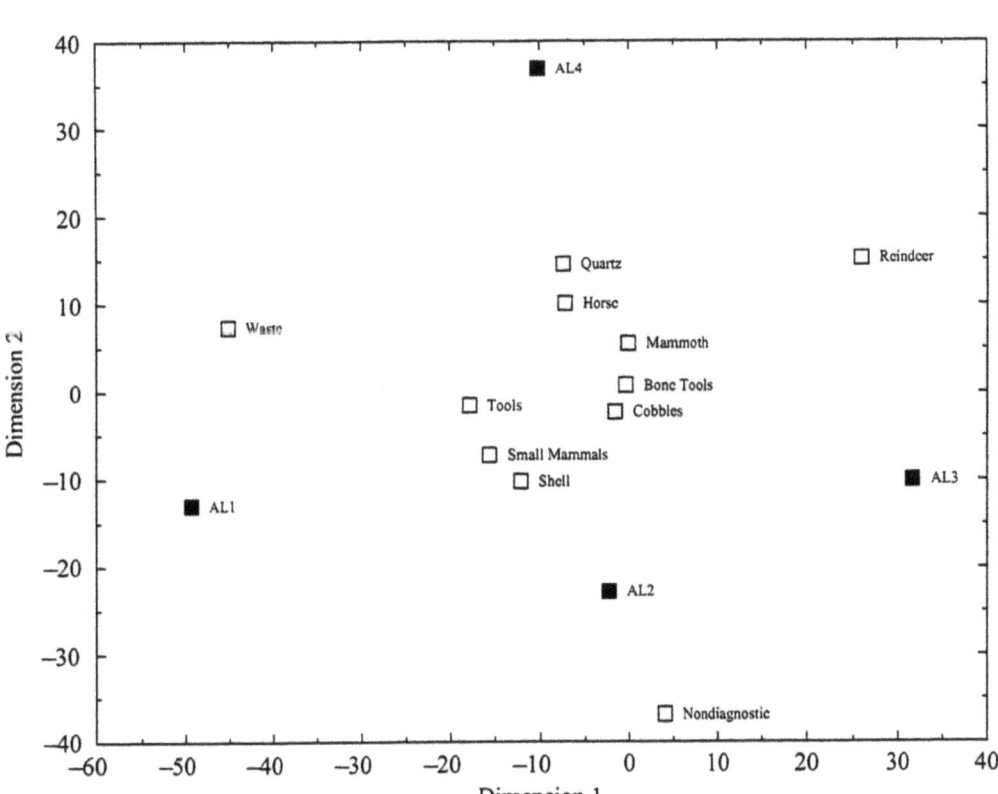

the third principle component explains a very small proportion of the total between-assemblage variance (3.23%) and can be omitted without a great loss of information. Efforts to display all three dimensions of variation yielded illustrations that were much less effective, and more difficult to comprehend visually, than the simpler two-axis diagram given in Figure 5.1. To facilitate comparison and discussion, the relations between variables and the relations between cases are displayed on a common pair of axes.

The various suites of covariantly related classes of remains elicited by the analysis are easily recognized in Figure 5.1 by examining the locations of the classes on the individual component axes. Dimension 1 represents the fundamental assemblage-structuring opposition between reindeer remains and all other classes of remains: reindeer and nondiagnostic faunal material are located on the positive aspect of Dimension 1 and the remaining classes are situated on the negative aspect. Lithic waste in particular contributes very strongly to the definition of the negative aspect of Dimension 1.

Dimension 2 introduces variation referable to tailoring and outfitting events (tools, small mammals, and shell on the negative aspect) and to the organization of subsistence fauna with elements of the lithic technology (reindeer and horse, quartz and lithic waste on the positive aspect). Nondiagnostic faunal material also contributes importantly to the definition of the negative aspect of Dimension 2.

Dimension 3 introduces little additional variation and is not depicted in Figure 5.1. As noted earlier, however, Dimension 3 primarily groups cobbles and quartz artifacts with nondiagnostic faunal material (negative aspect), and introduces reindeer into the context of clothing manufacture indicated by the grouping of small mammal remains, shell items, and tools (positive aspect).

The dimensions of variation depicted in Figure 5.1 represent *independently operating* organizational relations that structure interassemblage variability at Grubgraben. When these dimensions are examined individually as in Table 5.1.2, specific organizational relations between materials and activities can be recognized.

The dimensions of variation may also be regarded as new, composite variables that measure certain organizational properties of the assemblages. Each assemblage can then be plotted according to its values for these composite variables, providing a graphical assessment of how the individual archaeological deposits are structured and differentiated by the various organizational properties. This has been done in Figure 5.1, from which it is immediately evident that the assemblages from Grubgraben differ considerably when "measured" on the composite variables defined by the classes of remains in Table 5.1.1.

The character of the assemblage from AL1 is determined largely by events involving lithic waste, and by the organization of shell, small mammal remains, and tools. Level AL2 is distinguished mainly by events involving nondiagnostic faunal material, but also by the same suite of shell, small mammal remains, and tools that contributes to the structure of AL1. The assemblages from levels AL3 and AL4 are very different: horse remains and quartz artifacts are the important classes structuring AL4, whereas reindeer and nondiagnostic faunal material are the primary contributors to the character of the assemblage from AL3.

Many of the organizational relations discussed above could perhaps have been anticipated simply by inspecting the relative proportions of the classes of remains from level to level in Table 5.1.1, leading one to wonder if the quantitative method used here is strictly necessary, or even capable of detecting "unanticipated" patterning. Recall, however, from chapter 4 that the principle components analysis is performed not on the raw frequency data in Table 5.1.1, but on these data after they have been transformed to their chi-scores, i.e., to the frequencies that would be expected under a hypothesis of statistical independence of artifact category and archaeological level. There is no necessary relationship, however, between the magnitude of a class frequency and the magnitude of its chi-score; a small frequency that differs considerably from its expected value may yield a larger chi-score than a large frequency which differs only slightly from its expected value. Although a rough and ready "chi-by-eye" (Press et al. 1989:548) assessment of the interassemblage variation in Table 5.1.1 may suggest some kinds of patterning that are later confirmed by the principle components analysis, it can scarcely be relied upon to explore adequately a multivariate data set, gauge the strength of the covariant relations, and construct independent dimensions of variability through the data.

5.1.4 Summary

To develop some first impressions regarding the organizational relations that structure interassemblage variability at Grubgraben, the inventories of the archaeological levels were summarized using a small number of general classes of remains (Table 5.1.1). The data were first transformed to their chi-scores to eliminate the variance contributed by scale effects among the variables and to obtain a set of scaled deviations from the frequencies expected under the null hypothesis of independence between variables (classes of remains) and cases (archaeological levels). A scaled principle components analysis was then applied to elicit composite variables that operate independently and are indicative of organizational relations between the classes of remains. The results were presented both in the form of numerical definitions (Table 5.1.2) and graphical relations between the classes of remains and the archaeological cases (Figure 5.1). Three independent dimensions of variation were isolated, and several provocative suites of covariantly related classes of remains were recognized.

When the data on assemblage composition are conceptualized in terms of general classes of remains, the primary source of variability between assemblages is in the opposition between reindeer remains (reindeer and nondiagnostic faunal material) and all other classes of material (Dimension 1, Table 5.1.2). The opposition is strongest with lithic waste, but two additional groups of closely covariant classes of remains also emerge on the negative aspect. Shell and small mammal remains form one covariant grouping, suggesting their organization in events related to clothing and outfitting tasks. Events involving the use of tools made of high-quality non-quartz stone are also organized with the suite of shell and small mammal remains. Quartz artifacts and horse remains form a second group of closely covariant classes, isolating an aspect of the organization of stone tool technology with the main subsistence species. Because these three organizational relations (lithic waste; shell, small mammals, and tools; quartz and horse) are conflated on the negative aspect, however, Dimension 1 does not serve well as a monitor of any one of them individually, but monitors their collective effect in structuring assemblage composition.

The second dimension of variation defined by the assemblages is interpreted as a contrast between general outfitting tasks and the butchery and processing of reindeer and horse (Dimension 2, Table 5.1.2). The use of items of shell is organized with the exploitation of small mammals (fox and hare) in the context of clothing production, maintenance, and decoration (negative aspect). Reindeer, horse, and quartz items form another covariantly related suite of classes, organized in the context of animal butchery and processing (positive aspect).

The third and final dimension of variability among assemblages contributes very little of the total between-assemblage variability (Dimension 3, Table 5.1.2), and must also subsume any remaining "noise" in the data set. However, the classes of remains that exhibit the highest weights on Dimension 3 suggest additional organizational relations. Reindeer, shell, and small mammal remains are grouped on the positive aspect of Dimension 3, representing the introduction of reindeer into the context of hide tailoring, clothing production, and general outfitting tasks. Quartz pieces and cobbles are grouped with nondiagnostic faunal material on the negative aspect, suggesting their organized use in smashing bones for marrow extraction and bone grease production.

5.2 Analysis Stage 2: Classes of Lithic Items

The second stage in the analysis of interassemblage variability explores the organizational relations in the lithic component of the assemblages. Lithic material was included in stage 1 of the analysis, but was represented there only by the general classes of tools, waste, and quartz artifacts. Tools were discovered to always covary with shell and small mammal remains (negative aspect of Dimension 1 and Dimension 2, positive aspect of Dimension 3; Table 5.1.2). Lithic waste contributed strongly to the definition of Dimension 1 and was highly informative for distinguishing assemblages, but was not highly correlated with any other classes on the dimension. Quartz artifacts covaried closely with horse remains (negative aspect of Dimension 1), with horse, reindeer, and lithic waste (positive aspect of Dimension 2), and with cobbles and nondiagnostic faunal material (negative aspect of Dimension 3). These patterns call for a more detailed analysis of the covariation between lithic classes and between classes of faunal remains to isolate specific organizational relations within these two kinds of remains before undertaking an analysis of their joint variability. The present stage of analysis, therefore, addresses the structure of variability among archaeological levels in the lithic inventories, using a more detailed set of categories than was used in stage 1.

5.2.1 Description of the Data

Frequencies were tabulated in nineteen classes of lithic artifact for each of the four archaeological levels. The resulting array of class frequencies is shown in Table 5.2.1. The lithic categories are broadly defined to yield classes with good numerical representation across the four cases. Only chipped-stone artifacts and debitage made of cherts or radiolarites are considered; the small but consistently represented tool inventory in each level made from quartz, quartzite, and granulite (Montet-White 1990d:133–138; Hill 1993), and the small cobbles and hammerstones recovered from each level (Beck 1993), are not included.

The ten lithic tool classes used are: endscrapers; perforators; burins; truncations; marginally retouched blades; notches and denticulates; splintered pieces; side scrapers; backed bladelets; other tools. The relatively few combination tools [type numbers 17–22 in the Upper Paleolithic type list of de Sonneville-Bordes and Perrot (1954–56)] were doubly counted; a scraper-burin, for example, contributed a count of one to both the scraper and burin categories.

The category "other tools" contains frequencies for tool type number 92 in the Upper Paleolithic type list. This category comprises lithic fragments which are clearly retouched but, because they are broken pieces or atypically shaped, cannot otherwise be assigned to a specific tool type. At Grubgraben nearly all of the specimens classified as "other tools" are retouched fragments resulting from tool breakage rather than atypically shaped pieces. The remaining tool classes in Table 5.2.1 are conventionally defined (de Sonneville-Bordes and Perrot 1954–56).

Lithic waste was subdivided into nine classes: cores; shatter; spalls; crested pieces; blades; bladelets; chips; flakes; unidentifiable debitage. The distinction between chips, flakes, and unidentifiable debitage was made during the initial laboratory sorting of the lithics, and has been retained here because these categories can be expected to monitor different aspects of tool manufacture and use.

Chips are very small pieces, generally weighing less than 1 g, and are complete artifacts, having a visible striking platform and/or bulb of percussion. Chips are typically the byproduct of bifacial trimming, scraper resharpening, and similar fine retouching operations, and should be generally informative of tool finishing and tool maintenance activities. The chips are not small enough, however, to reliably monitor the fine retouch associated with backed bladelets.

Flakes are essentially large chips, but are produced at many stages in the lithic *chaîne opératoire* (Leroi-Gourhan and Brézillon 1966), from initial core preparation to production of tool preforms to final tool shaping. Flakes should approximately monitor the early and intermediate stages of tool production.

Unidentifiable debitage is lithic waste material that is fragmentary, irregularly shaped, usually very small, and completely lacking the landmarks which would allow it to be identified either as a chip or flake. On the basis of size, morphology, and quantity, unidentifiable pieces are more similar to chips than to flakes, and

Table 5.2.1. Analysis Stage 2: Frequencies in Classes of Lithic Items.

Level	End-scrapers	Burins	Perforators	Side scrapers	Marginally-retouched blades	Truncations
AL1	45	72	8	3	30	5
AL2	41	12	14	10	10	5
AL3	57	27	19	25	17	6
AL4	104	38	20	17	15	7

Level	Notches and denticulates	Splintered pieces	Backed bladelets	Other tools	Cores	Shatter
AL1	4	3	37	8	34	132
AL2	6	2	9	11	20	91
AL3	8	6	2	25	33	94
AL4	5	12	13	12	32	230

Level	Spalls	Crested pieces	Blades	Bladelets	Chips	Flakes	Unidentifiable lithic debitage
AL1	105	24	150	146	393	328	198
AL2	79	5	42	33	268	152	176
AL3	104	26	63	37	553	336	333
AL4	80	12	192	87	731	698	311

Combination tools (types 17–22) are counted once in each relevant category. The category "Cores" includes core tools (types 16 and 43): AL1: 6; AL2: 1; AL3: 1; AL4: 0.

may be expected to covary with the former in some contexts.

The only other category of waste needing clarification is that of crested pieces; these are typically blade-like items of triangular cross section which result from the initiation and rejuvenation of blade cores. Crested pieces could be included with burin spalls and tool spalls (e.g., the spalls produced by removing exhausted scraper edges), but were retained in a separate category because, together with cores, they are potentially informative regarding patterns of raw material reduction and tool manufacture.

5.2.2 Dimensions of Variability

The frequencies in Table 5.2.1 were transformed to chi-scores to eliminate the variance contributed by differences in the scale of measurement, and the transformed frequency array was subjected to a scaled principle components analysis. The results of the analysis are shown in Table 5.2.2. The first two dimensions of variation account for 92.86% of the total variation between assemblages in the lithic categories; the third component is relatively minor and explains only 7.14% of the variation in lithic frequencies.

The rank-order correlations of the scores on each principle component (Table 5.2.2) with sample sizes (variable totals summed across cases; Table 5.2.1) are given in Table 5.2.3. The probabilities for the coefficients are nonsignificant, therefore the principle component scores are unlikely to be indirectly correlated with sample size through an intermediate factor such as assemblage diversity.

On the positive aspect of Dimension 1 are grouped several classes of lithic waste as well as most of the categories of formal tools. Lithic waste is represented primarily by the unidentifiable debitage and chips, which are typically byproducts of tool retouch and rejuvenation. The category "other tools", which comprises fragmentary tools and should be indicative of tool breakage and discard, also covaries with these classes of resharpening waste. Spalls are another byproduct of tool manufacture and maintenance, but these are only weakly represented on the positive aspect of Dimension 1.

In addition to the categories of resharpening debris, nearly all of the formal tool classes are also grouped on the positive aspect of Dimension 1: side scrapers; perforators; endscrapers; notches and denticulates; splintered pieces; and truncations. With the possible exceptions of splintered pieces and truncations [which have much smaller weights on this dimension than do the other tools, and whose status as formal tools is debatable (White 1968; Eickhoff 1988:140; Hahn 1993:227, 249–250)], this suite of tools is broadly indicative of scraping, cutting, and perforating tasks. The specific contexts of use for many of these tool types have been elucidated by microwear analysis and experimental tool-use studies (Keeley 1980; Moss and Newcomer 1981; Moss 1983; Hahn 1993), suggesting that

Table 5.2.2. Analysis Stage 2: Scaled Principle Components for Classes of Lithic Items.

Dimension 1		Dimension 2		Dimension 3	
Unid. debitage	5.77	Spalls	6.24	Shatter	3.59
Chips	4.63	Unid. debitage	4.54	Spalls	1.83
Side scrapers	4.12	Crested pieces	2.90	Endscrapers	1.66
Other tools	3.03	Marg. ret. blades	2.62	Perforators	1.24
Perforators	2.35	Other tools	2.53	Backed bladelets	0.97
Endscrapers	1.54	Bladelets	2.35	Notch/Denticulate	0.76
Notch/Denticulate	1.36	Burins	2.33	Truncations	0.76
Splintered pieces	0.84	Cores	2.26	Cores	0.07
Truncations	0.46	Backed bladelets	2.23	Blades	0.02
Spalls	0.04	Notch/Denticulate	1.67	Unid. debitage	−0.16
Flakes	−0.16	Side scrapers	1.11	Bladelets	−0.17
Cores	−0.31	Perforators	0.93	Splintered pieces	−0.34
Crested pieces	−0.69	Truncations	0.75	Marg. ret. blades	−0.52
Shatter	−1.49	Chips	−0.51	Side scrapers	−0.61
Marg. ret. blades	−2.62	Endscrapers	−1.46	Other tools	−0.61
Blades	−6.20	Splintered pieces	−1.52	Chips	−1.20
Burins	−6.21	Shatter	−2.26	Flakes	−1.29
Backed bladelets	−6.54	Blades	−3.07	Burins	−1.74
Bladelets	−9.63	Flakes	−7.65	Crested pieces	−2.91
Singular value	17.71		13.62		6.20
Variance	313.66		185.58		38.41
% Variance	58.34%		34.52%		7.14%
Cumulative %	58.34%		92.86%		100.00%

Table 5.2.3. Analysis Stage 2: Correlation Coefficients between Principle Component Scores and Sample Sizes.

Principle Component	n	Spearman's Rho	Probability	Kendall's Tau	Probability
1	19	−0.0905	0.7124	−0.0651	0.6970
2	19	−0.0993	0.6858	−0.0059	0.9718
3	19	−0.0431	0.8610	−0.0059	0.9718

Probability values are two-tailed.

activities such as carcass butchering and hide working are the relevant contexts in which these tools were organized. The covariance of these formal tool classes with the products of tool resharpening (chips and unidentifiable debitage) but not with the products of tool production (cores, blades, flakes) implies that the tools were deposited during events of use and use-related breakage and reworking, and not during events related to their manufacture.

The negative aspect of Dimension 1 groups bladelets, backed bladelets, burins, blades, marginally retouched blades, shatter, crested pieces, cores, and flakes (Table 5.2.2). Except for burins, backed bladelets, and marginally retouched blades, these classes of lithic material are associated with the primary production of blades and flakes for eventual retouch into finished tools. Compared with the positive aspect, the structure of the negative aspect of Dimension 1 implicates the context of blank and tool production instead of a context of tool use and maintenance.

The strongest covariances on the negative aspect of Dimension 1 are those of backed bladelets, burins, and unretouched blades and bladelets, indicating that these items in particular were most directly and consistently organized. This suite of lithic classes (blades and bladelets, burins, backed bladelets) is especially suggestive of the manufacture of *armatures* and the preparation of grooved sagaies and bone and antler hafts for receiving the small backed forms (Keeley 1980, 1982, 1987; Moss and Newcomer 1981; Moss 1983). This interpretation is supported by the close correspondence between the spatial distributions of burins and antler fragments in each archaeological level at Grubgraben.

The production of *armatures* would involve the creation of lithic byproducts related to core preparation and reduction (cores, crested pieces, shatter), the production of unretouched blades and bladelets, the modification of unretouched blades and bladelets into their backed forms, and the use of burins and perhaps marginally retouched blades to fashion bone and antler hafts for receiving the backed pieces. Several examples of hafted bladelets have been recovered *in situ* from Upper Paleolithic contexts (Cheynier 1956; Allain and Descouts 1957; Allain 1979; Leroi-Gourhan 1983), and many other kinds of tools were also hafted in some way to facilitate their use, increase their efficiency, or extend their useful lifetimes (Deacon and Deacon 1980; Moss and Newcomer 1981; Keeley 1982, 1987; Moss 1983). In general terms, the negative aspect of Dimension 1 appears to group those classes of lithic items that were organized in the context of *retooling* operations (Keeley 1982, 1987; Torrence 1989).

An interesting feature of Dimension 1 is the indication of a different organizational context for burins than for the other formal tools; burins are an important class of formal tool in Paleolithic assemblages, but they are conspicuously absent from the tool-dominated positive aspect of Dimension 1 (Table 5.2.2). This dichotomy between burins and other tools (particularly scrapers) has frequently been observed in Upper Paleolithic lithic assemblages (e.g., Leroi-Gourhan and Brézillon 1966, 1972; Bosinski and Hahn 1973:192–227; Montet-White and Basler 1977; Otte 1981; Weniger 1982; Kozlowski 1986; Gamble 1986). It is also interesting to note that spalls, which are indicative of burin resharpening and rejuvenation, do not covary on Dimension 1 with the burins (some spalls were also produced by burinating endscrapers, but these "tool spalls" are much less numerous than the burin spalls). The small weight for spalls is an indication that these items were not organized to any appreciable degree with the events monitored by either the positive or negative aspects of Dimension 1, although this does not rule out the possibility that spalls may covary strongly with other lithic classes on the other dimensions of variability. In other words, whatever context of burin use is indicated by the negative aspect of Dimension 1 (rehafting and retooling operations have been suggested as the most likely contexts), it was evidently a context that did not involve burin resharpening and spall production.

In summary, the first dimension of lithic interassemblage variability is reporting a simple but significant structuring principle that essentially separates two main contexts of tool use, maintenance, and repair. This industrial dichotomy accounts for nearly 60% of the total variation between assemblages in the lithic inventories (Table 5.2.2).

The first context is monitored by the positive aspect of Dimension 1. Formal tool classes such as side scrapers, endscrapers, perforators, and notches and denticulates are grouped with classes of debitage indicative of tool use and resharpening (unidentifiable debitage, chips, and tool fragments). This suite of lithic items implicates general cutting, scraping, and perforating tasks, probably related to activities such as carcass processing, hide working, and other activities in which finished tools are used and resharpened as they become worn, resulting in the deposition of tools, resharpening waste, and breakage in positively covariant amounts.

The second context of tool use and manufacture is monitored by the negative aspect of Dimension 1. Lithic items indicative of core reduction, primary production of blades and bladelets, and the use of burins, backed bladelets, and marginally retouched blades, implicate the production of *armatures* and the maintenance of hafted and composite tools. More generally, the negative aspect of Dimension 1 is indicative of retooling and rehafting operations requiring the organized use of a suite of lithic items completely different from the one identified by the positive aspect of Dimension 1.

In marked contrast to Dimension 1, which accounts for 58.34% of the total interassemblage variation in lithic frequencies, the second dimension of variability in Table 5.2.2 explains only slightly more than one-half as much (34.52%) of the variation. Three features of Dimension 2 are particularly interesting and provide clues to the interpretation of this component.

The first characteristic is the marked asymmetry between the positive and negative aspects of the dimension. Only six lithic classes are found on the negative aspect; the remaining thirteen classes are located on the positive aspect. Secondly, the strongest covariation on both the positive and negative aspects is between classes of lithic waste: spalls, unidentifiable debitage, and crested pieces are heavily weighted on the positive aspect, and flakes, blades, and shatter are the most strongly weighted classes on the negative aspect. Cores and tool fragments (positive aspect) and chips and splintered pieces (negative aspect) enter this pattern with reduced weights. The waste items on the positive aspect are suggestive of tool use, breakage, and core reduction; those on the negative aspect implicate the retouching of flakes and blades and tool resharpening.

The third interesting feature of Dimension 2 is the presence of all classes of formal tools (except endscrapers) on the positive aspect with small and approximately equal weights. Endscrapers are grouped not with the other tools, but appear with small resharpening chips and splintered pieces on the negative aspect. This is a provocative trio of lithic items, because the small chips are typically the products of scraper and bifacial retouch, and because splintered pieces are morphologically similar to blade and flake endscrapers and are often combined with endscrapers as combination tools (Otte 1981; Hahn 1993:249). The covariance with endscrapers and splintered pieces of unretouched blades and flakes—the two blank forms upon which endscrapers are typically prepared—strengthens the appearance of the negative aspect of Dimension 2 as a suite of lithic forms related to the manufacture and use of endscrapers. Although most of the endscrapers recovered at Grubgraben are on blades (39–67% of the total endscraper inventory in each level), a significant proportion (11–23%) is manufactured on flakes.

Whereas Dimension 1 appeared informative of the differential organization of specific "tool kits" (Binford and Binford 1966; Binford 1983a:147) and their associated debitage or waste items, the second principle component in Table 5.2.2 is evidently differentiating events involving the production, use, and discard of endscrapers (negative aspect) from events involving the manufacture and use of all other tools (positive aspect). The negative aspect of Dimension 2 groups lithic items related to endscraper technology, and the positive aspect groups those classes related to the non-endscraper technology, e.g., burins and their associated spalls, cores and their associated crested pieces, and bladelets and backed bladelets. In other words, if Dimension 1 is said to monitor organizational relations between technology (lithic tool kits) and generic task categories (e.g., carcass processing, hide working, retooling, rehafting), Dimension 2 can be described as monitoring a purely industrial aspect of lithic variation, namely the intensity of endscraper technology relative to the technology involving other kinds of tools.

The third principle component in Table 5.2.2 is interpreted as a low-variance "noise" component of interassemblage variability. This conclusion is suggested by the small proportion of the total variation in lithic classes explained by Dimension 3 (7.14%, Table 5.2.2), and by the absence of large covariances on this dimension (most of the weights on this component are uniformly small). Despite the primary interpretation of Dimension 3 as a noisy residual component, however, it is still interesting to examine the classes that have the largest weights.

The strongest opposition on Dimension 3 is between two kinds of waste generally associated with core reduction: shatter (positive aspect) and crested pieces (negative aspect). Crested pieces are typically the byproduct of core rejuvenation and platform preparation, whereas shatter, which is abundant in all levels at the site, generally results from core breakage or from the breakage of a block of raw material during core fabrication. It is interesting, however, that neither of these two classes of core-related waste covaries strongly with cores themselves, even though the spatial distributions of shatter, cores, and crested pieces are similar and do not suggest a physical separation of activities involving these items. It seems likely that two industrial contexts of core modification are being reported by Dimension 3; one that involves typical core use and rejuvenation events and a second context that involves events related to extreme core reduction and eventual destruction. The information provided by Dimension 3, however, is insufficient to further evaluate or interpret this relationship.

The most significant relationship isolated by Dimension 3 is the strong opposition between spalls and burins, indicating that events involving spalls covaried inversely with events involving burins. This pattern was suggested earlier by the structure of Dimension 1, and it is now clear from Dimension 3 that the manufacture and resharpening of burins took place in contexts unrelated to their use and eventual discard. Relatedly, no burin spalls from Grubgraben have yet been refit to their burins, and preliminary intrasite spatial analysis of the lithic material from AL1 has also indicated that burins and burin spalls exhibit spatial distributions with relatively little overlap (Montet-White and Williams, unpublished data 1992), suggesting that burins were manufactured or rejuvenated in contexts unrelated to their use and eventual discard.

Finally, the relatively strong weight for backed bladelets on the positive aspect of Dimension 3 suggests that these items were organized not only with burins and with the primary production of blades and bladelets as indicated by Dimension 1, but also secondarily with a scraping, cutting, and perforating technology. The weights on Dimension 3 are small and its structure is therefore less convincing than that of Dimensions 1 and 2, but it appears that Dimension 3 is partially monitoring another context of use for backed bladelets, perhaps as cutting elements in composite tools used for working hides (Moss 1983:115–116).

5.2.3 Case/Variable Relations

A graphical representation of the interassemblage variability in lithic classes at Grubgraben is provided in Figure 5.2, in which the first and second principle components from Table 5.2.2 have been used as coordinate axes. The third principle component explains very little of the overall variation in lithic classes between assemblages and is not used for display purposes. Because the first two dimensions explain a total of 92.86% of the total variance (Table 5.2.2), Figure 5.2 accurately summarizes nearly all of the the variability in lithic classes between the assemblages.

The major organizational patterns identified by Dimension 1 and Dimension 2 are clearly visible in Figure 5.2. Dimension 1 represents the fundamental organizational dichotomy between events related to backed bladelet production, retooling, and rehafting (negative aspect), and events related to the use and maintenance of most of the formal tool categories (positive aspect). Burins, backed bladelets, and marginally retouched blades, together with unretouched blades and bladelets and some classes of primary production debris such as cores, crested pieces, and shatter, are grouped in the left part of the figure, corresponding to the negative aspect of Dimension 1. All formal tools (except burins), and the classes of debitage related to tool maintenance or resharpening, form a separate group in the right portion of the diagram, corresponding to the positive aspect of Dimension 1. As described earlier, Dimension 1 is interpreted as monitoring the differential organization of two kinds of lithic "tool kits" and their associated waste items.

Dimension 2 in Figure 5.2 represents an independently operating source of variability in lithic inventories, and essentially separates the endscraper component of each assemblage from the remainder of the lithic industry. The lower half of the figure (negative aspect of Dimension 2) is dominated by flakes, blades, shatter, endscrapers, and small retouch chips. All remaining formal tool categories and classes of lithic waste are located in the upper part of the figure along the positive aspect of Dimension 2.

The locations of the individual archaeological levels along each of the component axes are also shown in Figure 5.2 to illustrate how the lithic inventory in each level is differentially structured by the two most significant dimensions of lithic variability. It is immediately apparent, for example, that levels AL2 and AL3 are most similar to one another when "measured" by their lithic assemblages; the lithic inventories from levels AL1 and AL4 are markedly different, both from one another and from those of levels AL2 and AL3. If variation only along Dimension 1 is considered [the dimension that explains the greatest amount of interassemblage lithic variability (Table 5.2.2)], then AL4 is clearly similar to levels AL2 and AL3, although AL1 remains markedly different from the other levels. Variation along Dimension 2 does little to distinguish the lithic inventories of AL1, AL2 or AL3, but is largely responsible for the distinctive character of AL4.

Figure 5.2. Analysis Stage 2: Lithics.

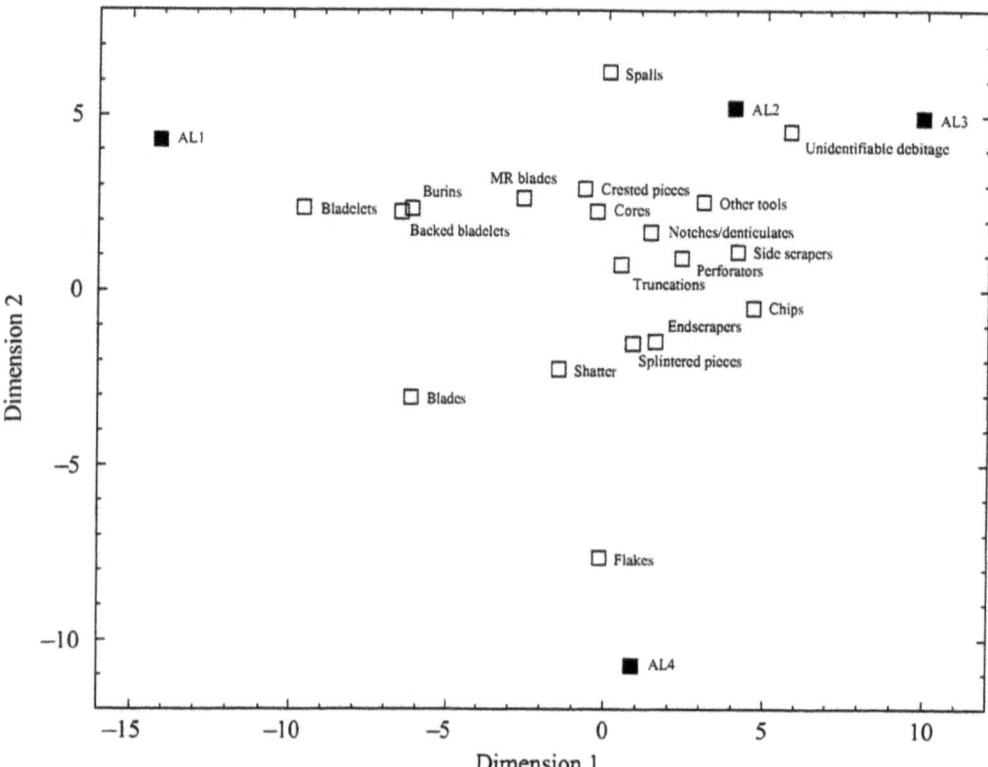

The position of AL1 in Figure 5.2 indicates that the assemblage from this level is dominated by a technology involving blades, bladelets (backed and unretouched), and burins, with relatively little structure contributed by the other lithic classes. The spatial distributions of burins and antler in this level also show a close correspondence. Thus the events involving stone tools that contribute most to the character of the assemblage from AL1 are oriented toward blade, bladelet, and burin usage, most probably associated with the manufacture and repair of composite tools, and with retooling and rehafting operations.

This "structural pose" (Gearing 1962:8) for the lithic assemblage from AL1 is completely consistent with the site framework recognized in the excavated portion of the level and with its interpretation as a portion of a larger domestic area (chapter 2; Montet-White 1990c, 1991b; Montet-White and Williams 1994). AL1 is characterized by two hearths and several extended stone features that may represent the remains of a pavement or possibly a series of tent rings. Hearths are acknowledged as "interpretive foci" for artifact distributions at Paleolithic campsites and as "centers" of site frameworks in general, and hearths frequently mark the centers of distributions of backed bladelets, burins, and debitage derived from retooling operations (Leroi-Gourhan and Brézillon 1966, 1972; Leroi-Gourhan 1976a, 1984; Binford 1983a; Moss and Newcomer 1983; Kind 1985; Gamble 1986:11–14, 1991; Audouze 1987; Stapert 1989, 1992:27; Olive and Taborin 1989).

The organization of lithic technology in levels AL2–AL4 is markedly different from that in level AL1. The lower levels are all located along the positive aspect of Dimension 1, indicating a focus on general scraping, cutting, and perforating tasks rather than on manufacturing, retooling, and rehafting operations. Levels AL2 and AL3 are most similar in this respect; each is characterized by greater than expected numbers of spalls, unidentifiable debitage, and broken tools, and by a relative abundance of all formal tools except endscrapers. Despite the demonstrable similarity of their lithic inventories, however, the site frameworks for AL2 and AL3 are very different (chapter 2): the presence of a pavement, hearth, and discrete activity areas in AL2 suggests that this level represents a domestic area similar to that in AL1; level AL3 is covered by a layer of stones that are not joined into a recognizable structure, and contains a variety of earthen pits covered with stone slabs. If the evidence from the lithic inventories is accepted, however, then levels AL2 and AL3 are more similar than their site frameworks would indicate, suggesting that the common excavation window at Grubgraben has simply exposed functionally differentiated portions of two levels that otherwise have much in common.

The lithic assemblage from AL4, although it is similar to the inventories from AL2 and AL3 with respect to the organizational properties isolated by Dimension 1, is markedly different from these levels when the organizational properties isolated by Dimension 2 are introduced. Dimension 2 was interpreted as monitoring the relative intensity of the endscraper technology in the lithic assemblages, and from Figure 5.2 it is clear that the assemblage from AL4 is more strongly structured by events involving the intensive use of blades, flakes, and endscrapers than are the other assemblages.

The site framework in AL4 is similar to that of AL3, and contains a number of trash- and earth-filled pits, although these are smaller and deeper than the pits in AL3, which may indicate their use in a different context (chapter 2). Level AL4 is also similar to AL3 in its high densities of bones and artifacts. The most significant difference in level AL4 is the overwhelming abundance of horse remains (Table 5.1.1), whereas the other levels are dominated by the remains of reindeer. Very likely the different structure of the lithic assemblage from AL4 was conditioned by differences in the relative exploitation of these two subsistence species; this interpretation will be further evaluated in the next stages of analysis.

A final comment regarding Figure 5.2 concerns those classes of lithic items which carry relatively the most information regarding assemblage structure. The most informative variables in a principle components analysis are those which are weighted most strongly on the individual components, and in Figure 5.2 these variables correspond to the lithic classes having the most extreme locations along the component axes: bladelets, backed bladelets, burins, blades, flakes, chips, unidentifiable debitage, and spalls. Thus it is seen that classes of lithic waste provide much greater information regarding organizational differences in lithic technology than do classes of lithic tools.

5.2.4 Summary

Stage 2 of the analysis of interassemblage variability at Grubgraben has been concerned with eliciting organizational relations between different classes of lithic items. Unlike stage 1 of the analysis in which lithic items were classified either as tools or as waste, the lithic inventories in this stage were summarized using ten classes of formal tools and nine classes of lithic waste and debitage (Table 5.2.1). The tool and waste classes were defined in general and broadly functional terms, not only to achieve adequate numerical representation in all the lithic classes but also to reduce the interpretive difficulties that can arise when examining a larger number of tool classes, many of which may be functionally ambiguous [see, for example, the study of Mousterian interassemblage variability by Binford and Binford (1966) in which 40 tool categories are employed]. Fewer and more broadly defined classes do not necessarily yield less ambiguity in interpreting the dimensions of variation, however, even if the function of each lithic class is well established.

When the data on assemblage composition at Grubgraben are conceptualized in terms of lithic items, a fundamental dichotomy in the organization of the tool and debitage categories is revealed (Dimension 1). The variation along this single dimension accounts for 58.34% of the total variance between lithic assemblages.

The positive aspect of Dimension 1 grouped side scrapers, perforators, endscrapers, denticulates, and the lithic waste associated with tool resharpening and breakage (chips, unidentified debitage, and tool fragments). This suite of lithic items was interpreted as a toolkit for generalized cutting, scraping, and perforating purposes. The probable contexts in which these lithic items were organized include the dismemberment of carcasses, the working of animal hides, and other processing tasks for which a variety of tools are used, broken, and resharpened during use.

The negative aspect of Dimension 1 grouped blades and bladelets, burins, backed bladelets, and several kinds of primary manufacturing waste such as cores, flakes, crested pieces, and shatter. This suite of lithic items was interpreted as representing events related to retooling and rehafting operations in which small backed pieces are manufactured, composite tools are repaired, and tools are rehafted.

The second dimension of variability defined by the lithic inventories explained 34.52% of the variance between assemblages and revealed the importance of the relative intensity of endscraper technology. Dimension 2 was markedly asymmetric, with lithic classes indicative of endscraper manufacture and use grouped on the negative aspect, and the remaining classes of tools and waste located on the positive aspect.

The structure of Dimension 3 was weak and the dimension appeared to represent primarily a "noise" component of interassemblage variability. The most interesting feature of Dimension 3 was the clear opposition of burins and burin spalls, indicating that burins were manufactured and resharpened (and spalls were produced) in contexts unrelated to the actual use of burins. Supporting evidence for the separation of events related to burin use and events related to spall production was also seen in the lack of refits between burins and spalls, and in the dissimilar spatial distributions of burins and spalls in level AL1.

5.3 Analysis Stage 3: Classes of Faunal Remains

Previous stages of analysis have examined the structure of interassemblage variability at Grubgraben when the assemblages are described using general classes of remains (stage 1) and classes of lithic tools and waste (stage 2). The third stage of analysis is concerned with elucidating the organizational relations that structure interassemblage variability when the assemblages are conceptualized strictly in terms of faunal remains.

Several broadly defined categories of faunal remains were used in stage 1 of the analysis: small mammals, reindeer, horse, mammoth, and nondiagnostic faunal remains (Table 5.1.1). The analysis resulted in the recognition of several strong and provocative patterns of covariation between faunal categories and between the faunal categories and other classes of remains such as shell items, stone tools, quartz artifacts, and cobbles (Table 5.1.2, Figure 5.1). The size and diversity of the faunal assemblages from Grubgraben, however, are sufficient to support many different descriptions of interassemblage variability; detailed information is available on more than 44,000 specimens of bone, representing at least seven genera of fauna (West 1995; Logan 1990b; Whitney 1992). An analysis of the faunal data using different faunal categories than were used in stage 1 can be expected to shed additional light on the organized use of animals at Grubgraben, and in particular on the organization of different segments of animal anatomy.

In the third stage of analysis attention is directed to the primary subsistence animals at the site, reindeer and horse, and the assemblages are described using anatomical part frequencies for these animals rather than frequencies in "whole animal" taxa as was done for stage 1. This approach allows the variability between assemblages to be understood in terms of the differential treatment and organization of various parts of reindeer and horse anatomy and, together with the results of the analysis of interassemblage variability in lithics (stage 2), provides a firm basis for interpreting the final stage of analysis in which the faunal and lithic data sets are combined and their jointly covariant structure is examined. It is not the purpose of the present analysis, however, to investigate the hunting strategies, butchering patterns, or subsistence-related economic decisions of the hunter-gatherer groups at Grubgraben; these subjects are examined in detail elsewhere (Logan 1990a,b; Whitney 1992; Montet-White 1994; West 1995).

An alternative approach to analysis that was considered involved the study of interassemblage faunal variability for the single taxon of Rangifer, using the anatomical part categories described by Binford (1978b:xiii, 1981:xxvii). The analysis would have enjoyed the advantages of a large corpus of information on reindeer ecology and economic anatomy from which to develop interpretations of the composite variables constructed by the analysis (e.g., Binford 1978b; Spiess 1979; Chase 1986; Gordon 1988; Leader-Williams 1988; Audouze and Enloe 1991; Enloe 1993). However, because climatic and environmental changes during the Last Glacial Maximum are expected to have affected different animal species in different ways (West 1995), it seems preferable to include the secondary subsistence species (horse) with reindeer as a means of recognizing and monitoring possible climatically conditioned shifts in the relative utilization of these two species (Straus 1987; Weniger 1990:177–179; Montet-White 1994:492–493; West 1995). In other words, by using data on both reindeer and horse it is possible to investigate shifts not only in the exploitation of parts within each subsistence species, but also shifts in the exploitation of parts between species.

The inclusion of horse, however, complicates the interpretation of the results because, unlike reindeer, there are at present no critical studies of the economic anatomy of horse upon which to base interpretations of patterning in the distribution and organization of horse remains [West, personal communication 1995; Spiess 1979:256; but see Spiess (1979:256–258, 270–274), West (1995), and studies of modern populations of wild horse by Mohr (1971), Tyler (1972), Bökönyi (1974), Boyd and Houpt (1994), and Mohr and Volf (1996)]. In addition, there are no contemporary hunter-gatherer groups whose subsistence strategy is based primarily on the hunting of wild horse, hence actualistic middle-range learning experiences cannot be pursued with horse as has been done with reindeer (Binford 1978b). In other words, our "knowledge of the moment" (Binford 1984b:9–17) regarding the economic anatomy of horse and the various decision paths and butchering strategies used by horse hunters is essentially nonexistent, even though horse is a significant component of the faunal material at many Paleolithic sites (Musil 1969; Teichert 1971; Combier 1976; Vörös 1982; Svoboda 1985, 1990; Chase 1986; Berke 1987, 1988, 1989; Soffer 1987c; Dobosi et al. 1988; Peterkin et al. 1993; West 1995).

Despite the interpretive difficulties that are introduced into the pattern recognition study by considering both horse and reindeer, both taxa are included in anticipation of recognizing organizational relations between the two that will exhibit patterned change in response to climatic change. This anticipatory belief does not constitute a formal hypothesis or prediction of expected relationships in the data; it is entirely an educated judgement (see Binford 1987a:465–466) as to the variables that are likely to be relevant for exploring the effect of climatic change on species exploitation.

5.3.1 Description of the Data

Stage 1 of the analysis included the following broadly defined classes of faunal remains established by West (1995) in her review of the faunal inventories at Grubgraben: small mammals (Alopex, Lepus, and cf. Lepus); reindeer (Rangifer and cf. Rangifer); horse (Equus and cf. Equus); nondiagnostic faunal remains (primarily highly fragmented reindeer bones); and mammoth (represented only by fragments of ivory). These categories provided an overview of interassemblage faunal variability at Grubgraben in terms of animal taxa and, together with other classes of remains, yielded several indications of organizational patterns between different animals and between animals and the technological component of the assemblages.

For the present analysis, frequencies were tabulated for 14 anatomical elements and groups of elements for reindeer [Rangifer and cf. Rangifer categories (West 1995)] and for horse [Equus and cf. Equus categories (West 1995)] from faunal data collected by West (1995) and Logan (1990a,b) and generously made available for this study. The following anatomical categories were used for both reindeer and horse: tooth (TTH); skull (SK); mandible (MAND); vertebra (VERT); pelvis (PELV); rib (RIB); scapula (SCAP); humerus (HUM); radio-cubitus (RC); carpal and tarsal (CRTR); metapodial (MPOD); femur (FEM); tibia (TIB); phalange (PHAL). For reindeer the frequency of antler (ANT) was also tabulated. The resulting data array (Table 5.3.1) contains 29 faunal categories for the four archaeological levels.

As with the species counts used in stage 1 of the analysis, the frequencies tabulated in each category in Table 5.3.1 are numbers of identifiable specimens (NISP). Despite the vigorous debate regarding the utility of NISP and other indices as summary measures of an archaeofauna (Binford 1978b:69–72, 1978b:478–479, 1981, 1982b, 1984b:48–51; Klein and Cruz-Uribe 1984; Grayson 1984; Ringrose 1993), NISP is used as a measure of faunal element abundance for reasons that were given in the discussion of the data for stage 1: these include its ease of collection; its utility as a gross indicator of species abundance; and the observations of Logan (1990a:71) and Whitney (1992:54) that MNI and NISP yielded comparable patterning for their studies of the faunal assemblages from Grubgraben. In practice, minimal animal units (MAU) are arguably the most appropriate quantity for study of the faunal assemblages (Binford 1984b:48–51; West, personal communication 1994). The use of NISP, however, ensures strict comparability of the results of the present stage of analysis with the patterns recognized in stage 1.

Selection of the anatomical element categories in Table 5.3.1 was guided by several considerations. A starting point was

Table 5.3.1. Analysis Stage 3: Frequencies of Skeletal Elements for Reindeer and Horse.

	Reindeer														
Level	ANT	TTH	SK	MAND	VERT	PELV	RIB	SCAP	HUM	RC	CRTR	MPOD	FEM	TIB	PHAL
AL1	7	55	5	21	29	9	41	29	26	67	31	161	27	40	40
AL2	33	49	16	73	60	12	71	22	31	67	16	347	52	77	20
AL3	133	210	54	332	264	44	473	82	130	293	60	1165	162	305	87
AL4	83	201	35	171	91	28	209	51	77	152	37	460	60	181	53

	Horse													
Level	TTH	SK	MAND	VERT	PELV	RIB	SCAP	HUM	RC	CRTR	MPOD	FEM	TIB	PHAL
AL1	12	2	0	0	2	2	0	0	1	0	11	3	2	12
AL2	16	0	3	2	1	0	1	4	2	0	3	1	8	1
AL3	34	2	8	7	6	5	14	6	20	2	8	7	18	3
AL4	45	8	35	8	15	11	18	18	23	7	29	10	42	1

Frequencies shown are NISP values. ANT: Antler; TTH: Tooth; SK: Skull; MAND: Mandible; VERT: Vertebra; PELV: Pelvis; RIB: Rib; SCAP: Scapula; HUM: Humerus; RC: Radio-cubitus; CRTR: Carpal/Tarsal; MPOD: Metapodial; FEM: Femur; TIB: Tibia; PHAL: Phalange.

provided by the list of categories used by West (1995) for tabulating the reindeer and horse material from Grubgraben, and by Binford (1978b:xiii, 1981:xxvii) for summarizing reindeer bone assemblages in general. However, because the data of Table 5.3.1 will be appended to those of Table 5.2.1 for the final stage of the analysis, producing a data array having many more variables than cases, the number of faunal elements for the present stage of analysis was reduced by combining proximal, distal, and diaphyseal portions of specific bones into single categories. For example, the femur category of Table 5.3.1 comprises all portions of the femur identified by West (1995). Similarly, the atlas, axis, cervical, thoracic, lumbar, and caudal vertebrae are combined into the single class of vertebrae, and the first, second, and third phalanges are grouped. Several elements with zero or very low frequencies for both horse and reindeer (the sternum, patella, and sesamoids) are excluded. The reduced data set has improved analytical properties and retains much of the information that can be expected from a more completely specified anatomical part frequency distribution. There are, however, two important limitations of the data as they have been summarized here.

First, the data in Table 5.3.1 are unlikely to contain sufficient information to adequately address complex patterns of animal procurement and utilization. An investigation of butchering practices, for example, should consider the differential treatment of proximal and distal portions of specific bones, in addition to ancillary information such as the presence and distribution of cut marks, types of breakage, evidence of natural transport, and so forth (West 1995; Logan 1990a,b; Binford 1981, 1984b). First phalanges might be tabulated separately, for example (West 1995), and the cervical, lumbar, and thoracic vertebrae might be distinguished because of their different meat yields.

Another limitation of the faunal data used here arises from the nature of the anatomical categories used to summarize the data. Nearly all of the bones from Grubgraben are broken and fragmentary, and although information on the fragmentation, state of preservation, and many other physical attributes of the bones has been collected (West 1995), this information is not incorporated into the data in Table 5.3.1. Instead, the bones have been summarized as if they were whole elements as found in living animals, and these are not classes that are particularly relevant for the study of taphonomic and formation processes, sorting agencies, and so on (Binford 1987b:83–84; Binford and Bertram 1977).

In summary, the data on faunal assemblage variability at Grubgraben have been conceptualized in terms that are hopefully relevant to the recognition of large-scale organizational patterns in the differential treatment of reindeer and horse. The data have not been summarized in terms that are particularly useful for the detailed study of animal procurement and butchering strategies or taphonomic and site formation processes (Binford 1978b, 1981; Scott 1980; Speth 1983; Chase 1986; Frison and Todd 1986; Logan 1990b; Audouze and Enloe 1991; Enloe 1993; West 1995).

5.3.2 Dimensions of Variability

The frequencies in Table 5.3.1 were transformed to chi-scores to eliminate the variance in the data contributed by scale effects among the variables. The transformed frequencies were then subjected to a scaled principle components analysis, with the results shown in Table 5.3.2. The first dimension of variability accounts for 52.53% of the total variance between assemblages in the chosen faunal classes; the first two dimensions together account for 93.63% of the variance. The third dimension is minor and explains the remaining 6.37% of the variance between faunal assemblages. These figures are in keeping with the results from previous stages of analysis (Table 5.1.2, Table 5.2.2) in which the first composite variable has explained more than one-half of the total interassemblage variability, and the first two composite variables have accounted for well over 90% of the total variance. Description and interpretation of the composite variables in Table 5.3.2 is facilitated by reference to Tables 5.3.3–5.3.5 in which the weights on the three dimensions have been grouped into separate reindeer and horse aspects.

Table 5.3.6 gives the rank-order correlation of the scores on each principle component (Table 5.3.2) with sample sizes (variable totals summed across cases; Table 5.3.1). The probabilities of these correlation coefficients for the second and third principle components are nonsignificant at the 0.10 level, indicating that these dimensions of variability are uncorrelated with sample size through some intermediate variable such as assemblage diversity or collection time (chapter 4). The probabilities of both rho and tau are significant, however, for the first principle component, suggesting that some of the structure of Dimension 1 is indirectly contributed by scale effects or sample sizes despite the transformation to chi-scores. A plot (not shown) of the scores on Dimension 1 versus the natural logarithm of sample size confirms a strong linear relationship between these quantities, with the weights for reindeer elements consistently greater than those for horse elements. Within each taxon, the correlation of principle component score with sample size also remains significant [reindeer ($n=15$): Spearman's rho = 0.5250, $p=0.0445$; Kendall's tau = 0.3714, $p=0.0536$; horse ($n=14$): rho = –0.5925, $p=0.0256$; tau = –0.4111, $p=0.0405$]. These facts suggest that Dimension 1 is partially weighting the faunal elements according to their relative abundance, both between and within the two taxa, via some indirect relationship with sample size such as assemblage diversity.

Table 5.3.2. Analysis Stage 3: Scaled Principle Components for Skeletal Elements for Reindeer and Horse.

Dimension 1		Dimension 2		Dimension 3	
r.MPOD	7.07	h.PHAL	9.17	r.MPOD	2.77
r.VERT	4.00	r.PHAL	5.71	h.TTH	1.84
r.F	2.92	r.CRTR	5.55	r.F	1.48
r.R	2.24	r.SC	3.49	h.H	1.43
r.MAND	1.34	r.RC	2.88	h.T	1.36
r.ANT	–0.26	h.MPOD	2.21	h.MAND	0.76
r.RC	–0.29	r.F	1.27	r.SK	0.70
r.SK	–0.30	r.H	0.77	h.VERT	0.29
r.T	–0.52	r.MPOD	0.66	h.MPOD	0.28
r.PELV	–0.66	r.TTH	0.58	r.PELV	0.23
r.H	–0.82	h.F	0.45	r.ANT	0.20
h.VERT	–1.23	h.TTH	0.45	r.T	0.17
r.SC	–1.44	r.PELV	0.39	r.SC	0.01
r.CRTR	–1.77	h.SK	0.28	h.PELV	–0.12
h.PHAL	–1.82	h.R	–0.35	r.CRTR	–0.21
r.PHAL	–2.03	r.VERT	–0.47	h.CRTR	–0.24
h.F	–2.41	h.PELV	–0.86	r.H	–0.30
h.SC	–2.69	r.SK	–1.46	h.SK	–0.32
h.RC	–2.71	h.VERT	–1.53	r.TTH	–0.34
h.CRTR	–2.94	r.T	–1.57	h.F	–0.41
h.R	–3.30	h.CRTR	–1.62	h.PHAL	–0.54
h.SK	–3.40	h.RC	–2.23	h.R	–0.65
h.H	–3.57	h.H	–2.35	r.PHAL	–0.74
h.TTH	–3.64	h.SC	–2.46	r.MAND	–0.77
h.PELV	–3.75	h.T	–2.79	r.VERT	–0.79
h.T	–5.23	r.R	–3.02	h.SC	–0.86
h.MPOD	–5.97	r.ANT	–3.34	h.RC	–0.89
h.MAND	–6.37	h.MAND	–3.51	r.RC	–0.91
r.TTH	–6.38	r.MAND	–4.06	r.R	–4.06
Singular value	18.24		16.14		6.35
Variance	332.87		260.44		40.37
% Variance	52.53%		41.10%		6.37%
Cumulative %	52.53%		93.63%		100.00%

Prefix "r." indicates reindeer parts; "h." indicates horse parts. See Table 5.3.1 for explanation of abbreviations.

Dimension 1 has a highly asymmetrical structure (Table 5.3.3). The positive aspect of the dimension consists of a small number of classes exclusively from reindeer: metapodial, vertebra, femur, rib, and mandible. These classes are also among those with the largest frequencies in Table 5.3.1. All remaining skeletal elements for reindeer and all of the horse elements are grouped together on the negative aspect of Dimension 1. With the exception of isolated teeth, however, those elements of reindeer that appear on the negative aspect have weights that are generally smaller in magnitude than the weights for the horse elements. In other words, although the negative aspect of Dimension 1 contains elements of both reindeer and horse, it is dominated by horse.

The overall structure of Dimension 1 clearly indicates a separation between the two primary subsistence taxa. This pattern is in part due to the indirect correlation with sample size discussed above, but the separation of events related to horse and events related to reindeer was also found to be one of the defining characteristics of Dimension 1 from stage 1 of the analysis (Table 5.1.2), and for which an autocorrelation with diversity was not evident. In stage 1 the contrast between reindeer and horse (among several other classes of remains) explained 60.27% of the total interassemblage variability. In the present stage, in which only the two focal subsistence taxa are considered, a comparable amount (52.53%) of interassemblage variability in the faunal inventories is also explained by the opposition of reindeer and horse. Thus the results of the present stage of analysis corroborate one of the patterns discovered earlier.

The specific anatomical elements that are responsible for the separation of the primary subsistence animals can now be identified from the construction of the composite variables in Table 5.3.3. The reindeer-dominated positive aspect of Dimension 1 is most strongly defined by the categories of metapodial, vertebra, femur, and rib. Collectively these elements are some of the most numerous in the faunal assemblages, but they are also among the highest utility parts of the reindeer anatomy and are exploited for several purposes: the metapodial elements have the highest marrow indices; the femur has the highest white grease index; the mandible and vertebrae have high yellow grease indices; and the vertebrae, ribs, femora, and mandibles are similar in having high meat utility indices (Binford 1978b: Tables 1.5, 1.9, 1.11, 1.12).

The positive aspect of Dimension 1 is evidently monitoring many of the most useable or highest yield parts of reindeer anatomy with respect to grease and marrow, and serves as a gross indicator of events related to reindeer exploitation. The juxtaposition of marrow-rich and grease-rich elements may seem odd, however, and one might have expected meat-rich elements to be weighted comparably with but oppositely to a suite of grease-rich elements. Thus mandibles and metapodials would have similar weights, and be weighted oppositely to ribs, vertebrae, and upper limbs. That this expectation is not met by Dimension 1 highlights the fact that different conceptualizations of the data will enable different organizational properties of the archaeological record to be studied; the variables chosen for use in this stage of analysis (Table 5.3.1) appear more relevant for monitoring gross levels of animal-part exploitation (independent of their resource, e.g., meat,

Table 5.3.3. Analysis Stage 3: Sorted Scores on Dimension 1.

Horse		Reindeer	
		r.MPOD	7.07
		r.VERT	4.00
		r.F	2.92
		r.R	2.24
		r.MAND	1.34
h.VERT	−1.23	r.ANT	−0.26
h.PHAL	−1.82	r.RC	−0.29
h.F	−2.41	r.SK	−0.30
h.SC	−2.69	r.T	−0.52
h.RC	−2.71	r.PELV	−0.66
h.CRTR	−2.94	r.H	−0.82
h.R	−3.30	r.SC	−1.44
h.SK	−3.40	r.CRTR	−1.77
h.H	−3.57	r.PHAL	−2.03
h.TTH	−3.64	r.TTH	−6.38
h.PELV	−3.75		
h.T	−5.23		
h.MPOD	−5.97		
h.MAND	−6.37		

Prefix "r." indicates reindeer parts; "h." indicates horse parts. See Table 5.3.1 for explanation of abbreviations.

grease, or marrow) than for monitoring differences in the processing of animal parts for specific resources.

The negative aspect of Dimension 1 groups parts from both reindeer and horse, but is most strongly defined by horse elements; with the exception of isolated teeth all elements of reindeer not present on the positive aspect are among the lowest weighted elements on the negative aspect. The classes of horse remains that most strongly structure the negative aspect of Dimension 1 are the mandible, metapodial, and tibia, although most of the horse elements are similarly weighted. As with the positive aspect, the horse elements with the greatest weights tend to be those having the greater frequencies in Table 5.3.1.

The large weight for isolated reindeer teeth on the negative aspect of Dimension 1 deserves comment but is not unusual. Binford (1987b:80, 1989b:451–453) has suggested that isolated teeth can in some contexts be used as indicators of "lag deposits" and "background events", i.e., deposits and events unrelated to the activities of humans and more likely related to natural animal deaths or taphonomic and site formation processes. In the present case, however, the positive aspect of Dimension 1 indicates that reindeer mandibles are covariant with other high-utility parts of the reindeer anatomy, implying that some of the isolated reindeer teeth were introduced to the site by human agency while socketed in the reindeer mandibles (Binford 1984b:104–106). [It is also likely that some teeth were introduced to the site in reindeer maxilla, but information on the maxillary or mandibular status of the isolated teeth was unavailable for this analysis. Reindeer maxillary bone fragments are very rare at Grubgraben, however, with only three specimens recorded in more than 44,000 bone fragments (one specimen in each of levels AL1, AL2, and AL4; these pieces were included with the skull fragments in Table 5.3.1). Evidently the maxilla and mandibles of reindeer were processed in different ways, or experienced differential preservation, leading to the near absence of maxillary fragments but an abundance of mandibular specimens. See West (1995) for a discussion of these patterns].

It is also known, however, that reindeer mandibles were deliberately smashed at Grubgraben to extract their marrow content (chapter 2; Montet-White 1990c: Figures V-7 and V-8; Montet-White and Williams 1994). This activity can be expected to have dislodged teeth from the mandibles and scattered them widely and uniformly across the site, as spatial distribution maps of reindeer teeth at the site clearly indicate. The resulting "background" distribution of isolated teeth would bear little relation to the distribution of mandibles, and would instead be expected to covary with other small and marginal parts of the reindeer anatomy, such as second and third phalanges, carpals and tarsals, that are also likely to accumulate as background deposits. Thus, although teeth and mandibles were introduced to the site as a unit, and could be expected to covary had no further processing occurred, teeth and mandibular fragments ultimately show little relation to one another as the result of experiencing different sequences of processing and deposition events.

In summary, Dimension 1 indicates that slightly more than one-half of the interassemblage faunal variability at Grubgraben is understandable in terms of the relative intensity of exploitation of reindeer versus horse. Essentially the same pattern was observed on Dimension 1 of stage 1 (Table 5.1.2). The present analysis has also indicated, however, that it is the higher utility parts of the reindeer (in terms of grease, marrow, and meat) that are most effective at monitoring the relative level of reindeer exploitation. More marginal reindeer parts are grouped with horse on the negative aspect of Dimension 1, but have weights that are considerably smaller than those for horse. Thus Dimension 1 monitors the relative exploitation of reindeer and horse as essentially whole animals, and does so by separating all horse elements from the more numerous and higher utility parts of the reindeer.

Unlike the results of stage 1 and stage 2, the proportion of variation explained by Dimension 2 (Table 5.3.4) in the present stage of analysis is nearly as high as the proportion explained by Dimension 1 (41.10% for Dimension 2 compared with 52.53% for Dimension 1; Table 5.3.2). An important clue to the interpretation of Dimension 2 is the indication that identical anatomical parts from horse and reindeer are often closely associated in terms of their weights on the principle component (this pattern is seen most clearly in Table 5.3.2). The phalanges, metapodials, isolated teeth, and femora of both horse and reindeer are paired on the positive aspect; the negative aspect pairs the mandibles, vertebrae, tibia, and ribs from both animals. The relatively few parts that are oppositely weighted (one positively and one negatively) are the carpals and tarsals, scapulae, radio-cubitus, humeri, pelves, and skull fragments. With the single exception of the skull, anatomical parts which are not paired on the same aspect of Dimension 2 are uniformly weighted positively for reindeer and negatively for horse.

Table 5.3.4. Analysis Stage 3: Sorted Scores on Dimension 2.

Horse		Reindeer	
h.PHAL	9.17	r.PHAL	5.71
h.MPOD	2.21	r.CRTR	5.55
h.F	0.45	r.SC	3.49
h.TTH	0.45	r.RC	2.88
h.SK	0.28	r.F	1.27
		r.H	0.77
		r.MPOD	0.66
		r.TTH	0.58
		r.PELV	0.39
h.R	−0.35	r.VERT	−0.47
h.PELV	−0.86	r.SK	−1.46
h.VERT	−1.53	r.T	−1.57
h.CRTR	−1.62	r.R	−3.02
h.RC	−2.23	r.ANT	−3.34
h.H	−2.35	r.MAND	−4.06
h.SC	−2.46		
h.T	−2.79		
h.MAND	−3.51		

Prefix "r." indicates reindeer parts; "h." indicates horse parts. See Table 5.3.1 for explanation of abbreviations.

In general terms, Dimension 2 groups those parts of the reindeer and horse anatomy that were similarly treated, and also indicates those parts that were differently organized. The positive aspect of Dimension 2 is defined primarily by the feet, upper and lower limbs, shoulders, and rear quarters of reindeer, and by the feet, lower legs, and skulls of horse. The negative aspect of this dimension is characterized by head parts of reindeer, the shoulders, upper front legs and rear quarters of horse, and by some of the choicer parts (ribs and vertebrae) from both horse and reindeer. Discussions of similar patterns of the differential representation of parts from the same animal and from different animals (Binford 1981, 1984b; Enloe 1993) suggest that Dimension 2 is separating the "gourmet" portions of horse, and to a lesser extent reindeer, on the negative aspect from the "marginal" elements of these animals on the positive aspect. These terms are used by Binford (1981, 1984b) to describe patterns of exploitation of animal anatomy; gourmet parts are those with high meat yield and marginal parts are ones with little useable meat. With regard to Dimension 2, however, the distinction appears to involve not only meat yield, but also marrow and grease yields; the contrast is better described in terms of high- and low-utility parts rather than in terms of meat-rich (gourmet) and meat-poor (marginal) parts.

Although the negative aspect of Dimension 2 groups several of the higher-utility parts of the reindeer such as the ribs, vertebrae, and mandibles, it may seem odd that several other choice, meat-rich parts such as the upper limbs (femur and humerus) and the shoulder (scapula) are not also present. Interestingly, the upper limbs and the shoulder of reindeer are also absent from the positive aspect of Dimension 1 (Table 5.3.3), which otherwise serves to group those parts that are most representative of the overall level of reindeer exploitation. The implication is not that these meat-rich parts of the reindeer were unimportant, but that they are relatively less informative than ribs, vertebrae, and mandibles for distinguishing the assemblages (chapter 4).

Also present on the negative aspect of Dimension 2 are the ribs, rear quarters, shoulders, and upper legs of horse, all of which are the choicer segments of the equid anatomy [West, personal communication 1995; these are also among the choicer parts of the bovid anatomy (Binford 1984b)]. In contrast, the positive aspect of Dimension 2 groups the more marginal parts from both reindeer and horse; these are most obviously represented by the bones of the feet and lower limbs.

In summary, Dimension 2 monitors the utilization of different suites of parts from reindeer and horse, and separates the anatomy of each animal into high- and low-utility aspects. The separation is most complete for horse; some "noise" in the separation of parts for reindeer is attributed to the fact that the distinction for reindeer was already partially revealed by Dimension 1 (Table 5.3.3).

As in the previous stages of analysis, the third composite variable (Table 5.3.5) explains only a small proportion of the total variance between assemblages (6.37%; Table 5.3.2). The weights on the third dimension are uniformly weak, and the dimension is primarily a residual "noise" component of the interassemblage variation in faunal material. The positive aspect contains metapodials and tibia from both horse and reindeer, and the negative aspect groups the radio-cubitus, phalanges, ribs, and carpals/tarsals from both reindeer and horse. Among the parts of reindeer and horse that are oppositely weighted, however, there is no systematic weighting of either animal on the positive or the negative aspect; this is additional evidence that Dimension 3 is reporting random, residual background noise in a data set which is almost completely summarized by its first two principle components (Table 5.3.2).

The major opposition on Dimension 3 is between reindeer limbs (metapodials and femora) on the positive aspect and reindeer ribs on the negative aspect. This opposition is suggestive of the dichotomy of marrow and meat as the primary food items obtained from reindeer, but could also be an indication of the differential processing, sequence of use, or storage of these parts. Thus, although the first two dimensions of variation are informative of the differential exploitation and treatment of segments of reindeer and horse anatomy, the third composite variable may be weakly indicative of the differential use of parts from the primary subsistence animal (reindeer).

5.3.3 Case/Variable Relations

The relationships between the cases (archaeological levels) and the variables (anatomical parts) used in this stage of analysis are displayed graphically in Figure 5.3 using the first two principle components from Table 5.3.2. Variation along the first and second principle components subsumes 93.63% of the total variation between assemblages (Table 5.3.2), therefore Figure

Table 5.3.5. Analysis Stage 3: Sorted Scores on Dimension 3.

Horse		Reindeer	
h.TTH	1.84	r.MPOD	2.77
h.H	1.43	r.F	1.48
h.T	1.36	r.SK	0.70
h.MAND	0.76	r.PELV	0.23
h.VERT	0.29	r.ANT	0.20
h.MPOD	0.28	r.T	0.17
		r.SC	0.01
h.PELV	−0.12	r.CRTR	−0.21
h.CRTR	−0.24	r.H	−0.30
h.SK	−0.32	r.TTH	−0.34
h.F	−0.41	r.PHAL	−0.74
h.PHAL	−0.54	r.MAND	−0.77
h.R	−0.65	r.VERT	−0.79
h.SC	−0.86	r.RC	−0.91
h.RC	−0.89	r.R	−4.06

Prefix "r." indicates reindeer parts; "h." indicates horse parts. See Table 5.3.1 for explanation of abbreviations.

5.3 summarizes nearly all of the information in the faunal data of Table 5.3.1.

Inspection of Figure 5.3 clearly reveals the major covariant patterns recognized above. Dimension 1 serves to distinguish the relative levels of reindeer and horse exploitation in the assemblages. The positive (right) aspect of the first principle component axis is completely defined by a small number of high-utility reindeer elements: metapodials, vertebrae, femora, ribs, and mandibles. All other anatomical parts for both reindeer and horse are located on the negative (left) aspect of Dimension 1. The horse parts have the more extreme values, indicating that they are more informative than the negatively weighted reindeer parts in defining the negative aspect of Dimension 1.

The second principle component axis in Figure 5.3 introduces variation referable to the differential treatment of high- and low-utility parts from reindeer and horse. Grouped on the negative (lower) aspect of Dimension 2 are several of the higher utility parts of the reindeer (ribs, vertebrae, and mandibles), and many of the meat-rich, gourmet parts of horse (ribs, rear quarters, shoulders and upper legs). In contrast, the positive (upper) aspect of Dimension 2 is defined by the lower utility parts, such as the bones of the feet and lower limbs, from both reindeer and horse.

The positions of the archaeological levels are also indicated in Figure 5.3, and it is evident that the four occupations differ considerably in the structure of their faunal assemblages. Archaeological levels AL2 and AL3 are most similar when measured by their faunal inventories; levels AL1 and AL4 differ markedly from each other and from levels AL2 and AL3.

The faunal assemblage from AL1 derives its distinctive character from its extreme location along the positive aspect of Dimension 2, indicating the greater-than-expected frequencies of the feet and lower legs of both reindeer and horse. The interpretation of the positive aspect of Dimension 2 as a monitor of the more marginal parts of horse and reindeer implies that the faunal assemblage in AL1 was structured by events in which these marginal parts were of greater importance than is seen in the other levels.

The faunal assemblages from AL2 and AL3 are similar in their greater-than-expected amounts of the higher utility parts of the reindeer anatomy such as metapodials, femora, vertebrae, ribs, and mandibles. The metapodials contribute strongly to the structure of AL3, whereas AL2 is somewhat less extreme in this respect and shows relatively greater contributions by the other elements. Both AL2 and AL3 have small scores on Dimension 2, implying less use of marginal parts in these levels, and both are displaced far to the right on Dimension 1, indicating the emphasis on reindeer instead of horse.

The faunal assemblage from AL4 is completely unlike the assemblages from AL1–AL3 and is structured predominantly by horse parts. The most informative elements are the mandible and parts of the limbs such as the metapodials, tibia, and humeri. The extreme position of AL4 in Figure 5.3 is not evidence for the exploitation of horse to the exclusion of reindeer in this level, but only an indication that horse remains provide relatively the most information for describing the structure of its faunal assemblage. In AL4 reindeer remains are still more abundant than horse remains (Table 5.1.1, Table 5.3.1), and concentrations of reindeer mandibles and bone fragments were identified during the excavation of the level (Montet-White 1990c: Figure V-15). The relationships in Figure 5.3 indicate, however, that the essential differences between AL3 and AL4 are not only in the focal subsistence animal—horse in AL4 as opposed to reindeer in AL3—but also in the parts of the anatomy that were exploited from each animal.

5.3.4 Summary

In stage 3 of the analysis of interassemblage variability at Grubgraben the structure of variation between the assemblages was investigated using classes of faunal remains for reindeer and horse, the two primary subsistence animals at the site. Several covariant relationships between the faunal classes were observed that confirmed general relationships recognized in stage 1, and additional organizational information was revealed by the more detailed classes of faunal remains.

Dimension 1 indicates that a large proportion (52.53%, Table 5.3.2) of the variability between assemblages at Grubgraben can be understood simply in terms of the relative intensity of events involving reindeer compared with events involving horse. This finding confirms a pattern first recognized in stage 1 of the analysis (Table 5.1.2). The positive aspect of Dimension 1 consists of a small number of exclusively reindeer elements with high marrow-, grease-, and meat-utility indices; the negative aspect of Dimension 1 is dominated by horse elements. Parts of reindeer not found on the positive aspect of Dimension 1 are grouped with horse on the negative aspect, but with weights that are generally much smaller than those for horse.

The second dimension of interassemblage faunal variability monitors the relative degree of utilization of higher and lower utility parts from horse and reindeer. The higher utility parts of both animals dominate the negative aspect of Dimension 2; these include the head parts of reindeer, the upper legs, shoulders, and rear quarters of horse, and some of the meat-rich parts from both horse and reindeer such as ribs and vertebrae. Grouped on the positive aspect of Dimension 2 and varying oppositely to the suite of higher utility parts are the more marginal, lower utility elements such as the limbs, shoulders, and rear quarters of reindeer, and the feet, lower legs, and skulls of horse. The distinction between high- and low-utility parts appears more complete for horse than for reindeer because of the previous partial separation by Dimension 1 of the marginal and higher utility parts for reindeer.

The structure of Dimension 3 is weak and, as in previous stages of analysis, the dimension represents primarily the noise in interassemblage variability that remains after the variation explained by the first two dimensions of variability is removed. The main opposition on Dimension 3 is between the limb parts (metapodials and femora) and ribs of reindeer, possibly indicating that some of the structure between faunal assemblages can be understood in terms of the differential use of reindeer elements for meat and for marrow.

5.4 Analysis Stage 4: Lithics and Fauna

At this point the structure of interassemblage variability at Grubgraben has been examined in terms of general classes of remains (stage 1), classes of lithic tools and debris (stage 2), and classes of faunal remains for reindeer and horse (stage 3). The latter two stages of analysis have resulted in the recognition of several provocative organizational relations *within* the classes of lithic and faunal remains.

Table 5.3.6. Analysis Stage 3: Correlation Coefficients between Principle Component Scores and Sample Sizes.

Principle Component	n	Spearman's Rho	Probability	Kendall's Tau	Probability
1	29	0.6066	0.0005	0.4296	0.0011
2	29	0.0665	0.7317	0.0346	0.7923
3	29	−0.0557	0.7742	−0.0642	0.6249

Probability values are two-tailed.

Figure 5.3. Analysis Stage 3: Faunal Remains.

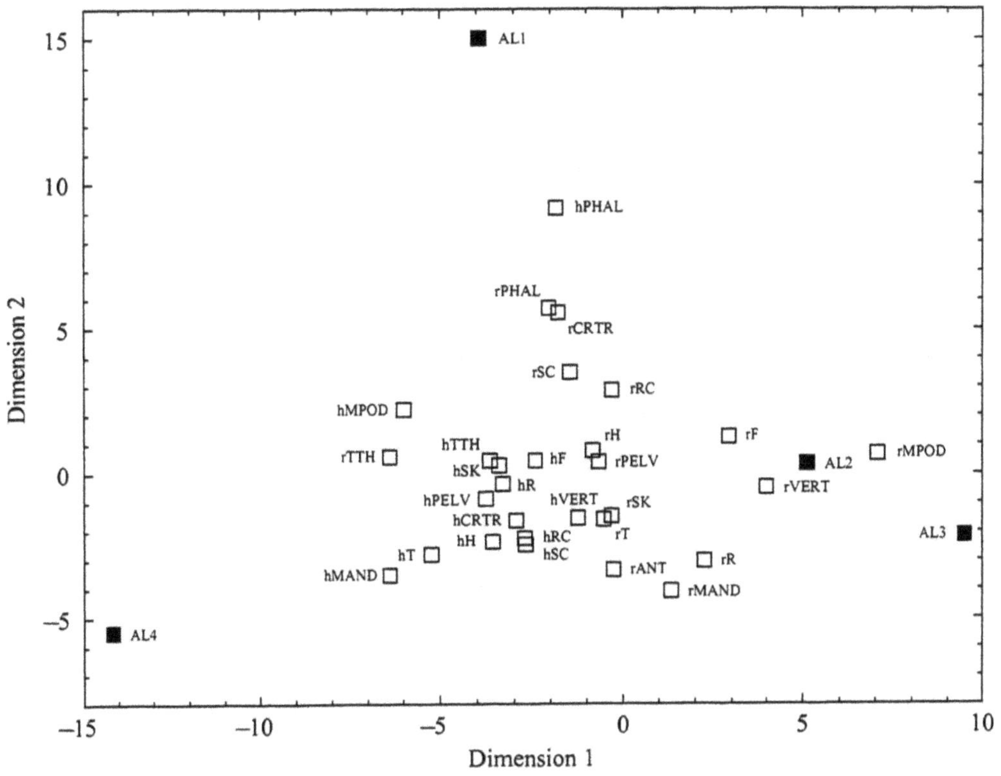

The purpose of the fourth and final stage of analysis is to seek evidence of organizational relations *between* these classes of remains, i.e., between the lithic items and the anatomical elements of the subsistence animals. In other words, which lithic tools and kinds of lithic waste covary with which reindeer elements, and which lithic classes covary with which elements of horse? Do the patterns of covariation that are discovered make sense in terms of what is known about the use of stone tools for the butchering and processing of these animals? It is reasonable to expect organizational relations to exist between tools, waste, and fauna because not only were tools used together with other tools (yielding the within-lithic organizational relations recognized in stage 2), but the exploitation of animals is expected to have been tool-assisted as well, yielding organizational relations between lithic and faunal classes.

5.4.1 Description of the Data

To elucidate the organizational relations between classes of lithic items and classes of faunal remains, a composite lithic/faunal data set is investigated using the same analytical procedure as in previous stages. The definitions of the various classes of lithic and faunal remains are unchanged, and the lithic and faunal data sets from stage 2 (Table 5.2.1, 19 lithic classes) and stage 3 (Table 5.3.1, 29 classes of faunal remains for reindeer and horse) are simply concatenated to form a single array. In view of the provocative covariation of quartz artifacts and cobbles with some classes of fauna (particularly horse remains and nondiagnostic faunal material) observed in stage 1, these two classes of remains from Table 5.1.1 are included with the lithics and fauna. Because the data for this stage are assembled from previously tabulated data, they are not repeated here in a separate table.

The composite data array for stage 4 of the analysis contains 4 cases and 50 variables, and the disparity in the number of cases and variables is much greater than for any of the arrays from earlier stages of analysis. Although the scaled principle components method described by Harpending and Rogers (1985) constructs dimensions of variation that are "best fits" in a least-squares sense, and does so irrespective of the numbers of cases and variables (Press et al. 1989:61–74; Horn and Johnson 1985: chapter 7), the nature of the data array may compromise the clarity and definition of the principle component results. Similar concerns have been voiced by Vierra (1975:90), Cowgill (1970), and Read (1985) with regard to factor analysis.

5.4.2 Dimensions of Variability

The frequencies in the composite data array were transformed to chi-scores to remove the variance contributed by scale effects and the transformed data were then subjected to a scaled principle components analysis. The results are given in Table 5.4.1. The first dimension of variability accounts for 70.82% of the total variance between assemblages in the combined lithic and faunal classes; the first two dimensions together explain 94.66% of the variance. As in previous stages of analysis, the third dimension is relatively uninformative and explains only 5.34% of interassemblage variability. These percentages are similar to those found in stage 1 of the analysis, where lithic and faunal information was also jointly analyzed, but with fewer and more coarsely defined categories. Description and interpretation of the composite variables in Table 5.4.1 is facilitated by reference to Tables 5.4.2–5.4.4 in which the weights on the three principle components have been separated to show the individual contributions by lithics (including cobbles and quartz), reindeer, and horse.

Table 5.4.5 gives the rank-order correlation of the scores on each principle component in Table 5.4.1 with sample sizes (variable totals summed across cases are from Table 5.1.1 for quartz and cobbles, Table 5.2.1 for lithics, and Table 5.3.1 for horse and reindeer). The probabilities of the correlation coefficients for the first and third principle components are non-significant at the 0.10 level, indicating that these dimensions of variability are uncorrelated with sample size.

The correlation coefficients for the second principle component, however, are very nearly significant at the 0.10 level. A plot (not shown) of the scores on Dimension 2 against the natural logarithm of sample size fails to confirm visually any strong linear relationship, but does reveal that reindeer elements consistently have larger weights than horse elements, and that weights for lithic items are not patterned with sample size. Within the categories of reindeer, horse, and lithics the correlation of principle component score with sample size is significant only for horse [reindeer ($n=15$): Spearman's rho $=0.1036$, $p=0.7134$; Kendall's tau $=0.0857$, $p=0.6560$; horse ($n=14$): rho $=-0.5176$, $p=0.0580$; tau $=-0.3445$, $p=0.0862$; lithics ($n=21$): rho $=-0.0571$, $p=0.8163$; tau $=0.0178$, $p=0.9154$]. These facts suggest that Dimension 2 is weakly structured by scale effects via an intermediate variable such as diversity or collection time, but the relationship is only within the faunal categories, and then primarily within the classes of horse remains.

Dimension 1 clearly separates reindeer from both horse and lithic items. The positive aspect of Dimension 1 is overwhelmingly defined by the anatomical elements of reindeer, and with few exceptions the lithic items and horse elements appear entirely on the negative aspect. The most strongly weighted parts of reindeer on the positive aspect are the metapodial, rib, mandible, vertebra, tibia, and femur; these are the same elements that defined the positive aspect of Dimension 1 in stage 3 (see Table 5.3.3) as a monitor of many of the higher utility parts of the reindeer anatomy. In fact, the entire weighted sequence of reindeer parts on this dimension corresponds closely to the order in which these parts appear on the combined positive and negative aspects of Dimension 1 from stage 3. The few lithic items and horse elements that appear on the positive aspect of Dimension 1 have weights that are much smaller than those for reindeer.

The negative aspect of Dimension 1 is defined by classes of horse remains and lithic items. Among the parts of horse on the negative aspect the phalanges, metapodials, and skull parts are weighted most strongly, which reiterates a pattern seen on the positive aspect of Dimension 2 in stage 3 (Table 5.3.4). The most strongly weighted lithic items are the retouched and unretouched blades and bladelets, flakes, shatter, burins and chips; this pattern is similar to the construction of the negative aspect of Dimension 1 in stage 2 (Table 5.2.2). As a group the lithic classes on the negative aspect are well separated from the elements of horse.

In summary, Dimension 1 reports essentially no new organizational information. The clear separation of events related to reindeer from events involving all other kinds of remains was first observed in stage 1 and detected again in stage 3, and the inclusion of lithic classes with the faunal classes in the present analysis clearly does not obscure or significantly modify this pattern.

It is interesting to note that the first dimension of variability does a remarkable job of separating the three major kinds of remains (reindeer, lithics, and horse). From Tables 5.4.1 and 5.4.2 it is easily seen that the absolute magnitudes of the weights for reindeer elements are consistently larger than those for lithics, which in turn are consistently larger than those for horse. If the magnitudes of the weights on Dimension 1 are taken as indicators of the classes of remains that are most informative for understanding interassemblage variability, then the rank-ordering is clearly reindeer followed by lithics and then by horse. Given the correlations in Table 5.4.5, this ordering of classes on Dimension 1 is unlikely to be an effect of variation in sample size.

Despite the nearly complete separation of lithics, reindeer, and horse on Dimension 1, there are a few instances of overlap between these groups (the overlaps are most easily detected by inspecting Table 5.4.1). The weights associated with the overlaps are small, however, and must be interpreted cautiously. On the positive aspect of Dimension 1 side scrapers, cobbles, and other tools (tool fragments) are grouped with the pelves, teeth, and scapulae of reindeer and the radio-cubitus, scapulae, and vertebrae of horse. The lithic classes are suggestive of scraping tasks, tool breakage, and percussion by hammerstones (Beck 1993), and it is conceivable that these actions were consistently performed with specific animal parts during butchering and disarticulation. The associated faunal elements, however, appear unrelated and do not represent specific anatomical segments, except perhaps for the shoulder.

On the negative aspect of Dimension 1, however, marginally retouched blades, quartz pieces, endscrapers, cores, crested pieces, and unidentifiable debitage covary closely with the feet, lower legs, and head parts of horse. The lithic classes are suggestive of core reduction and the use of endscrapers and expedient cutting tools (marginally retouched blades), and the faunal classes are provocative because they are exclusively from horse and represent well-defined anatomical segments such as the lower leg and head. The implication is that these parts of the horse anatomy were most closely or consistently organized with actions requiring heavy cutting implements (quartz, marginally retouched blades) and scraping tools (endscrapers).

Although these covariant relations between specific lithic items and classes of faunal remains are suggestive, they are poorly monitored by the dimension itself. Dimension 1 is foremost a measure of the variance contributed by the differences between assemblages in the broad categories of reindeer, horse, and lithic remains, and does not provide a useful monitor of the weak but potentially significant overlaps between items from these categories. The lack of any appreciable overlap between classes of lithics and classes of reindeer and horse remains on Dimension 1 does not indicate an absence of organizational relations between these different kinds of remains, but it is an indication that the relations between these classes contribute much less interassemblage variability than do the relations within these classes. In other words, the organizational rela-

Table 5.4.1. Analysis Stage 4: Scaled Principle Components for Lithic Items, Reindeer and Horse Elements, Quartz, and Cobbles.

Dimension 1		Dimension 2		Dimension 3	
r.MPOD	17.78	Bladelets	7.31	r.R	4.30
r.R	12.66	Spalls	6.62	Burins	2.73
r.MAND	10.41	Burins	5.78	Bladelets	2.16
r.VERT	9.65	r.MPOD	5.59	Crested pieces	2.14
r.T	7.64	Backed bladelets	5.33	Flakes	2.04
r.F	6.26	h.PHAL	4.29	Blades	2.03
r.ANT	6.10	Marg. ret. blades	4.16	r.TTH	1.99
r.RC	5.86	Crested pieces	3.86	r.RC	1.91
r.H	3.97	Unid. debitage	2.99	r.PHAL	1.89
r.SK	3.39	r.F	2.87	h.PHAL	1.62
r.PELV	2.14	Cores	2.75	h.RC	1.29
Side scrapers	2.05	r.VERT	2.64	r.CRTR	1.26
r.TTH	1.95	r.CRTR	2.30	h.R	1.20
h.RC	1.37	r.PHAL	2.27	h.SC	1.20
r.SC	1.33	r.RC	1.87	r.MAND	1.03
Cobbles	1.27	Cobbles	1.66	r.H	0.98
Other tools	1.22	Other tools	1.48	h.MPOD	0.95
h.SC	1.17	r.SC	1.32	h.SK	0.92
h.VERT	0.98	Notch/Denticulate	1.12	h.F	0.91
r.PHAL	0.25	Truncations	0.60	r.SC	0.89
Notch/Denticulate	0.03	Blades	0.43	r.VERT	0.85
Perforators	−0.14	r.R	0.17	h.PELV	0.73
r.CRTR	−0.29	r.H	0.16	h.CRTR	0.61
h.TTH	−0.33	Perforators	−0.04	r.T	0.56
h.H	−0.33	r.PELV	−0.07	Marg. ret. blades	0.51
h.T	−0.39	Side scrapers	−0.44	Backed bladelets	0.39
h.CRTR	−0.41	r.T	−0.92	Splintered pieces	0.29
h.F	−0.48	r.SK	−0.93	r.PELV	0.21
h.R	−0.78	Chips	−1.02	r.ANT	0.09
h.PELV	−0.83	r.MAND	−1.16	h.MAND	0.09
Splintered pieces	−0.87	h.F	−1.23	h.VERT	−0.10
Truncations	−1.01	Shatter	−1.28	r.SK	−0.42
h.MAND	−1.18	h.VERT	−1.65	h.T	−0.55
h.SK	−1.48	Splintered pieces	−1.70	Cores	−0.71
Crested pieces	−2.18	Endscrapers	−1.86	h.H	−0.91
Cores	−3.25	r.ANT	−1.91	h.TTH	−0.92
Unid. debitage	−3.32	h.SK	−1.99	Other tools	−1.06
h.MPOD	−3.35	h.TTH	−2.00	Side scrapers	−1.08
Endscrapers	−3.87	h.R	−2.28	Truncations	−1.13
h.PHAL	−4.29	h.MPOD	−2.49	Chips	−1.17
Quartz	−4.50	h.CRTR	−2.82	r.F	−1.20
Marg. ret. blades	−4.60	h.PELV	−2.87	Quartz	−1.45
Spalls	−5.02	h.RC	−2.96	Notch/Denticulate	−1.61
Backed bladelets	−8.54	h.SC	−3.10	Endscrapers	−2.08
Chips	−8.93	r.TTH	−3.47	r.MPOD	−2.15
Burins	−9.11	h.H	−3.67	Perforators	−2.27
Shatter	−9.65	h.T	−4.96	Shatter	−2.99
Blades	−13.13	h.MAND	−6.13	Unid. debitage	−3.31
Flakes	−13.31	Flakes	−6.15	Spalls	−3.55
Bladelets	−14.30	Quartz	−12.38	Cobbles	−3.67
Singular value	43.87		25.45		12.05
Variance	1924.13		647.75		145.10
% Variance	70.82%		23.84%		5.34%
Cumulative %	70.82%		94.66%		100.00%

Table 5.4.2. Analysis Stage 4: Sorted Scores on Dimension 1.

Lithics		Reindeer		Horse	
Side scrapers	2.05	r.MPOD	17.78	h.RC	1.37
Cobbles	1.27	r.R	12.66	h.SC	1.17
Other tools	1.22	r.MAND	10.41	h.VERT	0.98
Notch/Denticulate	0.03	r.VERT	9.65		
		r.T	7.64	h.TTH	−0.33
Perforators	−0.14	r.F	6.26	h.H	−0.33
Splintered pieces	−0.87	r.ANT	6.10	h.T	−0.39
Truncations	−1.01	r.RC	5.86	h.CRTR	−0.41
Crested pieces	−2.18	r.H	3.97	h.F	−0.48
Cores	−3.25	r.SK	3.39	h.R	−0.78
Unid. debitage	−3.32	r.PELV	2.14	h.PELV	−0.83
Endscrapers	−3.87	r.TTH	1.95	h.MAND	−1.18
Quartz	−4.50	r.SC	1.33	h.SK	−1.48
Marg. ret. blades	−4.60	r.PHAL	0.25	h.MPOD	−3.35
Spalls	−5.02			h.PHAL	−4.29
Backed bladelets	−8.54	r.CRTR	−0.29		
Chips	−8.93				
Burins	−9.11				
Shatter	−9.65				
Blades	−13.13				
Flakes	−13.31				
Bladelets	−14.30				

Prefix "r." indicates reindeer parts; "h." indicates horse parts. See Table 5.3.1 for explanation of abbreviations.

tions within classes of lithics (stage 2), and within classes of horse and reindeer remains (stage 3), are more significant contributors to interassemblage variability than the relations between lithics and fauna.

This situation might have been anticipated if the organizational relations between animal remains and lithic tools are primarily consequences of immutable physical properties of the objects themselves. For example, the mechanical requirements of carcass disarticulation and dismemberment, and the physical specifications of the tools, are expected to remain the same irrespective of environmental or climatic changes. Thus, if a marginally retouched blade is effective for disarticulating a carcass [a tool as expedient as a piece of broken glass is entirely adequate (Binford 1978b:62–63)], then it will remain effective for the task provided the physical properties of the tool and the carcass are unchanged. There is therefore no reason to expect that a marginally retouched blade was a less effective tool for butchering a fresh carcass in level AL1 than it was in level AL4, consequently the (hypothetical) organization of marginally retouched blades and animal carcasses should not be expected to contribute significantly to the variability between assemblages. Thus relations within the major categories of material (fauna and lithics) assume a greater importance for understanding interassemblage variability than relations between these categories.

Dimension 2 is presented in sorted order in Table 5.4.3. For the most part reindeer and horse remains continue to covary oppositely to one another: reindeer dominates the positive aspect and horse the negative aspect of this dimension. Lithic items, however, are separated into two suites by Dimension 2.

The positive aspect of Dimension 2 groups the metapodials, vertebrae, and most limb parts for reindeer; the negative aspect consists primarily of head parts. With minor variations this pattern is the same as that observed on the second dimension of stage 3 (Table 5.3.4), and interpreted there as a distinction between the higher and lower utility segments of the reindeer anatomy. The distinction was clearer in stage 3, however, presumably because of the smaller number of variables used for the same number of cases.

The negative aspect of Dimension 2 contains all of the horse elements with the exception of phalanges, and these elements (including the phalanges) also appear in much the same order as they did on the second dimension of stage 3. The more negatively weighted horse parts on Dimension 2 correspond well with the suite of higher utility parts from stage 3.

Lithic items are divided into two covariant groups by Dimension 2. The negative aspect comprises flakes, endscrapers, splintered pieces, shatter and chips, with quartz artifacts and unretouched flakes weighted most strongly. Most of the remaining classes of tools and waste are located on the positive aspect of Dimension 2. With minor differences these same groups of lithic items were observed earlier on the second dimension of stage 2 (Table 5.2.2), and interpreted there as monitoring the intensity of the endscraper technology relative to the remaining stone tool industry.

As with the first dimension of variability, Dimension 2 repli-

Table 5.4.3. Analysis Stage 4: Sorted Scores on Dimension 2.

Lithics		Reindeer		Horse	
Bladelets	7.31	r.MPOD	5.59	h.PHAL	4.29
Spalls	6.62	r.F	2.87		
Burins	5.78	r.VERT	2.64	h.F	−1.23
Backed bladelets	5.33	r.CRTR	2.30	h.VERT	−1.65
Marg. ret. blades	4.16	r.PHAL	2.27	h.SK	−1.99
Crested pieces	3.86	r.RC	1.87	h.TTH	−2.00
Unid. debitage	2.99	r.SC	1.32	h.R	−2.28
Cores	2.75	r.R	0.17	h.MPOD	−2.49
Cobbles	1.66	r.H	0.16	h.CRTR	−2.82
Other tools	1.48			h.PELV	−2.87
Notch/Denticulate	1.12	r.PELV	−0.07	h.RC	−2.96
Truncations	0.60	r.T	−0.92	h.SC	−3.10
Blades	0.43	r.SK	−0.93	h.H	−3.67
		r.MAND	−1.16	h.T	−4.96
Perforators	−0.04	r.ANT	−1.91	h.MAND	−6.13
Side scrapers	−0.44	r.TTH	−3.47		
Chips	−1.02				
Shatter	−1.28				
Splintered pieces	−1.70				
Endscrapers	−1.86				
Flakes	−6.15				
Quartz	−12.38				

Prefix "r." indicates reindeer parts; "h." indicates horse parts. See Table 5.3.1 for explanation of abbreviations.

cates the structure of previously examined principle components. However, Dimension 2 displays more extensive overlap between the lithic and faunal classes than is observed on Dimension 1; with the considerable variance subsumed by Dimension 1 having been removed, any structure contributed by lower-variance organizational relations between classes can be expressed more clearly.

The negative aspect of Dimension 2 contains two areas of overlap: quartz pieces and unretouched flakes covary with the mandibles, shoulders, and limb parts of horse, and the remaining lithic items (endscrapers, resharpening chips, splintered pieces, shatter) covary with the head parts of both reindeer and horse. If these covariant relations between specific lithic items and anatomical elements are organizationally relevant, then they imply the regular use of specific lithic equipment with particular segments of animal anatomy. Such relationships would not be unexpected: we may anticipate, for example, the use of scraping tools to remove adhering meat, tendons, or the periosteum (Binford 1981:134) prior to cracking and marrow extraction. The interassemblage variability contributed by these relationships, however, is unfortunately not expressed in unambiguous form on the available principle components.

On the positive aspect of Dimension 2 the technology indicative of rehafting and retooling events (blades, bladelets, burins, primary production waste) is interspersed with the limbs of reindeer. It is conceivable that this suite of lithic items was organized with events related to hide tailoring and general outfitting tasks in which delicate cutting operations, the manufacture of needles and awls, or even the preparation of dentalia and perforation of animal teeth involved the use of bladelets as cutting elements in composite tools (Moss 1983:115–116). Bones from the lower extremities of reindeer (and from the skulls and feet of small mammals, although these items are not considered in stage 4) could have remained attached to their skins and entered the archaeological record as "riders" during events related to clothing production (Binford 1978b:63–64, 1978b:74, 1981:42–43, 1981:234; Soffer 1985:271). An alternative interpretation is that the observed covariance is a consequence of the tendency for events involving these lithic and faunal elements to take place in a common spatial theater (see discussion of stage 1). In other words, a tendency for retooling, rehafting, and outfitting or tailoring operations to be conducted in similar places (e.g., around hearths, and in domestic spaces in general), could easily generate a depositional "covariation" between the material items involved in these events without these items being organized in any direct sense (Whallon 1973b, 1984; Binford 1983a; Kind 1985; Gamble 1991).

As is the case with Dimension 1, the overlaps on Dimension 2 are suggestive of organizational relations between specific lithic and faunal items, but the amount of interassemblage variation contributed by these relations is insufficient to be expressed over the much larger variance contributed by the relations within the categories of lithics, reindeer, and horse. Dimension 2 does not effectively monitor these weaker organizational patterns, and essentially reports a dimension of interassemblage variability that was recognized and described in previous stages of analysis.

Table 5.4.4. Analysis Stage 4: Sorted Scores on Dimension 3.

Lithics		Reindeer		Horse	
Burins	2.73	r.R	4.30	h.PHAL	1.62
Bladelets	2.16	r.TTH	1.99	h.RC	1.29
Crested pieces	2.14	r.RC	1.91	h.R	1.20
Flakes	2.04	r.PHAL	1.89	h.SC	1.20
Blades	2.03	r.CRTR	1.26	h.MPOD	0.95
Marg. ret. blades	0.51	r.MAND	1.03	h.SK	0.92
Backed bladelets	0.39	r.H	0.98	h.F	0.91
Splintered pieces	0.29	r.SC	0.89	h.PELV	0.73
		r.VERT	0.85	h.CRTR	0.61
Cores	−0.71	r.T	0.56	h.MAND	0.09
Other tools	−1.06	r.PELV	0.21		
Side scrapers	−1.08	r.ANT	0.09	h.VERT	−0.10
Truncations	−1.13			h.T	−0.55
Chips	−1.17	r.SK	−0.42	h.H	−0.91
Quartz	−1.45	r.F	−1.20	h.TTH	−0.92
Notch/Denticulate	−1.61	r.MPOD	−2.15		
Endscrapers	−2.08				
Perforators	−2.27				
Shatter	−2.99				
Unid. debitage	−3.31				
Spalls	−3.55				
Cobbles	−3.67				

Prefix "r." indicates reindeer parts; "h." indicates horse parts. See Table 5.3.1 for explanation of abbreviations.

The sorted scores on Dimension 3 are given in Table 5.4.4. The dimension is a minor one, however, and explains only 5.34% of the total interassemblage variance in the combined lithic/faunal data set. With few exceptions, the weights on this dimension are uniformly low among all categories of remains. However, any new organizational relations between the lithic, reindeer, and horse categories may not appear until the variation within these categories has been removed by the initial, large-variance principle components, so it is of interest to examine the dimension for patterning.

The individual reindeer, horse, and lithic contributions to this dimension are generally similar to those obtained in previous stages of analysis. The sequence of reindeer parts on Dimension 3 is nearly the same as on the third dimension from stage 3 (Table 5.3.5), especially among those parts having the larger weights, and the strongest opposition on the dimension continues to be between metapodials and ribs. The sequences for horse elements and for lithic items are also similar to previously obtained patterns (Tables 5.3.5 and 5.2.2, respectively).

The most interesting feature of Dimension 3 is the presence of most of the reindeer and horse parts on the positive aspect, whereas the lithic classes are more evenly distributed between the positive and negative aspects. The positive aspect of Dimension 3 groups burins with flakes and with all of the unretouched blade items (bladelets, crested pieces, and blades). The inclusion of crested pieces in this suite is reasonable, because these are typically unretouched, blade-like pieces with triangular cross-section. At much lower weights some retouched blade forms also appear (marginally retouched blades and backed bladelets). The negative aspect of Dimension 3 groups the remaining lithic items (all of the formal tool types and classes of debitage and waste).

It is evident from Table 5.4.4 that Dimension 3 is indicating that the burin and blade component of the lithic technology was most directly organized with events involving the subsistence animals. Unretouched blades are efficient cutting instruments and were probably well suited to the dismemberment and butchering of animal carcasses; Binford (1978b:62–63), for example, has documented the use of a small piece of broken glass for the "near complete butchering of a frozen caribou". If information were available on the frequencies of utilized and unutilized blades and flakes, this interpretation could be further evaluated; utilized flakes would be expected to covary most strongly with the subsistence taxa if they were indeed used in the cutting and butchering of carcasses, and unutilized flakes should covary strongly with the formal tools and the classes of primary production debris.

In summary, Dimension 3 is partially monitoring the use of a particular suite of lithic items—unretouched blades and flakes—in the exploitation of the subsistence animals. This organizational relation explains only a small proportion of the total interassemblage variability, however, and it must be remembered also that Dimension 3 is likely to contain most of the random "noise" in interassemblage variability, which will confound any efforts to use this dimension as a monitor of organizational change.

5.4.3 Case/Variable Relations

In Figure 5.4 the first two principle components are used to display the structural relationships between the cases and variables used in this stage of analysis. To avoid cluttering the figure only the most informative variables (those having the most extreme positions on the axes) are labeled; the identity of the unlabeled variables can be determined easily by reference to the definitions of the dimensions in Table 5.4.1. By using the first two dimensions of variation to display the relations between cases and variables, 94.66% of the information in the combined lithic/faunal data set is summarized in graphical form. Because the dimensions of variability elicited in this stage of analysis are essentially identical to those from stage 2 and stage 3, Figure 5.4 is very similar to the case/variable plots for those stages (Figure 5.2 and Figure 5.3).

The covariant suites of lithic classes and faunal elements discussed above are easily recognized in Figure 5.4. Dimension 1 is effectively separating reindeer remains, which are almost entirely located on the right side (positive aspect) of the figure, from the remains of horse and from the lithic classes, which are located on the negative aspect of Dimension 1. Dimension 2 does little to structure the horse remains, but is effective in separating the lithic classes related to endscraper production and use from other lithic items. The second dimension of variation also separates the reindeer remains into suites of higher and lower utility parts as was seen in the case/variable plot for stage 3 (Figure 5.3).

The locations of the archaeological levels are also shown in Figure 5.4, and correspond closely with their locations in the case/variable plots from stage 2 and stage 3. Level AL1 is characterized by a lithic assemblage oriented toward the use of burins with blades and bladelets, and by a faunal assemblage with an emphasis on the lower utility parts of the horse and reindeer anatomy. The structure of the assemblages from levels AL2 and AL3 is contributed largely by the greater-than-expected quantities of higher utility parts of reindeer and by a lithic inventory indicative of the manufacture and use of general cutting, scraping, and perforating tools. The greater-than-expected number of reindeer metapodials in AL3 is the single greatest factor in separating levels AL2 and AL3 along Dimension 2. The assemblage from level AL4 is structured primarily by the horse remains and the endscraper component of the stone tool technology. All of these aspects of assemblage structure were recognized in earlier stages of analysis (especially stage 2 and stage 3).

5.4.4 Summary

In stages 2 and 3 of the analysis of interassemblage variability at Grubgraben, organizational relationships were recognized within classes of lithics and within classes of faunal remains. In stage 4 of the analysis, the lithic and faunal data sets from stages 2 and 3 were combined and the composite data array was examined. The three dimensions of variability reported in Table 5.4.1 were found to be essentially identical to the corresponding dimensions from stages 2 and 3 of the analysis, and no new organizational patterns were recognized.

Dimension 1 reported an almost total separation of events involving reindeer from events involving lithics and events involving horse. The weighted sequence of items within the categories of lithic, reindeer, and horse remains closely paralleled the structure of the first dimension from stage 2 (lithics) and from stage 3 (reindeer and horse). Dimension 2 separated reindeer remains and lithics into positive and negative aspects that corresponded well with the patterns reported by the second dimension from stage 2 (lithics) and from stage 3 (reindeer). Horse remains were grouped almost entirely on the negative aspect of Dimension 2, and covaried most closely with the endscraper component of the lithic technology. Reindeer remains, and particularly the limb bones, were generally covariant with the rehafting and retooling component of the lithic assemblages. Dimension 3 was primarily a low-variance "noise" component that reiterated much of the information obtained from the third dimensions of stages 2 and 3. Dimension 3 also suggested, however, an organizational relation between the subsistence animals and the blade and flake component of the lithic technology. This relation was weak but well defined, and appeared to monitor the organized use of unretouched blades and flakes in events involving the dismemberment and butchering of animal carcasses.

The purpose in analyzing a composite lithic/faunal data set was to seek evidence of organizational relations between, rather than within, the categories of lithic items and anatomical elements for reindeer and horse. However, stage 4 of the analysis did not lead to the recognition of well-defined organizational relations between these kinds of remains. Instead, covariant groups within the lithics and within the fauna that had been observed in previous stages of analysis reappeared in stage 4. Some indications of the organization of particular faunal and lithic items were obtained in the form of overlapping lithic, reindeer, and horse categories, but the anticipated organizational relations between tools, waste, and fauna were not clearly expressed.

Table 5.4.5. Analysis Stage 4: Correlation Coefficients between Principle Component Scores and Sample Sizes.

Principle Component	n	Spearman's Rho	Probability	Kendall's Tau	Probability
1	50	0.0960	0.5072	0.1072	0.2720
2	50	0.2315	0.1058	0.1579	0.1056
3	50	–0.0243	0.8667	–0.0172	0.8602

Probability values are two-tailed.

Figure 5.4. Analysis Stage 4: Lithics and Fauna.

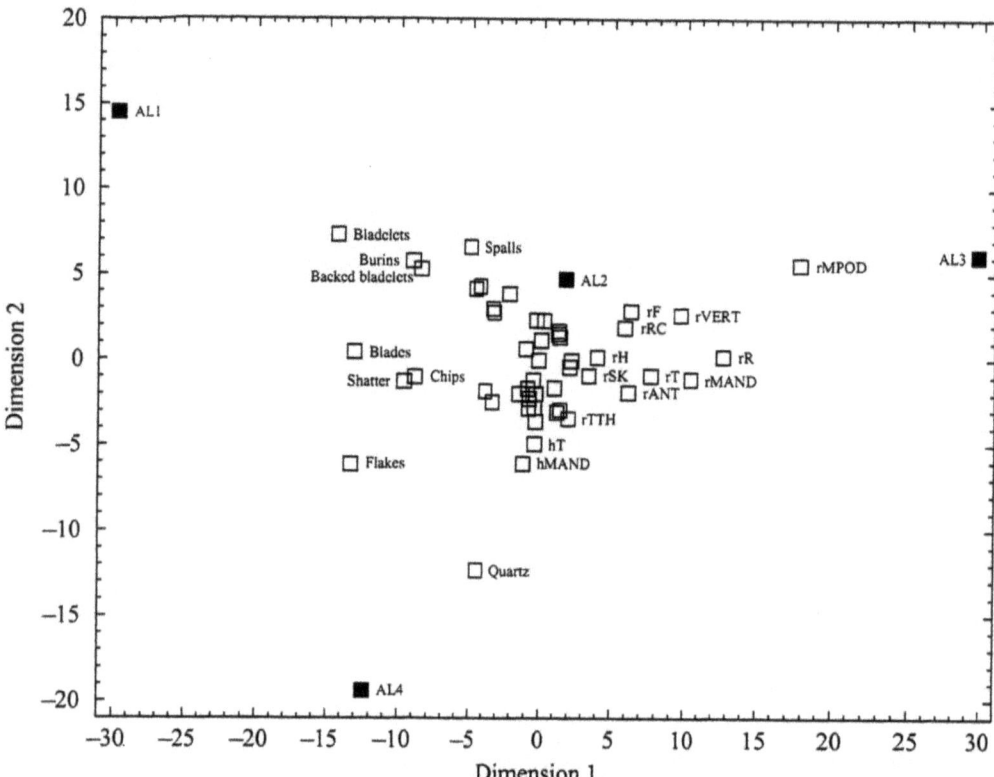

The failure to detect robust and detailed organizational relations in the present stage of analysis is believed to be due to the much larger number of variables used—nearly twice as many variables were used in stage 4 as in any of the previous stages—without a corresponding increase in the number of cases available for defining the dimensions of variation. The presence of additional cases (archaeological levels) would allow additional principle components to be defined and thus enable additional, low-variance organizational relations to be recognized. Even with the large number of variables used in this stage of analysis, however, the three available dimensions of variation were still able to monitor the same covariant patterns in lithic and faunal classes that were reported by earlier stages of analysis, which speaks well for the robusticity of both the patterns and the analytical technique used to detect them.

6.0 Diachronic Variability in Organizational Properties

The dimensional analysis of interassemblage variability presented in chapter 5 resulted in the recognition of several provocative organizational relations between different classes of remains in the archaeological deposits at Grubgraben. These organizational relations were manifested as suites of mutually covariant classes of remains, and were recognized using a principle components analysis of normalized frequency data on assemblage composition to elicit independent dimensions of interassemblage variability.

The task in this chapter is to examine the organizational relations recognized and interpreted in chapter 5 for patterned diachronic variation. How do the archaeological levels at Grubgraben differ when measured by their organizational properties? Do all organizational relations change in similar fashion from level to level, or are there multiple patterns of diachronic variability? In this chapter it is only the *form* of diachronic organizational variability at Grubgraben that is established; in the following chapter specific *causes* will be sought for diachronic variability in the organizational properties of the assemblages.

6.1 Method of Comparison

Each stage of analysis in chapter 5 yielded three principle components, or composite variables, representing independent dimensions of interassemblage variability. The definition of each composite variable was inspected and each variable was interpreted as monitoring some property of the assemblage sequence resulting from the organization of materials and activities in the cultural system that produced the assemblages. Examples of these organizational relations include the use of small mammals, shell, and tools in the context of meeting general outfitting needs (stage 1, Dimension 2; Table 5.1.2), the intensity of use of endscraper technology relative to the remaining stone tool industry (stage 2, Dimension 2; Table 5.2.2), and the relative levels of exploitation of the lower and higher utility parts from reindeer and horse (stage 3, Dimension 2; Table 5.3.4).

Because each principle component is essentially a new variable monitoring an organizational property of interassemblage variability, diachronic patterning in the organizational properties can be investigated by scoring the assemblages on these principle components and placing the scores in chronological (stratigraphic) order. This comparison was made implicitly in the case/variable plot for each stage of the analysis in chapter 5 by locating each assemblage on the diagram according to its scores on the first two composite variables. These data and patterns are now presented in a more appropriate form for comparison and discussion of diachronic trends.

In Figures 6.1–6.4 the scores on each principle component for each assemblage have been plotted for each of the four stages of analysis: general classes of remains (Figure 6.1); classes of lithic items (Figure 6.2); classes of anatomical elements for reindeer and horse (Figure 6.3); and combined lithic and faunal remains (Figure 6.4). Each figure illustrates the variation from archaeological level AL4 to level AL1 in the three principle components from the respective data set. The scores on the first dimension of variability are marked with open circles, scores on the second dimension are marked with open squares, and scores on the third dimension are marked with open triangles. The figures are most effectively viewed by orienting them to place the levels in their correct stratigraphic order, with AL4 at the bottom and AL1 at the top.

6.2 General Classes of Remains

In the first stage of the analysis of interassemblage variability the archaeological deposits were summarized in terms of a small number of broadly defined classes of remains (Table 5.1.1). Three dimensions of variability were elicited, the first two of which explained 96.77% of the total variability between assemblages (Table 5.1.2, Figure 5.1).

Dimension 1 was found to separate the classes of remains related to reindeer (reindeer and nondiagnostic faunal remains on the positive aspect) from all other classes of material. The negative aspect was dominated by lithic waste, but indicated two additional groups of closely covariant classes: shell, small mammals, and tools; and horse and quartz artifacts. Dimension 1 was interpreted as separating events related to the exploitation of reindeer from a generalized suite of "non-reindeer" events involving the deposition of lithic waste; the organized use of shell, small mammals, and tools; and the organization of quartz artifacts with the exploitation of horse.

The trajectory of Dimension 1 in Figure 6.1 indicates that the assemblage from AL4 is structured slightly more by the generalized suite of "non-reindeer" events than by events related to reindeer. Between AL4 and AL3 the character of the assemblage changes markedly, however. Level AL3 scores highly on the positive aspect of Dimension 1, indicating that the assemblage from this level is structured primarily by events related to the exploitation of reindeer. From level AL3 to AL1 the trajectory of Dimension 1 changes smoothly and toward increasingly negative values, indicating a gradual and steady shift in the relative roles of reindeer and "non-reindeer" events in structuring the deposits. The marked emphasis on reindeer exploitation in AL3 changes to nearly equal contributions by reindeer and "non-reindeer" events in AL2, and to a clear dominance in AL1 of events unrelated to reindeer exploitation.

Dimension 2 from stage 1 of the analysis monitored the organized use of shell items and small mammal remains on its negative aspect, and the organization of quartz artifacts with the primary subsistence animals (reindeer and horse) on its positive aspect. Dimension 2 was interpreted as a contrast between events related to tailoring and general outfitting tasks and events related to the subsistence effort and the use of quartz tools in the exploitation of horse and reindeer.

The trajectory of Dimension 2 in Figure 6.1 exhibits a pronounced increase with time, from a large positive value in AL4 to moderately negative values in the remaining levels. During the AL4 occupation the archaeological deposits were struc-

Figure 6.1. Analysis Stage 1: General Classes of Remains.

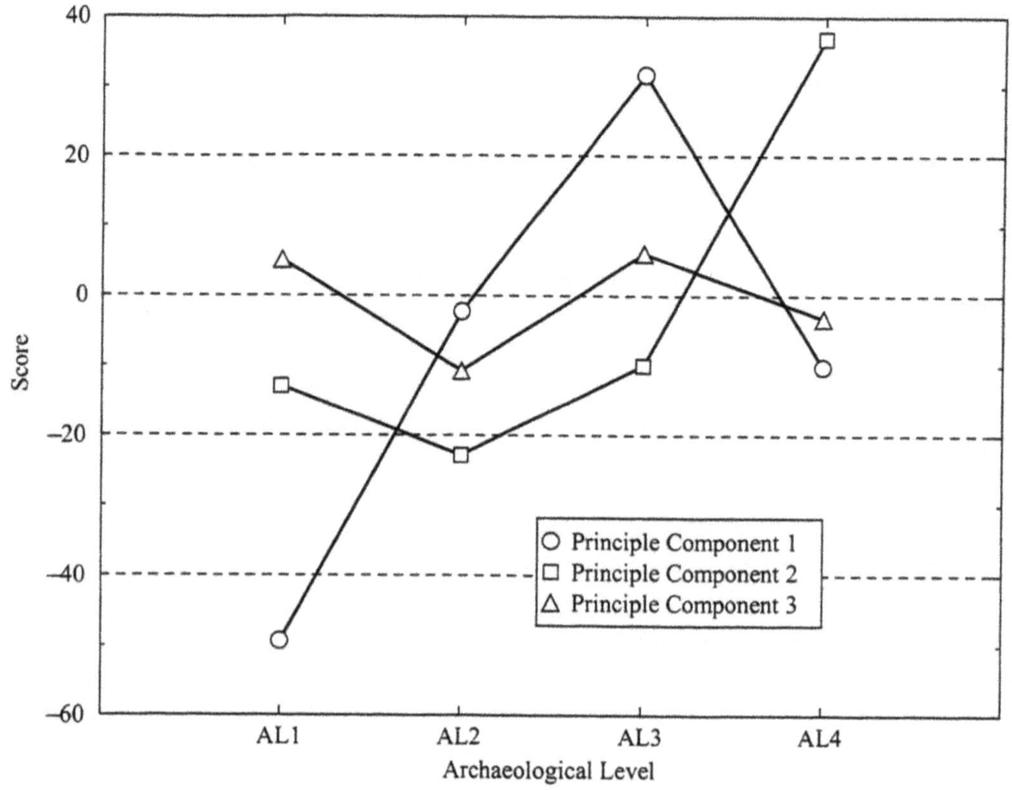

tured primarily by events related to the subsistence effort (the organized use of reindeer, horse, and quartz). The assemblages produced by subsequent occupations, however, all show a significant increase in the importance of events related to tailoring and outfitting (the organized use of shell and small mammals) [see also Soffer (1985:326–327)].

Dimension 3 from stage 1 explained only 3.23% of the total interassemblage variability in general classes of remains, but exhibited some weak organizational structure. The positive aspect of the dimension introduced reindeer into the context of hide tailoring, clothing production, and general outfitting tasks that was initially recognized on Dimensions 1 and 2. The negative aspect indicated an organization of quartz pieces and cobbles with nondiagnostic faunal material, probably in the context of smashing bones for marrow extraction or bone grease production.

The trajectory of Dimension 3 in Figure 6.1 is irregular and undirected, indicating that the interassemblage variability monitored by this dimension is diachronically unpatterned. It does not follow, however, that the organizational properties themselves are unpatterned; the appearance of the trajectory is instead attributed to the presence on Dimension 3 of a comparable amount of noise in the data on interassemblage variability that acts to obscure any genuine organizational patterning.

6.3 Classes of Lithic Items

The second stage of analysis examined interassemblage variability in lithic inventories using classes of formal tools and classes of lithic waste (Table 5.2.1). The first two dimensions of variation explained 92.86% of the total variability between assemblages (Table 5.2.2, Figure 5.2).

Dimension 1 separated two major industrial contexts of tool use and maintenance. The first context (positive aspect) involved the use of many formal tool classes such as side scrapers, endscrapers, perforators, and notches and denticulates, and included classes of debitage indicative of tool use, resharpening, and breakage (unidentifiable debitage, chips, and tool fragments). Organizationally this suite of lithic items implicated general cutting, scraping, and perforating tasks, probably in the contexts of animal processing and hide working. The second technological context, monitored by the negative aspect of Dimension 1, involved lithic items indicative of core reduction, the primary production of blades and bladelets, and the use of burins, backed bladelets, and marginally retouched blades. This suite of items implicated the production of *armatures* and the maintenance of hafted and composite tools in events related to retooling and rehafting tasks.

The trajectory of Dimension 1 in Figure 6.2 indicates that the assemblage from AL4 is characterized by approximately equivalent contributions by each aspect of this industrial dichotomy. Thus, events related to general utility tool use and events related to retooling and rehafting operations contribute equally to the character of the lithic assemblage from AL4. Following AL4 the assemblage from AL3 shows a slight increase in the importance of events related to general tool use. From level AL3 to AL1 the proportion of events related to general tool use declines, however, and events related to rehafting

Figure 6.2. Analysis Stage 2: Lithics.

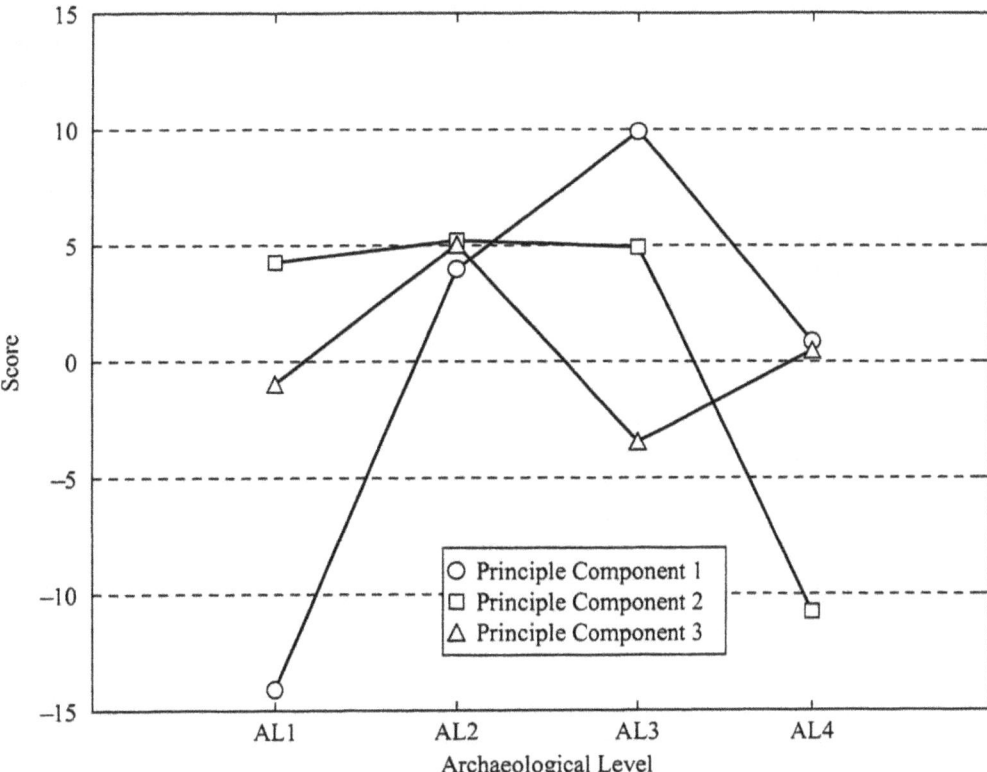

and retooling become increasingly important until the assemblage from AL1 is predominantly structured by such events.

Dimension 2 from stage 2 of the analysis was found to monitor the intensity of endscraper technology relative to the technology involving other kinds of tools. The negative aspect of this dimension was defined by lithic items related to endscraper manufacture, use, and maintenance, and the positive aspect comprised all remaining tools and debitage classes.

The trajectory of Dimension 2 in Figure 6.2 initially parallels that of Dimension 1, and the assemblage from AL4 is structured mostly by events related to the endscraper component of the lithic industry. From AL4 to AL3 the relative intensity of endscraper technology declines markedly; the proportions of endscraper and non-endscraper technology become more equable and remain so from AL3 to AL1 (there is actually a slight emphasis on the non-endscraper technology for levels AL3–AL1).

Dimension 3 from stage 2 explained a small amount (7.14%) of the interassemblage variability in lithic items, but two weak organizational properties were tentatively recognized in its structure: the opposition of shatter and crested pieces suggested an industrial dichotomy in the contexts of core modification and reduction; and the opposition of burins and burin spalls indicated that the manufacture and resharpening of burins occurred in contexts unrelated to their use and eventual discard.

Figure 6.2 illustrates that the trajectory of Dimension 3 from stage 2 of the analysis is unpatterned across archaeological levels. As with Dimension 3 from stage 1, any organizational structure on the third principle component is evidently confounded with the noise component of interassemblage variability, yielding an overall unpatterned trajectory.

6.4 Classes of Faunal Remains

In the third stage of analysis the assemblages were summarized in terms of anatomical part frequencies for reindeer and horse (Table 5.3.1). These are the two primary subsistence animals at Grubgraben and are therefore the faunal taxa most likely to reveal climatically conditioned organizational changes in faunal exploitation (Straus 1987; Weniger 1990:177–179; Montet-White 1994:492–493; West 1995). Three dimensions of variability were elicited, the first two of which were comparable in the proportion of variance explained. Together the first two components accounted for 93.63% of the total interassemblage variability in reindeer and horse frequencies (Table 5.3.2, Figure 5.3).

Dimension 1 of stage 3 reiterated and refined some of the structure of Dimension 1 from stage 1 (Table 5.1.2) by indicating a strong separation of events related to reindeer from events related to horse. The positive aspect grouped a small number of higher utility parts of reindeer (metapodials, vertebrae, femora, ribs, mandibles), whereas the negative aspect of Dimension 1 grouped all horse elements and the remaining parts of reindeer. Overall, Dimension 1 monitors the intensity of reindeer exploitation relative to horse.

The trajectory of Dimension 1 in Figure 6.3 indicates that level AL4 is characterized by a greater relative exploitation of horse than reindeer, after which a shift toward relatively greater rein-

Figure 6.3. Analysis Stage 3: Faunal Remains.

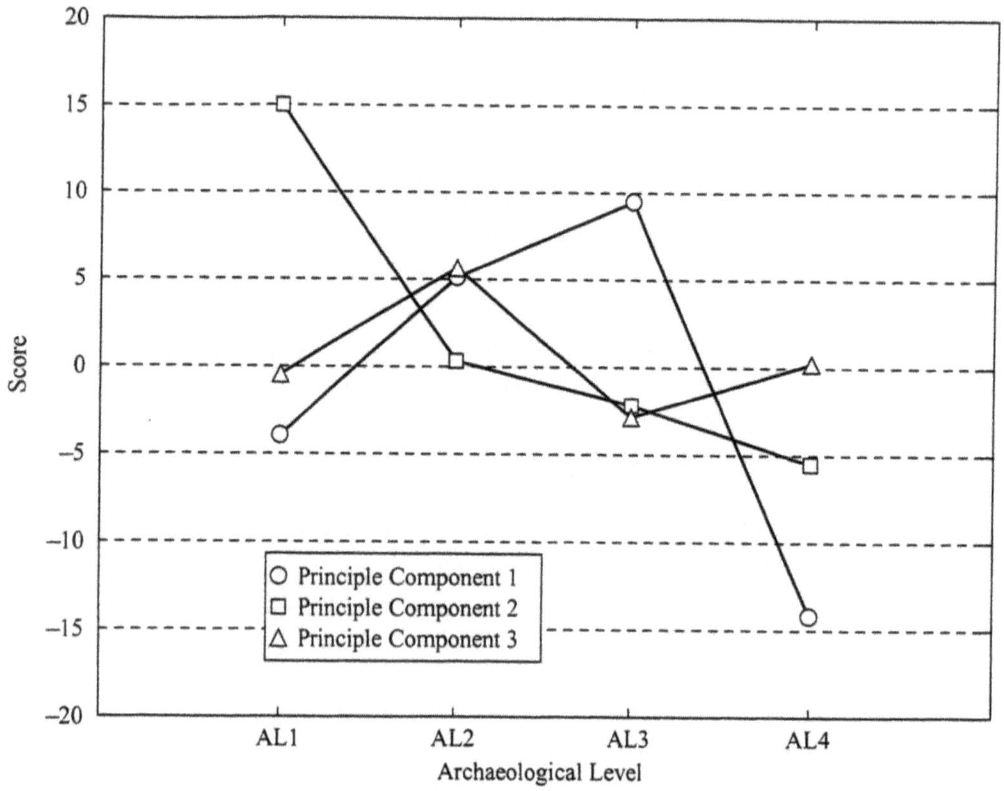

deer exploitation is observed. From AL3 to AL1 a gradual increase in the exploitation of horse is observed, although horse exploitation does not return to the level that characterizes AL4.

Dimension 2 from stage 3 was interpreted as a monitor of the use of different suites of parts from horse and reindeer. In particular, the negative aspect of Dimension 2 grouped the higher utility parts of horse and reindeer (parts with high meat, grease, and marrow indices), whereas the positive aspect was defined by the more marginal, lesser utility parts of these animals. The distinction between high and low utility parts was found to be more complete for horse than for reindeer, which was attributed to the earlier partial separation by Dimension 1 of the higher and lower utility parts of reindeer.

The trajectory of Dimension 2 in Figure 6.3 exhibits a steady increase from a small negative score for AL4 to a large positive score for level AL1. Thus level AL4 is characterized by a moderate emphasis on the higher utility parts of horse (and of reindeer, although reindeer is not as intensively exploited in AL4). The use of more marginal parts of the subsistence animals increases steadily, however, and by the time of the occupation of level AL1 the structure of the faunal assemblage clearly indicates a marked emphasis on the use of more marginal parts from both reindeer and horse. The shift from higher to lower utility parts is relative, however, and animal parts with any utility at all were presumably used. The trajectory of Dimension 2 points to the increasing importance of lesser utility parts from AL4 to AL1, but does not indicate that the use of marginal parts gradually replaced the use of higher utility parts.

Dimension 3 of stage 3 explained a small proportion (6.37%) of interassemblage variability, but appeared weakly indicative of the differential use of reindeer elements for meat and for marrow. This organizational information is obscured, however, by comparable amounts of variance contributed by the noise component of interassemblage variability, and the resulting trajectory of Dimension 3 in Figure 6.3 is diachronically unpatterned.

6.5 Classes of Lithics and Fauna

In the fourth and final stage of analysis the data sets from stage 2 (classes of lithics; cobbles and quartz were included from stage 1) and stage 3 (classes of reindeer and horse remains) were combined and their joint covariant structure was studied. The purpose in analyzing the combined data set was to seek evidence of organizational relations between, rather than within, these different kinds of material remains. Three dimensions of variability were elicited, the first two of which accounted for 94.66% of the total interassemblage variability in the lithic, reindeer, and horse inventories (Table 5.4.1, Figure 5.4).

Dimension 1 of stage 4 reiterated the organizational information provided by the first dimensions of stages 2 and 3. A separation between events related to reindeer and events related to horse was clearly indicated, and the lithic component of the assemblages was grouped into aspects indicative of events related to general utility tool use and events related to retooling and rehafting. Very little overlap among the lithic, reindeer, and horse categories was observed. Not surprisingly, the trajectory of Dimension 1 from stage 4 in Figure 6.4 is essentially identical to the trajectory of Dimension 1 from both stage 2

(Figure 6.2) and stage 3 (Figure 6.3).

Dimension 2 of stage 4 was found to reproduce the dimensions of interassemblage variability initially recognized as Dimension 2 of stage 2 (lithics) and Dimension 2 of stage 3 (fauna). Horse and reindeer were separated into suites of higher and lower utility parts, and the blade and endscraper component of the lithic technology was separated from the remaining lithic items. Consequently, the trajectory of Dimension 2 in Figure 6.4 is essentially the sum of the trajectories of the second dimension of variability from stage 2 (Figure 6.2) and stage 3 (Figure 6.3). The small overlaps observed on Dimension 2 between specific lithic and faunal items do not influence the trajectory of the dimension to any observable extent.

Finally, Dimension 3 from stage 4 of the analysis (Table 5.4.4) explained only 5.34% of interassemblage variability but appeared to monitor a weak but well structured organizational relation between the subsistence animals and the blade and flake component of the lithic technology. It is clear from Figure 6.4, however, that the interassemblage variability contributed by this relation is either diachronically unpatterned or, more likely, insufficient to rise above the comparable level of variation contributed by random noise in the data.

6.6 General Observations

Several recurring patterns are immediately apparent in the diachronic trajectories of the principle components shown in Figures 6.1–6.4. The score on the first principle component from each stage of analysis is small (near zero) for AL4, but has increased markedly to a moderate or high positive value for AL3. From AL3 to AL1 the score on the first principle component decreases steadily and smoothly and in most cases regains and eventually exceeds the value in AL4. The overall effect is for the first principle component to exhibit a sharp bend and reversal of direction at AL3, indicating a marked change between the occupations of AL4 and AL3 in the factors conditioning assemblage variability that are reported by this dimension.

The trajectories of the second principle components in Figures 6.1–6.4 are less uniformly patterned than are the first principle components but still have several features in common. The trajectories from stages 2–4 begin with moderately negative values in AL4 and increase steadily but unevenly to moderately positive values in AL1. An interesting deviation from this pattern in seen in Dimension 2 for classes of lithics (Figure 6.2, open squares); there is a marked increase in the score on this dimension from AL4 to AL3, after which the scores decrease only slightly.

The trajectory of Dimension 2 from stage 1 (Figure 6.1, open squares) appears to deviate radically from the pattern established by the other second principle components. The difference is due partly to the magnitude of the scores on this dimension (they are much greater), but also to the orientation of the trajectory; whereas the second principle components from stages 2–4 increase from AL4 to AL1, the second principle component from stage 1 decreases in like manner. However, if the second principle component from stage 1 is reversed by negating its scores for AL4–AL1, then the resulting trajectory is more obviously similar to those of the other second principle components. Reflecting the trajectory in this way amounts only

Figure 6.4. Analysis Stage 4: Lithics and Fauna.

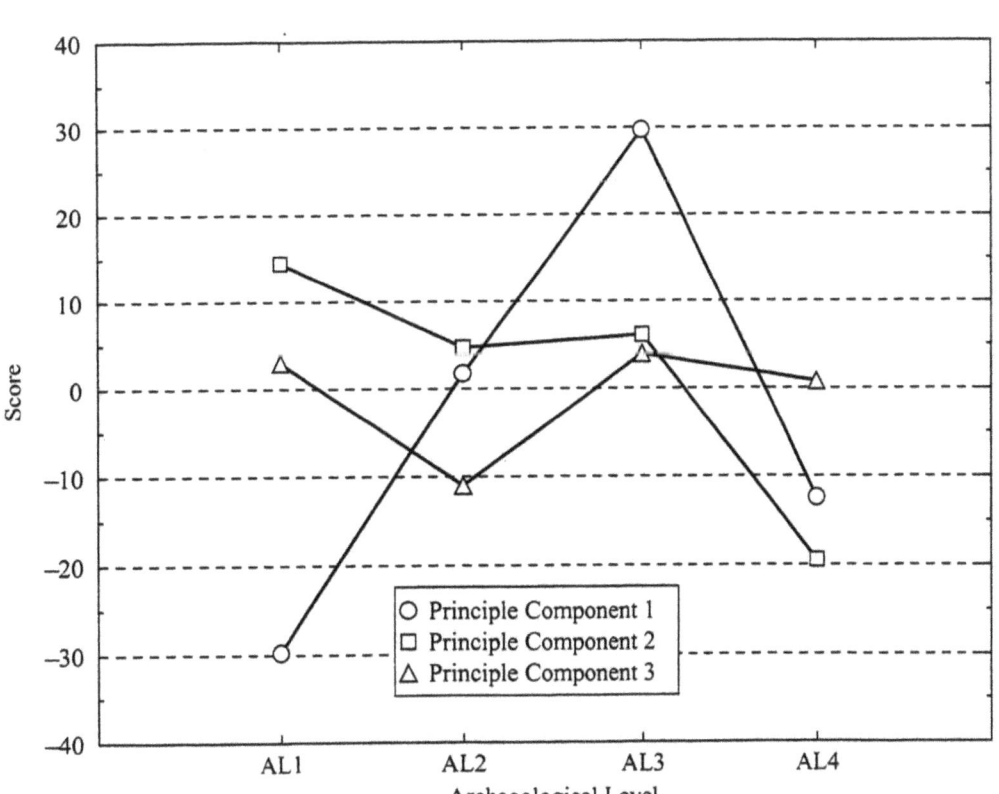

Figure 6.5. Comparison of 1st Principle Components.

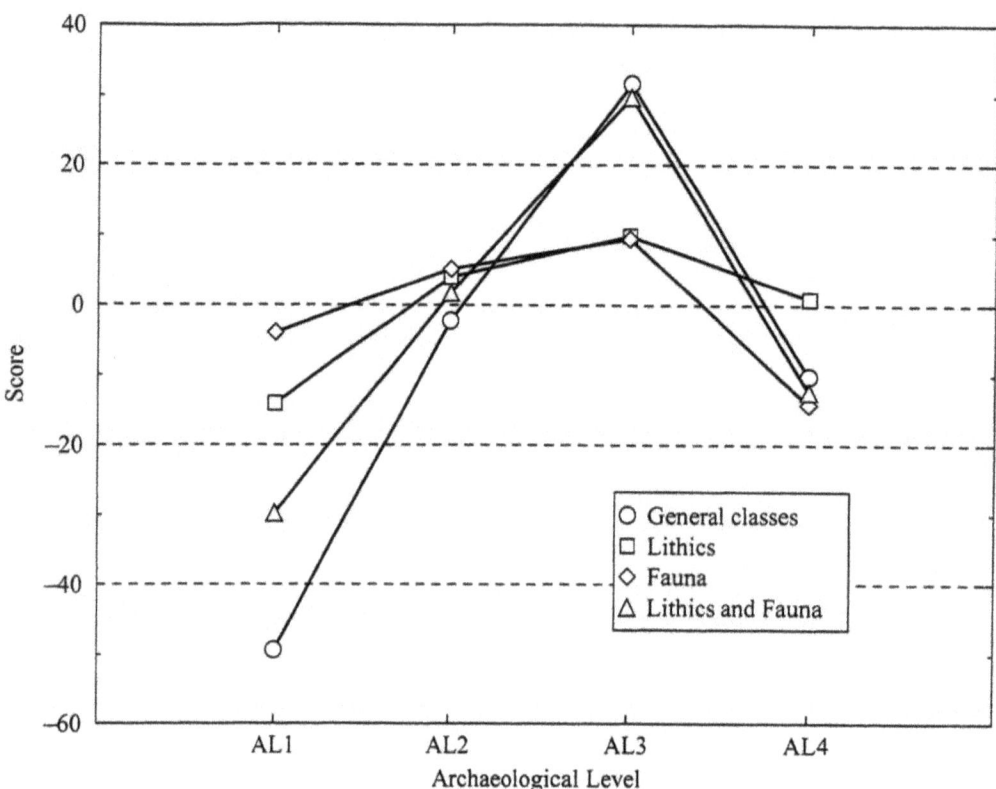

Figure 6.6. Comparison of 2nd Principle Components.

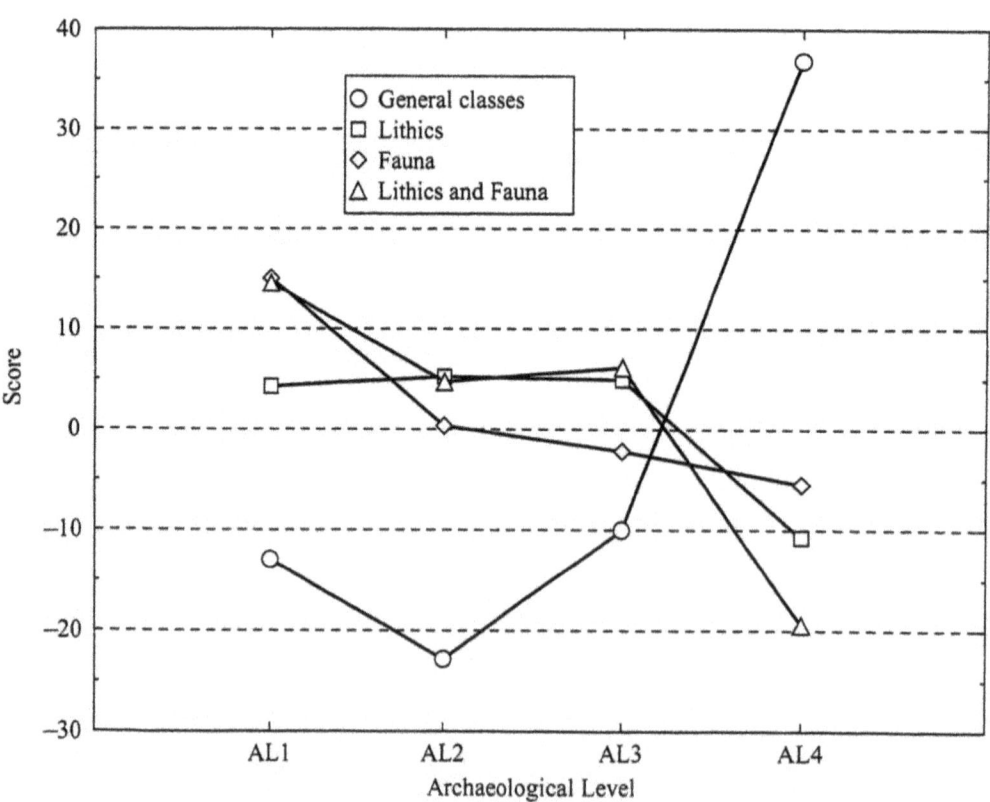

to a reversal of the roles of the positive and negative aspects of the principle component, and does not change the information reported by the dimension. Thus, the second principle component from stage 1 differs from those of the other stages mainly in the sense (orientation) rather than the pattern of its change.

The third principle component summarizes the interassemblage variability that remains after variation explained by the first two principle components has been removed. In every stage of analysis this component exhibits an undirected fluctuation about the zero line. This behavior is entirely consistent with the earlier interpretations of the third dimensions of variability as conflations of low-variance organizational structure with random "noise" components of interassemblage variability. Although the third principle component from each stage of analysis was found to contain some weak but organizationally relevant structure, the information is obscured by comparable amounts of undirected noise, yielding composite trajectories that are diachronically unpatterned.

It is instructive to compare corresponding principle components across stages of analysis as is done in Figures 6.5–6.7. The comparison in Figure 6.5 illustrates clearly that the first principle components from stages 1 and 4 are very similar, as are those from stages 2 and 3. All four first principle components, however, exhibit the same basic pattern of diachronic change. In Figure 6.6 the second principle components are compared, and the general similarity of stages 2–4 is apparent. Although the second principle component from stage 1 varies oppositely to the others and over a greater range, it still has many points of similarity to the second principle components from the other stages. Figure 6.7 shows that the third principle components from stages 2 and 3 are nearly identical, and vary inversely to those from stages 1 and 4, which also correspond closely.

The considerable similarity of corresponding principle components from each stage of the analysis is remarkable. Figures 6.5–6.7 illustrate unequivocally that similar structural patterns in interassemblage variability at Grubgraben are discovered irrespective of the classificatory language used to conceptualize and summarize the archaeological deposits. In other words, whether the deposits are described in terms of general classes of remains, lithic items, faunal remains, or jointly in terms of lithic and faunal categories, comparable patterns of interassemblage variability are elicited. Thus all four first principle components are similarly patterned across archaeological levels, as are the four second and the four third principle components. The similarities are most pronounced for the first and third principle components (Figures 6.5 and 6.7); the family of second principle components (Figure 6.6) exhibits the greater internal variability.

The similarity of corresponding principle components across the four stages of analysis does not imply, however, that the composite variables have similar meanings. For example, the first principle component from stage 2 (lithics) and from stage 3 (faunal elements), though nearly identical in their pattern of diachronic change, have completely different interpretations and are informative of different organizational relations (chapter 5). Instead, the fact that totally different organizational properties undergo very similar changes through time is an empirical indication that these properties monitor "extra-assemblage" processes that condition interassemblage variability (chapter 3; Binford 1973:248). This statement anticipates the discussion of the next chapter, however, in which the causes of diachronic variability in the organizational properties of the assemblages are explored.

Figure 6.7. Comparison of 3rd Principle Components.

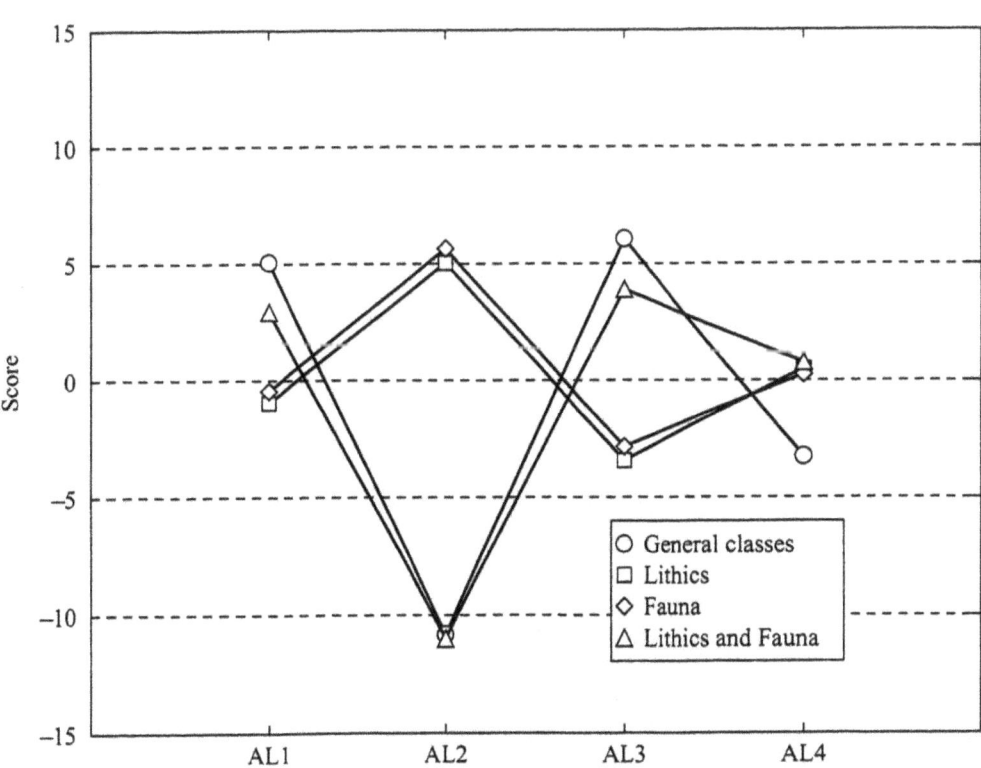

7.0 Explaining Organizational Change

It should now be evident that organizational relations exist between different classes of remains at Grubgraben and that these relations can be recognized in the structure of interassemblage variability (chapter 5). It is also clear that most of these organizational properties are diachronically patterned in a remarkably consistent and stable fashion, irrespective of the particular classificatory language used to summarize the archaeological deposits (chapter 6). The challenge now is to understand why these changes with time in the organizational properties of the assemblages should occur. In particular, do the diachronic trajectories established in chapter 6 for the various organizational relations make sense as adaptive responses to long-term climatic change? Several of the patterns of change in organizational relations seem plausible as adaptive responses to a changing environmental situation; other trajectories, however, appear unrelated to climatic dynamics and may instead monitor other sources of interassemblage variability.

7.1 Sources of Variation

The dimensions of variability discussed in chapters 5 and 6 were elicited through the use of principle components analysis to achieve structural simplification of a data set comprising multiple archaeological assemblages. The construction of the composite variables, the recognition of mutually covariant classes of remains, and the interpretation of organizational relations, were therefore based on the patterns existing between rather than within the assemblages. It follows that the organizational properties recognized by the analysis are not unique to any individual assemblage, but crosscut all the assemblages and monitor sources of variation that were active between assemblages deposited over several millennia (Figure 2.2). The design of the analysis therefore leads to the conclusion that sources of interassemblage variation at Grubgraben are most reasonably sought in "extra-assemblage" processes, or processes that were operative external to and independent of the behavioral system responsible for producing the assemblages:

> ...those sets of tools [and other classes of remains] exhibiting strong patterns of mutual co-variation *across* assemblage variants should be related to consistent features of the environment playing conditioning roles in human behaviour (Binford 1973:248, original emphasis).

In other words, the organizational properties that structure interassemblage variability at Grubgraben were recognized not on the basis of a single assemblage, but by using a collection of processually related assemblages. Therefore, when changes through time in these organizational properties are demonstrated, the causes for such changes are most reasonably sought in interassemblage processes such as environmental change and its corollaries. The demonstration in chapter 6 that unrelated organizational properties of interassemblage variability experience remarkably similar changes through time provides empirical support for this conclusion.

The experimental conditions under which the analysis was conducted also have implications for the sources of interassemblage variability. The archaeological cases chosen for analysis were not unrelated assemblages from various sites, representing different time periods, dissimilar environmental situations and climatic dynamics, variable site types, and inconsistent excavation and recovery methods. The dimensions of variation were derived instead from the temporal sequence of assemblages from the single site of Grubgraben, a site that appears to have been a stable residential site during the Last Glacial Maximum and that has many desirable processual and analytical properties (chapters 2 and 3). Grubgraben offers within the context of a single site a previously unavailable degree of control over variation in geography and environment, chronology and timing of climatic change, site type, seasonality of occupation, agents responsible for the archaeological deposits, and excavation methodology and data recovery (chapter 2).

These lines of reasoning, one theoretically and the other experimentally motivated, converge to implicate two specific "extra-assemblage" sources of interassemblage variability and of diachronic change in its organizational properties: long-term climatic and environmental variation, and intrasite functional variation resulting from excavation sampling bias.

Climatic deterioration and increasingly dry and cold environmental conditions during the Last Glacial Maximum are expected to explain a significant portion of interassemblage variability at Grubgraben. Exact relationships among lithic, faunal, and other classes of remains have not been proposed, however, that would unambiguously implicate climatically conditioned adaptations, nor can the magnitude of any climatically conditioned interassemblage variability be accurately predicted. The position was argued in chapters 1 and 3 that expectations for such relationships cannot be developed actualistically, and that those relationships between interassemblage variability and climatic change that can be articulated on the basis of other sources of knowledge (e.g., generalizations from modern hunter-gatherer societies) have consequences that are not currently observable at Grubgraben (e.g., specific patterns of change in housing, mobility, and storage).

The second and possibly most significant potential source of interassemblage variability at Grubgraben is believed to be intrasite functional variation resulting from the limited horizontal exposure of the site and the corresponding potential for excavation sampling bias. Thus some of the patterning in the organizational properties of interassemblage variability may only reflect differences in the function of the specific area of the larger residential site that was exposed by the excavations. As discussed in chapter 2, domestic spaces were evidently revealed in AL1 and AL2, but areas of intensive animal processing were exposed in AL3 and AL4. There is no effective control over this situation, but the variability contributed by intrasite sampling variation should be recognizable in the form of organizational changes that are both large (explaining a large proportion of interassemblage variability) and uncorrelated with climatic change. For instance, the assemblages may consistently be grouped in a certain way (e.g., AL1 with AL2, and AL3 with AL4), reflecting their functional similarity within the framework of the larger residential site. Many factors are likely to be involved, however, and the exact form of the interassemblage variability contributed by intrasite functional differences will probably be complex.

7.2 Linking Climate and Organization

Without prior knowledge of the mechanisms linking climate, environment, and the organizational properties of cultural systems, it is not possible in advance to do more than guess as to which organizational relations will "track" the pattern of climatic change. Identifying the causal links between climate and organization is a concern that middle-range research can in principle address (chapters 1 and 3), but in the absence of such knowledge it is reasonable to expect only that some organizational properties of hunter-gatherer systems will be more sensitive than others to environmental and climatic changes. This supposition is more reasonable than assuming that no organizational changes at all will occur, or that all organizational properties are equally sensitive and respond in kind.

If a given organizational change does not track the pattern of climatic change, however, then observed changes in the given organizational property of interassemblage variability cannot be convincingly referred to climate change. In other words, if climatic variability and interassemblage variability are uncorrelated, then claims for a causal relationship between them cannot be realistically supported. Of course, organizational change and climatic change may not be causally related in the first place, and demonstrating a statistical correlation between them will not establish causality. It makes no sense, however, to argue for a causal relationship between events which are demonstrably uncorrelated, i.e., without establishing correlation there can be no strong arguments regarding causality. Thus, a first step in linking climate and organization must be that of exploring the correlation between climatic change and the trajectories of organizational change (Figures 6.5–6.7).

Recall from chapter 2 that the climate at Grubgraben changes markedly from AL4 to AL3, corresponding to the onset of a colder and drier climatic regime following a relatively warm and humid oscillation. Although it is not well monitored by the proxy data used to prepare Figure 2.6, the climate then continues to become colder and more arid following AL3, with conditions after AL1 possibly too extreme for human occupation (Haesaerts 1990b; Pawlikowski 1990a; Montet-White et al. 1990:160).

Comparison of Figures 6.5–6.7 with the pattern of climatic change reconstructed from proxy data in Figure 2.6 suggests that some of the trajectories of organizational change do indeed track the climatic trend, either directly or inversely. Many of the principle components displayed in Figures 6.5–6.7 exhibit a marked change from AL4 to AL3, followed by monotonic and often steady change from AL3 to AL1.

At first glance the patterns displayed by the first principle components (Figure 6.5) appear especially well correlated with the pattern of climatic change at Grubgraben. The first principle components exhibit a marked change between AL4 and AL3, perhaps corresponding to the climatic oscillation, and they change steadily from AL3 to AL1, ostensibly in response to the increasing aridity and colder temperatures after AL4. These changes in the first principle component, however, are oppositely directed: there is a marked *increase* from AL4 to AL3, yet a gradual *decrease* after AL3. If the arguments presented in chapter 2 for the monotonicity of climatic change at Grubgraben are correct, however, these segments of the overall trajectory should have the same sense, either uniformly increasing or decreasing. Evidently the first principle components are monitoring a property of interassemblage variability unrelated to climatic change.

The second principle components, summarized in Figure 6.6, do not respond to climatic change in the same manner as the first principle components, and the correspondence between climatic change and organizational variability is more exact. Most of the second principle components show a marked change from AL4 to AL3, followed by more gradual change from AL3 to AL1, and these changes have the same sense, either increasing or decreasing. Thus the second principle components are more promising candidates for monitoring climatically conditioned organizational changes than are the first principle components.

The third and final principle components, which express the interassemblage variability that remains after the information from the first two dimensions has been removed, follow random, irregular trajectories (Figure 6.7). As discussed in chapter 6, this behavior is consistent with the interpretation of the third principle components as sums of low-variance organizational properties and comparable amounts of undirected noise in the data on interassemblage variability. Although all stages of analysis gave some indication of organizational relations on the third dimension of variability (chapter 5), these relations are conflated with the noise component and their diachronic variability is consequently poorly monitored by the dimension.

These qualitative statements regarding the correlation between the organizational trajectories in Figures 6.5–6.7 and the proxy pattern of climatic change in Figure 2.6 are corroborated by the results given in Table 7.1. For each stage of the analysis, two rank-order correlation coefficients [Spearman's rho and Kendall's tau (Snedecor and Cochran 1980:191–193; Press et al. 1989:532–543)] are determined between the assemblage scores on each principle component and an ordinal measure of climatic severity. The use of rank-order statistics allows a valid correlation to be assessed between climate and organizational relations, even though the climate during each episode of occupation cannot be quantified on a ratio or interval scale using continuous environmental variables such as mean annual temperature or effective temperature.

Relative climatic severity was determined from the results of the stratigraphic and paleoenvironmental studies summarized in chapter 2 (Haesaerts 1990b; Pawlikowski 1990a; Montet-White et al. 1990). According to these studies, the climate at Grubgraben became increasingly dry and cool from AL4 to AL1. Thus level AL4, as the occupation during which the climate was least severe, was assigned a rank of 1 for climatic severity; AL3 a rank of 2; AL2 a rank of 3; and AL1, during which conditions were most severe, a rank of 4. This ordinal measure of climatic severity was then correlated with the principle component score for each archaeological level, with the

Table 7.1. Correlation Coefficients between Principle Component Scores for Archaeological Levels and an Ordinal Measure of Climatic Severity.

Principle Component	n	Spearman's Rho	Probability	Kendall's Tau	Probability
Stage 1: General Classes					
1	4	−0.4000	0.6000	−0.3333	0.4969
2	4	−0.8000	0.2000	−0.6667	0.1742
3	4	0.0000	1.0000	0.0000	1.0000
Stage 2: Lithic Items					
1	4	−0.4000	0.6000	−0.3333	0.4969
2	4	0.4000	0.6000	0.3333	0.4969
3	4	0.0000	1.0000	0.0000	1.0000
Stage 3: Reindeer and Horse					
1	4	0.2000	0.8000	0.0000	1.0000
2	4	1.0000	0.0000	1.0000	0.0415
3	4	0.0000	1.0000	0.0000	1.0000
Stage 4: Lithics and Fauna					
1	4	−0.4000	0.6000	−0.3333	0.4969
2	4	0.8000	0.2000	0.6667	0.1742
3	4	0.0000	1.0000	0.0000	1.0000

Probability values are two-tailed.

results shown in Table 7.1. Probability values for the correlation coefficients are also given in Table 7.1, but because the correlations are based on only four data points these probabilities should not be interpreted strictly. They are entirely suitable, however, as guidelines for judging the similarity of patterns of organizational change and climatic change.

Inspection of the probabilities for the correlation coefficients in Table 7.1 indicates that the first principle component from every stage of analysis is only weakly correlated with climatic change. The third principle component from each stage of analysis is perfectly uncorrelated with climatic change (the correlation coefficients are identically zero with associated probabilities of one). The second principle component, however, is clearly correlated with climatic severity. The correlation is perfect for the second principle component from stage 3 (fauna), and is strong for stage 1 (general classes) and stage 4 (combined lithics and fauna), but is unremarkable for stage 2 (lithics). Although the second principle component for lithics is not strongly correlated with climatic severity, the correlation rises considerably when lithics and fauna are jointly analyzed, indicating that faunal patterns dominate the structure of variability in the joint data set.

In summary, three families of trajectories of organizational change have been recognized in the data on interassemblage variability at Grubgraben, yet only one family of curves—the second principle components—is closely correlated with the pattern of climatic change at the site. The first principle components are clearly and consistently patterned, but are weakly correlated with changes in the climate. The third principle components are diachronically unpatterned and completely uncorrelated with climatic change, and are not considered further. In the remainder of this chapter the trajectories of the first two dimensions of variability from each stage of the analysis are reviewed and the causal relationships between these organizational relations, intrasite functional variation, and a changing climate are explored.

7.3 Intrasite Functional Variation

The family of first principle components (Figure 6.5) is believed to represent the interassemblage variability resulting from intrasite sampling bias, i.e., variation in the spatial placement of the excavation units relative to the larger, internally structured residential campsite. Of 92 m^2 of horizontal exposure at Grubgraben, approximately one-half of the excavated units (48–50 m^2) were extended to the deeper levels AL3 and AL4 (chapter 2). Because these excavation units are spatially fixed, however, any variation between occupations in the arrangement of features within the camp or in the placement of the campsite in the ravine could result in the exposure of functionally different areas of the larger residential camp in each archaeological level. To judge from the feature and assemblage content, domestic spaces were exposed in AL1 and AL2 (hearths, pavements and pavement-like stone structures, discrete activity areas), and extensive animal processing areas were exposed in AL3 and AL4 (pits of various design and construction, large quantities of smashed animal bones, thick homogeneous deposits).

The functional variation between archaeological levels is probably more complicated than this impressionistic and feature-based judgement would suggest, however, and it may well be that all four levels are dissimilar in terms of their functional integration within the framework of the larger residential site. As described in chapter 2, for example, the pavements and stone structures in AL1 and AL2 appear to have been differently maintained, and there are important variations in the construction and content of the pit-like features in AL3 and AL4 as well as in the composition of the faunal assemblages from these levels (Montet-White 1990c,d; West 1995). Thus the archaeological levels that initially seem similar are found on closer inspection to exhibit important and possibly functional differences.

The variability in feature and assemblage inventories, even among occupation levels which are clearly similar in many respects, and the lack of good instruments for measuring (even at a nominal level) the "function" of discrete and differentiated areas within the overall site context, means that the ascription of function to the exposed portions of the individual archaeological levels is very difficult, even to the simple extent of equating particular levels on the basis of function. Consequently an independent determination of the form and magnitude of intrasite functional variation is unavailable with which to directly evaluate the assertion that the first principle components report the component of interassemblage variability due to excavation sampling bias. It was demonstrated above, however, that the first principle components are weakly correlated with climatic severity, and there is good circumstantial evidence that they are in fact measuring an "artificial" source of interassemblage variability such as excavation bias.

By construction, the first principle component explains the greatest possible proportion of total interassemblage variability, subject to certain numerical constraints and analytical relationships to the other principle components (Manly 1986:61–63). Assuming that any interassemblage variability due to excavation sampling bias and intrasite functional variation would be greater than the variability contributed by climatic change (as certainly seems likely at Grubgraben), then such intrasite functional variability would be expected to appear on the first principle component.

Furthermore, each of the first principle components describes a radical division of assemblage content into two large and oppositely covarying suites of variables. Thus Dimension 1 of stage 1 separates reindeer from all other classes of remains; Dimension 1 of stage 2 separates formal tools and resharpening waste from blades, bladelets and primary production debris; in stage 3 the first dimension separates a few numerous and higher utility parts of reindeer anatomy from the remaining reindeer parts and from all of the horse elements; and in stage 4 the first dimension of variability clearly separates reindeer from both horse remains and lithic items. Although specific expectations for the organizational changes conditioned by long-term climatic change have not been postulated, it is difficult to accept that these changes could be expressed in such comprehensive terms as reindeer versus horse exploitation, or the use and resharpening of formal tools versus blade/bladelet production. Thus the coarse construction of the first principle components indirectly suggests that they monitor a coarse (i.e., large variance) dimension of interassemblage variability such as that contributed by intrasite sampling bias and functional variation. Interestingly, the first principle components are not significantly correlated with variables that might be imagined as "measures" of intrasite sampling bias and functional variability, such as horizontal exposure, assemblage size, or collection diversity (these correlations are not shown). Nor do the first principle components group the assemblages in the way that might have been expected based on their feature inventory (AL1 with AL2 and AL3 with AL4): Figure 6.5 shows instead that AL2 and AL4 are most similar, with AL1 and AL3 having extreme values to either direction. These facts imply that neither assemblage size, nor collection diversity, nor feature inventory is singly and directly a useful measure at Grubgraben of the intrasite sampling bias and functional variability reported by the first principle components.

7.4 Climatic Change

The second major source of interassemblage variability at Grubgraben is expected to be the climatic change that took place during the sequence of occupations at the site: an episode of increasing aridity, decreasing temperatures, and the onset of severe ice-age conditions (chapter 2). The process of climatic change is expected to contribute less significantly to interassemblage variability than excavation sampling bias and intrasite functional variation, and the form of the variability explained by climatic change is expected to involve finer contrasts in assemblage content than are observed as the result of excavation bias and functional variation. These expectations are not based on any special knowledge of the relationships between climate and interassemblage variability, but are intuitively plausible, particularly at Grubgraben where the variability between levels in assemblage and feature content is pronounced. These expectations also imply that variation due to climatic change is most likely to appear on the second principle components.

In each stage of the analysis, the second principle components explain, by construction (Manly 1986), smaller proportions of the total interassemblage variability than do their corresponding first principle components. The second principle components therefore monitor a numerically less significant source of variability between archaeological levels, although Figure 6.6 clearly illustrates that the second dimensions of variability are diachronically no less patterned. In other words, the second principle components report a source of interassemblage variability that is smaller in its effect, but no less patterned, than the variability contributed by intrasite functional variation and monitored by the first principle components.

The family of second principle components is also closely correlated with the pattern of climatic change at the site (Table 7.1), whereas the first principle components were only weakly correlated with an ordinal index of climatic severity. The correlation is strong in all stages of analysis except stage 2, in which the interassemblage variability in lithics was examined. Other studies have also found, however, that conventionally summarized lithic inventories can be insensitive to significant structural changes in cultural systems (Vierra 1975; Binford 1978b, 1982a), so that the weaker correlation of the second principle component from stage 2 is not without precedent.

These features of the second principle components suggest that they are indeed monitoring the interassemblage variability at Grubgraben that is contributed by the organizational responses to long-term climatic change. The final task is that of examining the specific organizational relations defined by the second principle components and determining if their diachronic trajectories make sense as adaptive responses to climatic change.

The events of AL4 transpired during the relatively warmer and more humid conditions associated with a climatic oscillation during the Last Glacial Maximum. During this period the assemblage was structured mainly by events related to the quartz-tool- and flake-assisted exploitation of horse and reindeer (Figure 6.6, stages 1 and 4). Corresponding to the relatively greater importance in AL4 of events related to subsistence animal exploitation (stage 1) is a lithic industry that is structured primarily by the intensive use of flake, blade, and endscraper technology (stage 2) and by events involving heavy-duty quartz tools and both quartz and non-quartz flakes (stages 1, 4). The covariance of these lithic and quartz items with reindeer and horse was discussed in stage 1 of the analysis, and understood in terms of the technological requirements for butchering and processing the animal carcasses (West 1995; Hill 1993). During AL4 a slight emphasis on the higher utility (meat, marrow, and grease yielding) parts of horse and reindeer is also observed (stage 3), suggesting that there was less need to exploit the more marginal, lower yield parts of the subsistence animals during the relatively more hospitable climatic conditions.

Following the climatic oscillation and the events of AL4 the climate became markedly colder and more arid. Biodiversity and biomass declined as larger and slower species such as mammoth and bovids were forced by changes in the vegetation to leave the region and seek new foraging grounds (Weniger 1982, 1990; West 1995). Gregarious and highly adaptable species such as the reindeer and horse remained, although herd size may have declined and foraging ranges probably increased as these species responded to changes in environmental patterns such as the duration of snow cover, the length of the summer growing season for the tundra vegetation, and other phenological phenomena. Consequently, the seasonal movements and migratory routes for horse and reindeer may have become less predictable (Sturdy 1975; Weniger 1982; Stewart and Jochim 1986; Straus 1987; Jochim 1991; Peterkin et al. 1993).

Because of differences in the digestive systems of these animals, reindeer probably fared better than horse under the vegetational spectrum of the colder and drier landscape (West 1995). Both horse and reindeer are efficient herbivores, but horse feed on high-fiber, low-protein content vegetation and would need to move more often and consume more forage to meet their dietary needs in a colder and drier environment (Spiess 1979; Weniger 1982; West 1995). Reindeer, however, are highly adaptable mixed feeders and are able to subsist on grasses, sedges, shrubs, and lichens. The ability of reindeer to digest lichens enables them to exploit an ecological niche unclaimed by other cervids (Leader-Williams 1988:92–122).

These climatically conditioned changes in the vegetational and faunal background prompted adaptive organizational responses in cultural systems. At Grubgraben, important shifts are observed between AL4 and AL3 in several organizational properties. Events related to general clothing and outfitting tasks assume greatly increased importance in structuring the archaeological deposits (stage 1). Events involving the use of the non-endscraper technology (armatures, burins and spalls, and other formal tools) also increase (stages 2, 4), probably in response to the relatively greater importance of tasks involving hide tailoring and outfitting [recall from stage 1 (Table 5.1.2) the strong covariation of lithic tools with shell and small mammal remains]. Interestingly, the trajectory that exhibits the least change from AL4 to AL3 is from stage 3 (faunal remains). The change in this dimension, though small, is significant in reporting an increase in events involving the more marginal parts of both reindeer and horse [see West (1995) for similar observations].

From AL3 to AL1 the climate at Grubgraben became progressively drier and cooler, with conditions after AL1 perhaps too severe to support a continuous human presence (Montet-White et al. 1990:160). Concomitant with the steady deterioration of the climate is a smooth and regular change in three of the four organizational properties illustrated in Figure 6.6. The importance of events related to clothing and outfitting increases further and remains high (stage 1). Regular and steady increase is also observed in the use of the more marginal parts of the subsistence animals (stages 3, 4). By the time of the occupation of level AL1, and during the time of greatest climatic and environmental stress, the more marginal parts of reindeer and horse contribute most to the structure of the assemblage [see also West (1995)].

Unlike the organizational relations from stages 1, 3, and 4, however, the lithic technology at Grubgraben remains exceptionally stable from AL3 to AL1; the assemblages are approximately equally structured by events related to the flake, blade, and endscraper technology and by events involving the non-endscraper lithic technology such as armatures, burins and spalls, and formal tools (stages 2, 4). In fact, there is actually a slight emphasis on the non-endscraper technology for levels AL3–AL1, probably because the positive aspect of Dimension 2 monitors much more of the overall lithic industry than does the negative aspect.

The lack of sensitivity of conventionally summarized lithic inventories to major organizational changes in cultural systems has been examined by others (Vierra 1975; Binford 1978b, 1982a), and the failure of the second dimension of interassemblage variation in lithics (Figure 6.6) to track climatic change appears to be a further example of this lithic-typological insensitivity. It is nevertheless peculiar that the lithic technology at Grubgraben evidently responds to the climatic transition between AL4 and AL3, yet remains essentially constant from AL3 to AL1 despite an increasingly dry and cold climate. As none of the organizational relations defined by any of the other principle components also exhibits this pattern (the second principle component from stage 1 is most similar), it is difficult to determine whether the change in the lithic assemblage between AL4 and AL3 represents a genuine response to climatic change, or is perhaps instead an additional dimension of intrasite functional variation not removed by the first principle component. As suggested above, the organizational change in lithics from AL4 to AL3 may be most directly a response to changes in the importance of events related to hide tailoring and outfitting (stage 1, second principle component; Figure 6.6). This organizational property also increases markedly from AL4 to AL3 and thereafter remains comparatively stable.

The possibility of a "cultural" or "ethnic" explanation for the change in lithic organization from AL4 to AL3 can be discounted. Although changes in the frequencies of some kinds of tools (e.g., backed pieces or perforators) as well as in the technique used to manufacture tools (e.g., burins on truncations versus dihedral burins) have been used to define and then recognize various "cultural" changes in the Upper Paleolithic (Bosinski and Hahn 1973:192–227; Hemingway 1980; Otte 1981; Hahn 1981a,b, 1988a, 1993; Weniger 1982; Gamble 1986), it is unlikely that any "cultural" factor responsible for a change in the relative intensity of endscraper technology during the half-millennium between AL4 and AL3 would produce no further changes in the subsequent 1300 years from AL3 to AL1 (Figure 2.2). Instead, changes in the relative intensity of endscraper technology are most likely to be conditioned by changes in the activity structure of the archaeological levels, which in turn may be expected to vary in response to seasonal and environmental factors. Alternatively, a variety of environmentally independent, technological factors may be at work, such as the differential frequency of breakage of the endscraper and non-endscraper technologies (perhaps due to differences in raw material or the mechanics of use), or an unusual excavation bias resulting from sampling an area of endscraper production or use.

7.5 Summary

Diachronic patterns in the organizational properties of interassemblage variability at Grubgraben have been examined, and causes of the observed changes with time have been sought in the processes of excavation sampling bias and intrasite functional variation, and protracted climatic change during the Last Glacial Maximum.

The family of first principle components from stages 1–4 of the analysis monitored coarsely defined, large-variance aspects of interassemblage variability: the separation of reindeer from all other classes of remains (stage 1); the separation of formal tools and resharpening waste from blades, bladelets and primary production debris (stage 2); the separation of a few numerous and higher utility parts of reindeer anatomy from the remaining reindeer parts and from all of the horse elements (stage 3); and the separation of reindeer from both horse remains and lithic items (stage 4). These dimensions of variability were weakly correlated with an ordinal index of climatic severity, and variability between levels in the first principle components was argued to represent the intrasite functional variation produced by the differential spatial placement of the large and internally structured residential camp relative to the fixed excavation units.

The family of second principle components was found to be highly correlated with an ordinal measure of climatic severity, and variability between archaeological levels in these components was attributed to the process of long-term climatic deterioration that transpired during the sequence of occupations at the site. The diachronic changes in organizational properties described by the second principle components were entirely consistent with the kinds of adaptations one would sensibly expect in response to an increasingly dry and cold climate. Thus events related to clothing and outfitting assume increased importance; increased use is made of the more marginal parts of the subsistence animals; and the lithic inventory changes in a manner that reflects the revised technological requirements of the cultural system.

8.0 Concluding Remarks

During the Last Glacial Maximum from 22,000 to 14,000 years BP, human groups in central Europe were subjected to a previously unexperienced suite of climatic and environmental selection pressures as the last major advance of the ice sheets brought about the most severe ice-age conditions of the Pleistocene epoch. Conditions were especially severe in central Europe where the northern Fennoscandian and southern Alpine ice masses advanced to within 500–600 km of each other, leaving only a narrow periglacial corridor from central and southern Germany through Poland, Bohemia, Moravia, and Lower Austria. These facts have motivated a particular view of the past; namely, the expectation that the widespread and severe climatic and environmental modifications associated with the Last Glacial Maximum in central Europe precipitated local and organizational adaptive responses by hunter-gatherer systems. The present research has enabled a partial evaluation of this view of the past by addressing the problem of recognizing the variability between archaeological assemblages that is conditioned by the responses of hunter-gatherer systems to climatic change and the onset of ice-age conditions.

8.1 Review of Methods and Results

The strategy used to investigate climatically conditioned organizational responses was a pattern recognition study of interassemblage variability. The potential for recognizing adaptive responses that are local in nature was maximized by investigating archaeological variability at the single site of Grubgraben in Lower Austria. The site dates to the Last Glacial Maximum and has good evidence for multiple residential occupations during an episode of monotonically increasing aridity and decreasing temperatures. Arguments were presented to the effect that factors such as site type and season of habitation were stable during the sequence of occupations of Grubgraben, further improving the potential for climatically conditioned adaptations to be documented in interassemblage variability. Variation in the function of the specific area of the larger residential site revealed by the fixed excavation window was acknowledged as a potential contributing source of interassemblage variability, the effects of which could not be securely postulated in advance but proved recognizable upon inspection of the resulting organizational patterns.

Interassemblage variability at Grubgraben was decomposed using a principle components analysis of normalized frequency data to elicit organizational relations between different classes of remains. The analysis was conducted in four stages, using a different "observational language" and conceptualization of the assemblage inventories in each stage, to determine the extent to which recognized patterns depended on the properties selected for manipulation. The organizational relations were interpreted by appeal to "knowledge of the moment" (Binford 1984b:9–17), i.e., ideas regarding the form and function of stone tools, principles of the economic anatomy of animals, ethnographic analogy, and ethnoarchaeological observation. These interpretations were developed without prior knowledge of any diachronic patterning in the organizational properties.

Following the recognition and interpretation of organizational relations between various classes of remains, the change between archaeological levels in these organizational properties was examined, and three recurring patterns of diachronic variability were discovered.

The first principle components from all stages of the analysis monitored coarse, large-variance aspects of interassemblage variability and were not significantly correlated with an ordinal index of climatic severity. Variability between levels in the first principle components was argued to represent the intrasite functional variation produced by the differential spatial placement of the residential camp relative to the excavation units.

The family of second principle components was highly correlated with an ordinal measure of climatic severity, and variability between archaeological levels in these components was attributed to the adaptive response of the hunter-gatherer systems at Grubgraben to the climatic deterioration that transpired during the sequence of occupations at the site. Events related to clothing and outfitting assumed increased importance; increased use was made of the more marginal parts of the subsistence animals; and changes in the lithic inventory were made that reflected revised technological requirements.

The third principle components from each stage of analysis appeared to monitor several weakly developed organizational properties, but these were conflated with the variance contributed by undirected noise in the data on assemblage composition. Consequently the organizational relationships on the third principle components were diachronically unpatterned.

8.2 Discussion

In retrospect the research has been more successful than might have been expected; the view of the past that motivated the research has received some support, and the utility of the theory and method used to address the issue has been demonstrated. At the beginning of the study no firm expectations had been formulated as to the organizational properties that would be recognized in interassemblage variability, nor was it known whether these properties would prove responsive to the climatic and environmental modifications experienced during the Last Glacial Maximum. On the basis of general ideas about culture as a system it was anticipated only that the organizational properties of the hunter-gatherer adaptation would be the most likely components of the cultural system to respond to prolonged and severe climatic modification. This expectation has been vindicated, and some knowledge of the specific kinds of organizational changes made has been acquired as well.

From the results and discussion presented in chapter 7 one obtains the impression that the local organizational modifications in hunter-gatherer systems at Grubgraben in response to severe climatic stress were relatively minor. If this impression is accurate, and assuming of course that any responses to climatic change would be organizational in nature, then several interesting implications follow.

First, a minimal amount of organizational adjustment in

response to marked climatic change may indicate that the hunter-gatherer systems at Grubgraben were "preadapted" and therefore relatively stable. In other words, the systems may already have possessed a degree of cultural and technological latitude or pliancy that was entirely adequate for coping with the stresses imposed by conditions during the Last Glacial Maximum. Thus the adaptation of cultural systems in general to severe ice-age conditions may be much less spectacular than expected, and entail organizational adjustments no greater than those involved in accommodating seasonal environmental extremes. This implication of the research is in keeping with recent suggestions that human groups were much less affected by the Last Glacial Maximum than has been suspected (Gamble 1983; Valoch 1989; Oliva 1989; Weniger 1989, 1990; Svoboda 1990; Kozlowski 1990; Montet-White et al. 1990; Montet-White 1994; Simán 1990; Dobosi 1991a; West 1995), and arguments for a hiatus in the human occupation of parts of Europe and for the emergence of "Pleistocene refugia" in protected regions such as the Périgord, the Ukraine, or the Hungarian Basin, may be superfluous (Hahn 1976, 1983; Valoch 1980; Gamble 1983, 1986; Jochim 1983, 1987; Soffer 1987b, 1990; Weniger 1989, 1990; Kozlowski 1990; Otte 1990; Straus 1991). Alternatively, a limited organizational response to climatic change may imply that the cultural systems at Grubgraben, although pliant enough to accommodate some climatically conditioned stresses, had neared their maximum adaptive potential. Support for this interpretation comes from the absence of identifiable occupations above AL1 at Grubgraben, provided the absence is genuine and not a consequence of the deep terracing that has modified much of the loess overburden (Montet-White et al. 1990; Haesaerts 1990b).

In addition, if the cultural systems were nearing the limits of their adaptive potential by the time of the occupation of AL1, then the process of adaptation is likely to have started long before the occupation of AL4. The excavated levels at Grubgraben do not document the onset or the earliest stages of the Last Glacial Maximum (Figure 2.4), but the prospect of additional cultural levels below AL4 (level AL5 is indicated at least, and still earlier deposits are likely) may eventually enable a more extensive investigation of the stages in adaptation to an ice-age environment.

Unfortunately, the perception that the observed adaptive responses of the systems at Grubgraben are "minor" is exceedingly difficult to evaluate because of the lack of any baseline for comparison. How does one address the question of how large were the adaptive responses of hunter-gatherer systems to the onset of an ice age, and is this question even meaningful? There are at least two aspects to the problem: quantifying and measuring the degree of adaptation, and establishing a scale for the comparison of various adaptive states.

The best evaluation that can be made at present is to compare the percentages of interassemblage variance that are explained by intrasite functional variation (the first principle components) and by adaptation to climatic change (the second principle components). These percentages were given in Tables 5.1.2, 5.2.2, 5.3.2, and 5.4.1 and are presented again in Table 8.1 together with their means, standard deviations, and coefficients of variation. The ratio of climatic to intrasite variation is also given. Depending on the observational language used to summarize assemblage content, the organizational adaptive responses to climatic change at Grubgraben account for 24% to 41% of the total variability between assemblages, and are typically 34% to 78% of the variation due to excavation bias. Excluding the figures for stage 4 (joint lithic/faunal data), the ratio of climatic- to excavation-conditioned interassemblage variability is highest when assemblages are described by their faunal content, and lowest when assemblages are summarized in terms of their lithic inventories. These numbers suggest that the magnitude of the adaptive response made by the systems at Grubgraben is appreciable (contributing more than half as much variability between assemblages as does excavation bias), but even in these terms the magnitude of the adaptive response is difficult to comprehend or understand in "biological" or "cultural" terms.

8.3 Criticism

Several ostensible criticisms of the study are easily anticipated. Some of these are irrelevant and readily dismissed, but other objections are more serious and point out areas in need of additional research and the need to develop more sophisticated archaeological methodology. Attention is restricted here to four pedagogically valuable criticisms: these are directed against the interpretations offered for the organizational relations; the scale at which human adaptation and the dynamics of the Last

Table 8.1. Comparison of Interassemblage Variability at Grubgraben Explained by Adaptation to Climatic Change (C) and by Intrasite Functional Variation due to Excavation Sampling Bias (E).

Source of Variation	Stage of Analysis				Mean	SD	CV
	General Classes	Lithics	Fauna	Lithics & Fauna			
Climate (C)	36.51%	34.52%	41.10%	23.84%	33.99	6.33	0.19
Excavation (E)	60.27	58.34	52.53	70.82	60.49	6.61	0.11
Ratio C/E	0.61	0.59	0.78	0.34	0.56		

Percentages for C (the second principle components) and E (the first principle components) are taken from Tables 5.1.2, 5.2.2, 5.3.2, and 5.4.1.

Glacial Maximum should be investigated; the problem of studying long-term change and the evolution of systems in archaeology; and against the arguments proposing climatic change as a major source of interassemblage variability at Grubgraben.

Probably the most obvious target for criticism is found in the interpretations proposed for the various organizational relations recognized in chapter 5. Arguments are of course inevitable as to the correct interpretation and meaning of the patterns elicited in any pattern recognition study, but these arguments can become gratuitous if they fail to appreciate that the more critical issue is simply the demonstration that *the patterns exist*. In other words, the patterned organizational changes between assemblages are demonstrably real and exist independently of any inaccuracy in or disagreement over the interpretations postulated for the individual organizational relations:

> ...consistent patterns of mutual co-variation as demonstrable between tool classes, cross cut the recognized forms of assemblage variation. This is a fact and not an inference or an interpretation. It is clearly as much a fact as are the summary proportional frequencies of the various tool classes. ....
> Any criticism of the approaches I have taken must seek to destroy the factual character of this observation, and/or offer an alternative explanatory argument with clear test implications (Binford 1973:248).

Thus the dimensions of variability recognized in any stage of the analysis in chapter 5 may be interpreted as A, B, and C, for example, and it simply does not change the fact that A, B, and C are patterned as shown in Figures 6.1–6.7. Accurate interpretation of the organizational relations is of course desirable if the causes of their variability are to be investigated, but the existence of diachronic patterning in these relations is clearly independent of their interpretation and is in itself a real phenomenon to be understood.

A second point needing clarification concerns the potential misperception that the present study has treated the Last Glacial Maximum as a singular and monolithic climatic event, both preceded and followed by glacial conditions that were less than maximal, when in reality it was a complex and finely structured event:

> ...it is meaningless to consider [the Last Glacial Maximum (LGM)] a simple 'time-spike' for the purposes of studying past human behaviour—a hurdle which required a little extra effort for human populations to surmount. Rather, the LGM 'spike' was ... a palimpsest of smaller-scale, independent climatic events. Their sum total added up to the LGM, which varied in impact and severity between and within regions (Gamble and Soffer 1990b:8).

> [T]he LGM was a complex event made up of different phases of ice advances and retreats....
> By characterizing this period as one big undifferentiated event rather than what it was in reality—a series of smaller scale, independent events—we bias our interpretations of human adaptations. This is because a series of rapid climatic changes would have given both the natural environments and people time to make adequate adaptive responses (Weniger 1990:179).

It should be obvious that the relevance of these arguments is dependent entirely upon the temporal scale at which adaptive responses to the Last Glacial Maximum are investigated. If the period of time over which cultural modification is investigated is sufficiently large, then the Last Glacial Maximum is for all intents and purposes "one big undifferentiated event" and it is analytically presumptuous and meaningless to treat the Last Glacial Maximum as a complex series of smaller-scale climatic fluctuations. However, if human behavioral adaptation is investigated for a period of time comparable in magnitude to the duration of the Last Glacial Maximum itself, then it is clearly necessary to consider the small-scale dynamics of this event. The discussion in chapter 2 should make it clear that the totality of the Last Glacial Maximum is *not* considered in this study; instead, a single episode of climatic change, occurring during the latter stages of the Last Glacial Maximum and lasting slightly more than 2000 years, has been examined. Within this episode of climatic change smaller-scale fluctuations in the climate are likely to have occurred, but these events are not resolvable at the scale of paleoclimatological reconstruction discussed in chapter 2.

Mention should also be made of the selectionist-evolutionist school of thought in anthropology and its position regarding the study of long-term change and the evolution of cultural systems (Dunnell 1980, 1982, 1989; Rindos 1985, 1986, 1989). Proponents of this school have argued that the strategy of middle-range research advocated by Binford (e.g., 1977a, 1981, 1987a) for learning about the past is inherently unsuited to the study of processual variability and systemic evolution. If this position has any validity, then studies such as the present one are misdirected and cannot possibly lead toward an understanding of past processes, diachronic change, and systemic evolution. The following comments are primarily in response to arguments presented by Dunnell (1982, 1989); it is clear that Rindos (1989:21–22) subscribes to the Mertonian conception of middle-range research, introduced into archaeology by Raab and Goodyear (1984), as the development of "general theory" by the progressive accumulation and synthesis of "special-purpose" theories having greater empirical content than general theories (Merton 1948, 1968; Williams 1988). However, middle-range research *sensu* Binford (1983c:18–19, 1987a, 1990:149) is not especially concerned with the construction of "special-purpose" theories, nor with "formation processes" of the archaeological record (Schiffer 1976, 1985), but with the study of contemporary variability and the recognition of relationships between process and pattern that can support uniformitarian projection into the past.

Dunnell (1982, 1989) argues that the study of change through time differs fundamentally and perhaps irreconcilably from the study of change across space. The difference is concisely expressed by considering the following dualities inherent in the two approaches:

discrete—continuous
things exist—things are in a state of becoming
difference—change
space-like conception of reality—time-like conception of reality
synchronic studies—diachronic studies
essentialist metaphysic—materialist metaphysic
ahistorical—historical

Of relevance to the present study of adaptation to long-term climatic change is Dunnell's assertion that the investigation of change across time using contemporary ahistorical methods involves discretizing a continuous process. In so doing, change is converted into difference, states of becoming are replaced by the existence of things, and a diachronic process becomes reduced to a set of synchronic system states. Thus, a strategy for learning about the past that is based on contemporary synchronic spatial variability (i.e., middle-range research) is fundamentally inappropriate for learning about past diachronic processes. More generally, methods that presume the existence of "things" (such as artifacts) are theoretically (but not necessarily methodologically) unsuited to the study of process, in which "things" do not exist but are forever in a state of becoming (Dunnell 1989:148–149). The replacement of the materialist metaphysic by an essentialist one leads to interpretive difficulties when trying to explain the causes of patterned variation with time (Dunnell 1989:149).

Dunnell's position is objectionable on theoretical, methodological, and pragmatic grounds. Most importantly, perhaps, scientific disciplines are replete with examples of the use and utility of discrete approximations to continuous phenomena. Information and communications theory have developed the methods of time-sampling to a high degree, and diachronic systemic change ("evolution") is successfully investigated by sampling the state of the system at discrete intervals. In the present research, modifications through time in the cultural systems at Grubgraben have been "sampled" in the form of discrete archaeological levels, with each level containing information on the state of the system at the time it was deposited. By investigating the variability between these assemblages clear evidence for change emerges and certain temporal processes are implicated. Of course, information is lost when a process is sampled, and a smaller sampling interval (finer discretization) of the continuous process of adaptation could provide greater resolution of past events, but these issues are beside the point.

The arguments of the selectionist-evolutionist school are of philosophical interest, but it is unwise to accept them as strictures for metaphysically consistent and acceptable scientific inquiry. To paraphrase Shott (1989:313), we can either throw up our hands in disgust and despair at the task before us, or we can roll up our sleeves and try to account for organization and change in the archaeological record. Uncritical acceptance of Dunnell's arguments could only lead one to take the former action; the research presented here has obviously endorsed the latter posture.

The most significant criticism of the present study must certainly be directed at the arguments used in chapter 2 to establish Grubgraben as a test site at which many alternative sources of archaeological variability are controlled, or at least operative at reasonably constant rates and therefore contribute minimally to the totality of interassemblage variability. These arguments were intended to support the claim that climatic change and intrasite functional differences due to excavation sampling bias should be the primary factors conditioning interassemblage variability at the site.

There is, however, no disguising the fact that the arguments in support of the experimental controls on interassemblage variability have many characteristics of an "argument from elimination" (Binford 1981:83). Thus it was essentially argued that climatic change and intrasite functional differences must be the primary factors conditioning interassemblage variability because other understood and expected sources of variability (e.g., site type, season of occupation, agents responsible for the deposits) are held approximately constant by the remarkable archaeological situation at Grubgraben. To what extent, however, can all of the possible situations and agents have been considered that might account for the observations at Grubgraben? Obviously it cannot be claimed that all possible causes of interassemblage variability have been identified, and that all but climatic change and sampling bias are controlled and need not be considered. The excellent correspondence, demonstrated in chapter 7, of the trajectories of diachronic change in organizational relations with an independently documented pattern of site-specific climatic change and with properties characteristic of intrasite functional differences suggest that the arguments of chapter 2 were generally accurate, but a more secure *frame of reference* (Binford 1984b:65–77, 1987a) against which to project the results of the pattern recognition study would strengthen the analysis and the logical construction of its conclusions.

8.4 Directions for Further Research

It is often the case that the results of a study fare better as departure points for new research than as ivory pillars of truth and knowledge. The present research is no exception, and its contribution is perhaps best judged by considering the extent to which questions have been raised and directions for future study indicated.

At a methodological level, the interassemblage variability introduced by excavation bias and the exposure of functionally differentiated areas of a large, internally structured site needs to be better understood. Most importantly, variables need to be developed that can quantify this form of variability (Renfrew 1987), and the analysis of intrasite spatial patterning needs to move beyond its recent fixation on "thick description" (e.g., Whallon 1973a,b, 1974, 1978, 1984; Leroi-Gourhan 1976a; Leroi-Gourhan and Brézillon 1966, 1972; Jochim 1976; Yellen 1977; Kintigh and Ammerman 1982; Simek 1984; Carr 1984; Julien 1988; Olive 1988; Kintigh 1990; Gamble and Boismier 1991; Kroll and Price 1991) and pursue the development of explicitly inferential procedures (Binford 1978a:357, 1983a, 1987a, 1991b; Kind 1985; Gamble 1991; Whitelaw 1983, 1989, 1991). The discussion of chapter 7 demonstrated the utility of principle components analysis in this regard, but in the present case there was a need for independent monitors of intrasite functional variation with which the principle component scores could be correlated.

One means of dealing with intrasite functional differences at Grubgraben would involve exposure of the site in its entirety at all levels, but the size of the site makes this an unlikely development (Haesaerts 1990b: Figure III-7). An alternative to total site exposure would be to analyze interassemblage variability within those sets of assemblages that are equivalent according to some feature- or inventory-based conventions for judging their function. This approach is compromised, however, by requiring the investigator to impose *a priori* judgements of functional similarity on the assemblages, and is in any case a totally impractical approach at Grubgraben because of the small number of assemblages. It would require, for example, that AL1 and AL2 (as examples of domestic areas) be analyzed together and independently of a second set of assemblages comprising AL3 and AL4 (as examples of intensive animal carcass processing areas). The use of principle components analysis, however, to explore the structure of interassemblage variability, is absurd with only two cases from which to construct composite variables.

A further direction for additional research involves applying the methods described here to data on interassemblage composition from other sites where the requisite analytical conditions are approximately met. There are at present, however, no sites in central Europe other than Grubgraben that can support this kind of study. Other sites have yielded evidence for occupations at or near the Last Glacial Maximum (Figure 2.4)—well-known examples include Ságvár (Hungary), Arka (Hungary), Madaras (Hungary), Stránská skála IV (Moravia), Spadzista C (Poland)—but these sites do not provide the sequence of deposits necessary to investigate diachronic variability in organizational relations. The site of Willendorf in the Wachau of Lower Austria contains rich deposits and a long sequence of occupations, but the Gravettian levels at Willendorf are considerably older than those at Grubgraben, and date to the very onset of the last glacial advance: approximately 30,500 BP for Willendorf II/5 and 25,800 BP for level II/8 (Brandtner 1956–59; Otte 1981:261–299, 1991:47; Haesaerts 1985b, 1990a). Thus, sites in central Europe that date to the Last Glacial Maximum are not deeply stratified or do not have abundant deposits, and the deposits at rich, well-stratified sites do not date to the Last Glacial Maximum. In every respect Grubgraben is an exceptional site without which the specialized analysis presented here would have been impractical.

The most promising direction for further inquiry stems from the main criticism of the present study: although the research has provided new observations of the archaeological record, the absence of directly relevant middle-range knowledge makes these observations less meaningful than they could be:

> It is quite true that archaeologists can expand our potential for learning about the past by identifying properties and characteristics of the archaeological record not previously given systematic descriptive attention by previous workers. This is akin to expanding our exploration of relationships only at the primary observational level. Just as in the case of discovering new and previously unseen relationships, the new properties observed do not carry self-evident meaning. We must conduct hardheaded middle-range research in order to understand any generalizations made from these "new" observations or from any patterns recognized through second- and third-derivative pattern-recognition studies. In the absence of methodological research, the "new" observations stand only as potential sources of knowledge going beyond our current level of either ignorance or knowledge, depending upon one's evaluations of the state of our art (Binford 1989a:277).

Binford's assessment of the results of pattern recognition work in general is insightful and entirely relevant to the results of the present study. The diachronic patterning in organizational properties demonstrated at Grubgraben is robust and provocative, and stands as a potential source of knowledge about how hunter-gatherer systems responded to the climatic modifications associated with a severe ice age. However, although the demonstrable correlation of certain patterns of organizational change with climatic change is compelling, and although the observed diachronic changes in organizational properties are plausible as adaptive responses to ice-age conditions, it does not necessarily follow that climate is the causal agent.

To establish causality, a program of relevant middle-range research is advisable. As discussed in chapters 1 and 3, however, actualistic middle-range research examining the archaeological consequences of the response of human groups to the onset of an ice-age does not appear accessible at present. Nevertheless, some promising alternatives are available, such as using environmental variation with latitude as a proxy for climatic change, and studying the organizational consequences of historical episodes of climatic change. A reasonable course of action would be to pursue these alternatives, using the results of the present study to suggest relevant observations and to guide the research in appropriate directions, and seek to increase our knowledge of the uniformitarian relationships between environmental processes, the organization of cultural systems, and archaeological patterns.

...archaeologists are simply free to make up the past as they go along. We need hardheaded analytical study of the variable characteristics remaining for us to see; only with some understanding of the causes of the observed variation can we make accurate statements about the past and sort out the interactions of variables necessary for the successful building of robust theory.

Lewis Binford

General impressions are never to be trusted. Unfortunately when they are of long standing they become fixed rules of life, and assume a prescriptive right not to be questioned. Consequently those who are not accustomed to original inquiry entertain a hatred and a horror of statistics. They cannot endure the idea of submitting their sacred impressions to cold-blooded verification. But it is the triumph of scientific men to rise superior to such superstitions, to desire tests by which the value of beliefs may be ascertained, and to feel sufficiently masters of themselves to discard contemptuously whatever may be found untrue.

Francis Galton

Bibliography

Albrecht, Gerd
1979 *Magdalénien-Inventare vom Petersfels: Siedlungsarchäologische Ergebnisse der Ausgrabungen 1974–1976.* Tübinger Monographien zur Urgeschichte 6. Tübingen, Germany: Archaeologica Venatoria.

1981 Die neuen Ausgrabungen in Munzingen 1976/1977. *Archaeologica Venatoria e.V. Mitteilungsblatt* 2:21–23.

Albrecht, G., J. Hahn, W. von Koenigswald, H. Müller-Beck, W. Taute, and W. Wille
1976 Die klimatische Veränderung des terrestrischen Lebensraumes und ihre Rückwirkung auf den Menschen. *Zentralblatt für Geologie und Paläontologie, Teil II, Paläontologie, Heft 5/6,* pp. 449–479.

Aldenderfer Mark S., and Roger K. Blashfield
1978 Cluster Analysis and Archaeological Classification. *American Antiquity* 43(3):502–505.

Allain, Jacques
1979 L'industrie lithique et osseuse de Lascaux. In *Lascaux Inconnu,* edited by Arlette Leroi-Gourhan and Jacques Allain, pp. 87–120. Paris: CNRS.

Allain, J., and J. Descouts
1957 A propos d'une baguette a rainure armée de silex découverte dans le Magdalénien de Saint-Marcel. *L'Anthropologie* 61(5–6):503–512.

Andersen, Björn G.
1981 Late Weichselian Ice Sheets in Eurasia and Greenland. In *The Last Great Ice Sheets,* edited by George H. Denton and Terence J. Hughes, pp. 1–65. New York: Wiley.

Audouze, François
1987 Deux modèles et des faits: les modèles de A. Leroi-Gourhan et de L. Binford confrontés aux résultats recents. *Bulletin de la Société Préhistorique Française* 84:343–352.

Audouze, François, and James Enloe
1991 Subsistence Strategies and Economy in the Magdalenian of the Paris Basin, France. In *The Late Glacial in North-West Europe: Human Adaptation and Environmental Change at the End of the Pleistocene,* edited by N. Barton, A.J. Roberts, and D.A. Roe, pp. 63–71. Council for British Archaeology Report 77. London: Council for British Archaeology.

Bailey, Harry P.
1960 A Method of Determining the Warmth and Temperateness of Climate. *Geografiska Annaler* 42(1):1–16.

Bailey, Geoff, and Clive Gamble
1990 The Balkans at 18 000 BP: The View from Epirus. In *The World at 18 000 BP, Volume 1: High Latitudes,* edited by Olga Soffer and Clive Gamble, pp. 148–167. London: Unwin Hyman.

Bánesz, Ladislav
1969 Gravettské súvrstvia s obsidiánovou a pazúrikovou industriou v Kasove a Cejkove. *Archeologické rozhledy* 21(3):281–290.

Bánesz, Ladislav, and Lubomíra Kaminská
1984 Vyskum archeologickej lokality v Hrceli. *Historica Carpatica* 15:255–281.

Bánesz, Ladislav, and Karol Pieta
1961 Vyskum v Cejkove I Roku 1960. *Studijné Zvesti Aúsav* 6:5–30.

Barner, Wilhelm
1959 Renjäger am Aschenstein im Selter bei Freden. *Alt-Hildesheim* 30:5–9.

1962 Die würmeiszeitliche Renjägerstation am Aschenstein bei Freden, Kreis Alfeld. *Nachrichten aus Niedersachsens Urgeschichte* 31:115–120.

Bárta, Juraj
1966 *Einige beachtenswerte paläolithische Fundstellen in der Westslovakei.* Nitra: Archeologicky ústav SAV.

1970 Zur Problematik der gravettezeitlichen Besiedlung der Slowakei. *Slovenská Archeológia* 18(2):207–215.

1980 *Vyznamné paleolitické lokality na strednom a západnom Slovensku.* Nitra: Archeologicky ústav SAV.

1982 La Periode du Gravettien en Slovaquie. In *Aurignacien et Gravettien en Europe,* Fascicule III, pp. 31–44. ERAUL 13. Liège, Belgium: ERAUL.

Beck, Margaret
1993 *An Introductory Analysis of the Grubgraben Cobbles.* Manuscript.

Bergthórsson, Páll
1969 An Estimate of Drift Ice and Temperature in Iceland in 1000 Years. *Jökull* 19:94–101.

Berke, Hubert
1987 *Archäozoologische Detailuntersuchungen an Knochen aus südwestdeutschen Magdalénien-Inventaren.* Urgeschichtliche Materialhefte 8. Tübingen, Germany: Archaeologica Venatoria.

1988 Butchering Marks on Horse Bones from the Magdalenian Site Petersfels, Southwestern Germany. In *Recent Developments in Environmental Analysis in Old and New World Archaeology,* edited by R. Esmée Webb, pp. 105–116. BAR International Series 416. Oxford, England: British Archaeological Reports.

1989 Archeozoology and Site Catchment in the Magdalenian: Solutre, Petersfels, Pekarna Cave,

Kniegrotte. A Preliminary Report. *Early Man News* 14:15–31.

Binant, Pascale
   1991 *La Prehistoire de la Mort: Les premières sépultures en Europe.* Paris: Editions Errance.

Binford, Lewis R.
   1962 Archaeology as Anthropology. *American Antiquity* 28(2):217–225.

   1965 Archaeological Systematics and the Study of Culture Process. *American Antiquity* 31(2):203–210.

   1968 Post-Pleistocene Adaptations. In *New Perspectives in Archeology,* edited by Sally R. Binford and Lewis R. Binford, pp. 313–341. Chicago: Aldine.

   1969 Comments to "Culture Traditions and the Environment of Early Man" by Desmond Collins. *Current Anthropology* 10(4):297–299.

   1972 *An Archaeological Perspective.* New York: Seminar Press.

   1973 Interassemblage Variability—The Mousterian and the 'Functional' Argument. In *The Explanation of Culture Change: Models in Prehistory,* edited by Colin Renfrew, pp. 227–254. London: Duckworth.

   1977a General Introduction. In *For Theory Building in Archaeology: Essays on Faunal Remains, Aquatic Resources, Spatial Analysis, and Systemic Modeling,* edited by Lewis R. Binford, pp. 1–10. New York: Academic Press.

   1977b Olorgesailie Deserves More Than the Usual Book Review. *Journal of Anthropological Research* 33(4):493–502.

   1978a Dimensional Analysis of Behavior and Site Structure: Learning From an Eskimo Hunting Stand. *American Antiquity* 43(3):330–361.

   1978b *Nunamiut Ethnoarchaeology.* New York: Academic Press.

   1979 Organization and Formation Processes: Looking at Curated Technologies. *Journal of Anthropological Research* 35(3):255–273.

   1980 Willow Smoke and Dogs' Tails: Hunter-Gatherer Settlement Systems and Archaeological Site Formation. *American Antiquity* 45(1):4–20.

   1981 *Bones: Ancient Men and Modern Myths.* New York: Academic Press.

   1982a The Archaeology of Place. *Journal of Anthropological Archaeology* 1(1):5–31.

   1982b Comments to "Rethinking the Middle/Upper Paleolithic Transition" by Randall White. *Current Anthropology* 23(2):177–181.

   1982c Objectivity—Explanation—Archaeology—1981. In *Theory and Explanation in Archaeology: The Southampton Conference,* edited by Colin Renfrew, Michael J. Rowlands, and Barbara Abbott Segraves, pp. 125–138. New York: Academic Press.

   1982d Meaning, Inference and the Material Record. In *Ranking, Resource, and Exchange: Aspects of the Archaeology of Early European Society,* edited by Colin Renfrew and Stephen Shennan, pp. 160–163. Cambridge: Cambridge University Press.

   1983a *In Pursuit of the Past.* London: Thames and Hudson.

   1983b Long Term Land Use Patterns: Some Implications for Archaeology. In *Lulu Linear Punctated: Essays in Honor of George Irving Quimby,* edited by Robert C. Dunnell and Donald K. Grayson, pp. 27–53. Ann Arbor, MI: Anthropological Papers, Museum of Anthropology, University of Michigan, No. 72.

   1983c *Working at Archaeology.* New York: Academic Press.

   1984a Bones of Contention: A Reply to Glynn Isaac. *American Antiquity* 49(1):164–167.

   1984b *Faunal Remains from Klasies River Mouth.* Orlando: Academic Press.

   1986a Reply to "Systematic Butchery by Plio/Pleistocene Hominids at Olduvai Gorge, Tanzania" by Henry T. Bunn and Ellen M. Kroll. *Current Anthropology* 27(5):444–446.

   1986b Reply to "Further Comment on Fauna From Klasies River Mouth" by J.F. Thackerey. *Current Anthropology* 27(5):512–515.

   1987a Researching Ambiguity: Frames of Reference and Site Structure. In *Method and Theory for Activity Area Research: An Ethnoarchaeological Approach,* edited by Susan Kent, pp. 449–512. New York: Columbia University Press.

   1987b Were There Elephant Hunters at Torralba? In *The Evolution of Human Hunting,* edited by Matthew H. Nitecki and Doris V. Nitecki, pp. 47–105. New York: Plenum.

   1989a *Debating Archaeology.* San Diego: Academic Press.

   1989b Technology of Early Man: An Organizational Approach to the Oldowan. In *Debating Archaeology,* by Lewis R. Binford, pp. 437–463. San Diego: Academic Press.

1989c Isolating the Transition to Cultural Adaptations: An Organizational Approach. In *The Emergence of Modern Humans: Biocultural Adaptations in the Later Pleistocene*, edited by Erik Trinkaus, pp. 18–41. Cambridge: Cambridge University Press.

1990 Mobility, Housing, and Environment: A Comparative Study. *Journal of Anthropological Research* 46(2):119–152.

1991a There is Always More We Need to Know. In *The First Americans: Search and Research*, edited by Tom D. Dillehay and David J. Meltzer, pp. 275–286. Boca Raton, FL: CRC Press.

1991b When the Going Gets Tough, the Tough Get Going: Nunamiut Local Groups, Camping Patterns and Economic Organization. In *Ethnoarchaeological Approaches to Mobile Campsites*, edited by Clive S. Gamble and William A. Boismier, pp. 25–137. International Monographs in Prehistory, Ethnoarchaeological Series 1. Ann Arbor, MI: International Monographs in Prehistory.

1993 Bones for Stones: Considerations of Analogues for Features Found on the Central Russian Plain. In *From Kostenki To Clovis: Upper Paleolithic—Paleo-Indian Adaptations*, edited by Olga Soffer and N.D. Praslov, pp. 101–124. New York: Plenum.

Binford, Lewis R., and Jack B. Bertram
    1977 Bone Frequencies—And Attritional Processes. In *For Theory Building in Archaeology: Essays on Faunal Remains, Aquatic Resources, Spatial Analysis, and Systemic Modeling*, edited by Lewis R. Binford, pp. 77–153. New York: Academic Press.

Binford, Lewis R., and Sally R. Binford
    1966 A Preliminary Analysis of Functional Variability in the Mousterian of Levallois Facies. *American Anthropologist* 68(2), Part 2, Recent Studies in Paleoanthropology, edited by J. Desmond Clark and F. Clark Howell, pp. 238–295.

Binford, Lewis R., and Jeremy A. Sabloff
    1982 Paradigms, Systematics, and Archaeology. *Journal of Anthropological Research* 38(2):137–153.

Binford, Lewis R., and Nancy M. Stone
    1986 Zhoukoudian: A Closer Look. *Current Anthropology* 27(5):453–468.

Bíró, K.T. (editor)
    1987 *Proceedings of the International Conference on Prehistoric Flint Mining and Lithic Raw Material Identification in the Carpathian Basin. Budapest–Sümeg 1986*. Budapest: Magyar Nemzeti Múzeum.

Bíró, K.T.
    1988 Distribution of Lithic Raw Materials on Prehistoric Sites. An Interim Report. *Acta Archaeologica Academiae Scientiarum Hungaricae* 40(1–4):251–274.

Bíró, K.T., I. Pozsgai, and A. Vladár
    1986 Electron Beam Microanalyses of Obsidian Samples from Geological and Archaeological Sites. *Acta Archaeologica Academiae Scientiarum Hungaricae* 38(1–2):257–278.

Bökönyi, Sándor
    1974 *The Przewalski Horse*. London: Souvenir Press.

Bosinski, Gerhard
    1981 *Gönnersdorf: Eiszeitjäger am Mittelrhein*. Köln: Rhenania-Verlag.

    1988 Upper and Final Paleolithic Settlement Patterns in the Rhineland, West Germany. In *Upper Pleistocene Prehistory of Western Eurasia*, edited by Harold L. Dibble and Anta Montet-White, pp. 375–386. Philadelphia, PA: The University Museum, University of Pennsylvania.

Bosinski, Gerhard, and Joachim Hahn
    1973 Der Magdalénien-Fundplatz Andernach (Martinsberg). *Rheinische Ausgrabungen*, Band 11.

Boyd, Lee, and Katherine A. Houpt (editors)
    1994 *Przewalski's Horse: The History and Biology of an Endangered Species*. Albany: State University of New York Press.

Bradley, Richard
    1995 Fieldwalking Without Flints: Worked Quartz as a Clue to the Character of Prehistoric Settlement. *Oxford Journal of Archaeology* 14(1):13–22

Brandtner, Friedrich
    1954–55 Kamegg, eine Freilandstation des späteren Paläolithikums in Niederösterreich. *Mitteilungen der Prähistorischen Kommission der Österreichischen Akademie der Wissenschaften*, Band 7.

    1956–59 Die geologisch-stratigraphische Position der Kulturschichten von Willendorf i.d. Wachau, N.Ö. In *Willendorf in der Wachau*, Mitteilungen der Prähistorischen Kommission der Österreichischen Akademie der Wissenschaften, Band 8/9, Teil 1, edited by Fritz Felgenhauer, pp. 173–198.

    1989 Die Paläolithstation "Grubgraben" bei Kammern. Vorläufige Ergebnisse neuerer Grabungen. *Fundberichte aus Österreich* 28:17–26.

Brooks, C.E.P.
    1922 *The Evolution of Climate*. London: Benn Brothers.

Butzer, Karl W.
    1964 *Environment and Archeology: An Introduction to Pleistocene Geography*. Chicago: Aldine.

    1982 *Archaeology as Human Ecology*. Cambridge: Cambridge University Press.

Carr, Christopher

1984 The Nature of Organization of Intrasite Archaeological Records and Spatial Analytic Approaches to Their Investigation. In *Advances in Archaeological Method and Theory, Volume 7*, edited by Michael B. Schiffer, pp. 103–222. New York: Academic Press.

1985 Getting Into Data: Philosophy and Tactics for the Analysis of Complex Data Structures. In *For Concordance in Archaeological Analysis: Bridging Data Structure, Quantitative Technique, and Theory*, edited by Christopher Carr, pp. 18–44. Kansas City, MO: Westport.

1991 Left in the Dust: Contextual Information in Model-Focused Archaeology. In *The Interpretation of Archaeological Spatial Patterning*, edited by Ellen M. Kroll and T. Douglas Price, pp. 221–256. New York: Plenum.

Chambers, F.M.
1993 *Climate Change and Human Impact on the Landscape: Studies in Palaeoecology and Environmental Archaeology*. London: Chapman and Hall.

Chase, Philip G.
1986 *The Hunters of Combe Grenal: Approaches to Middle Paleolithic Subsistence in Europe*. BAR International Series 286. Oxford, England: British Archaeological Reports.

Chatters, James C.
1987 Hunter-Gatherer Adaptations and Assemblage Structure. *Journal of Anthropological Archaeology* 6:336–375.

Cheynier, André
1939 Le Magdalénien Primitif de Badegoule—Niveaux à raclettes. *Bulletin de la Société Préhistorique Française* 36:354–396.

1956 Feuille de laurier emmanchée à Badegoule. *Bulletin de la Société Préhistorique Française* 53:94–95, 446.

Childe, V. Gordon
1952 *New Light on the Most Ancient East*. London: Routledge and Kegan Paul.

Christenson, Andrew L., and Dwight W. Read
1977 Numerical Taxonomy, R-Mode Factor Analysis, and Archaeological Classification. *American Antiquity* 42:163–179.

Christensen, Ronald
1991 *Linear Models for Multivariate, Time Series, and Spatial Data*. New York: Springer-Verlag.

CLIMAP
1976 The Surface of the Ice-Age Earth. *Science* 191(4232):1131–1137.

1981 *Seasonal Reconstructions of the Earth's Surface at the Last Glacial Maximum*. Geological Society of America, Map and Chart Series, MC-36.

COHMAP
1988 Climatic Changes of the Last 18,000 Years: Observations and Model Simulations. *Science* 241(4869):1043–1052.

Combier, J.
1976 Solutré. In *Livret-guide de l'excursion A8: Bassin de Rhône*. UISPP Congrès IX, Nice. Paris: CNRS.

Conkey, Margaret W.
1980 The Identification of Prehistoric Hunter-Gatherer Aggregation Sites: The Case of Altamira. *Current Anthropology* 21(5):609–630.

Cook, Eva
1993 *The Dentalia Shell Collection from the Epigravettian Site of Grubgraben, Austria*. Manuscript.

Cowgill, George L.
1968 Archaeological Applications of Factor, Cluster, and Proximity Analysis. *American Antiquity* 33(3):367–375.

1970 Some Sampling and Reliability Problems in Archaeology. In *Archéologie et Calculateurs: Problèmes sémiologiques et mathématiques*, edited by M. Jean-Claude Gardin, pp. 161–172. Paris: CNRS.

1986 Archaeological Applications of Mathematical and Formal Methods. In *American Archaeology Past and Future: A Celebration of the Society for American Archaeology 1935–1985*, edited by David J. Meltzer, Don D. Fowler, and Jeremy A. Sabloff, pp. 369–393. Washington, DC: Smithsonian Institution Press.

1989 The Concept of Diversity in Archaeological Theory. In *Quantifying Diversity in Archaeology*, edited by Robert D. Leonard and George T. Jones, pp. 131–141. Cambridge: Cambridge University Press.

Cox, G.W.
1980 *Laboratory Manual of General Ecology*. 4th edition. Dubuque: William C. Brown.

Crowley, Thomas J., and Gerald R. North
1991 *Paleoclimatology*. New York: Oxford University Press.

Dansgaard, W., S.J. Johnsen, N. Reeh, N. Gundestrup, H.B. Clausen, and C.U. Hammer
1975 Climatic Changes, Norsemen and Modern Man. *Nature* 255(5503):24–28.

Davidson, I.
1983 Site Variability and Prehistoric Economy in Levante. In *Hunter-Gatherer Economy in Prehistory: A European Perspective*, edited by Geoff Bailey, pp. 79–95. Cambridge: Cambridge University Press.

Davis, Richard S.
　1985 Upper Pleistocene Climatic Fluctuations and Palaeolithic Settlement Distributions in Soviet Central Asia and Surrounding Territories. In *Proceedings of the International Workshop on the Late Cenozoic Palaeoclimatic Oscillations in Kashmir and Central Asia*, edited by D.P. Agrawal, pp. 215–221. New Delhi: Today and Tomorrow's Printers and Publishers.

　1990 Central Asian Hunter-Gatherers at the Last Glacial Maximum. In *The World at 18 000 BP, Volume 1: High Latitudes*, edited by Olga Soffer and Clive Gamble, pp. 266–275. London: Unwin Hyman.

Deacon, H.J., and Janette Deacon
　1980 The Hafting, Function and Distribution of Small Convex Scrapers with an Example from Boomplaas Cave. *South African Archaeological Bulletin* 35(131):31–37.

Denton, George H., and Terence J. Hughes (editors)
　1981 *The Last Great Ice Sheets*. New York: Wiley.

Dewez, Michel
　1982 Comments to "Rethinking the Middle/Upper Paleolithic Transition" by Randall White. *Current Anthropology* 23(2):182.

　1987 *Le paléolithique supérieur recent dans les grottes de Belgique*. Publications d'histoire de l'art et d'archéologie de l'Université Catholique de Louvain, LVII. Louvain-La-Neuve, Belgium: Société Wallonne de Palethnologie.

Dobosi, Viola T.
　1991a Discontinuity in the Upper Paleolithic of Hungary. In *Les bassins du Rhin et du Danube au paléolithique supérieur: environnement, habitat et systèmes d'échange*, edited by Anta Montet-White, pp. 18–25. ERAUL 43. Liège, Belgium: ERAUL.

　1991b Economy and Raw Material: A Case Study of Three Upper Palaeolithic Sites in Hungary. In *Raw Material Economies Among Prehistoric Hunter-Gatherers*, edited by Anta Montet-White and Steven Holen, pp. 197–203. Lawrence, KS: University of Kansas, Publications in Anthropology 19.

Dobosi, Viola T., Béla Jungbert, Arpád Ringer, and István Vörös
　1988 Palaeolithic Settlement in Nadap. *Folia Archaeologica* 39:13–39.

Dobosi, V.T., E. Kövecses-Varga, E. Krolopp, I. Vörös, I. Magyar, I. Varga, and E. Hertelendi
　1991 Upper Palaeolithic Site at Esztergom-Gyurgyalag. *Acta Archaeologica Academiae Scientiarum Hungaricae* 43(3–4):233–271.

Dobosi, V.T., I. Vörös, E. Krolopp, J. Szabó, A. Ringer, and F. Schweitzer
　1983 Upper Palaeolithic Settlement in Pilismarót-Pálrét. *Acta Archaeologica Academiae Scientiarum Hungaricae* 35:287–311.

Dolukhanov, Pavel M., Janusz K. Kozlowski, and Stefan K. Kozlowski
　1980 *Multivariate Analysis of Upper Palaeolithic and Mesolithic Stone Assemblages*. Warszawa: Nakladem Uniwersytetu Jagiellonskiego.

Doran, J.E., and F.R. Hodson
　1975 *Mathematics and Computers in Archaeology*. Cambridge, MA: Harvard University Press.

Dumond, Don E.
　1972a Prehistoric Population Growth and Subsistence Change in Eskimo Alaska. In *Population Growth: Anthropological Implications*, edited by Brian Spooner, pp. 311–328. Cambridge, MA: MIT Press.

　1972b Population Growth and Political Centralization. In *Population Growth: Anthropological Implications*, edited by Brian Spooner, pp. 286–310. Cambridge, MA: MIT Press.

Dunnell, Robert C.
　1980 Evolutionary Theory and Archaeology. In *Advances in Archaeological Method and Theory, Volume 3*, edited by Michael B. Schiffer, pp. 35–99. New York: Academic Press.

　1982 Science, Social Science, and Common Sense: The Agonizing Dilemma of Modern Archaeology. *Journal of Anthropological Research* 38(1):1–25.

　1989 Diversity in Archaeology: A Group of Measures in Search of Application? In *Quantifying Diversity in Archaeology*, edited by Robert D. Leonard and George T. Jones, pp. 142–149. Cambridge: Cambridge University Press.

Eickhoff, S.
　1988 Ausgesplitterte Stücke, Kostenki-Enden und "retuschierte Bruchkanten": Einige Aspekte zur Untersuchung der Artefakte aus westeuropäischem Feuerstein auf dem Magdalénien-Fundplatz Gönnersdorf. *Archäologische Informationen* 11:136–144.

Enloe, James G.
　1993 Subsistence Organization in the Early Upper Paleolithic: Reindeer Hunters of the Abri du Flageolet, Couche V. In *Before Lascaux: The Complex Record of the Early Upper Paleolithic*, edited by Heidi Knecht, Anne Pike-Tay, and Randall White, pp. 101–115. Boca Raton, FL: CRC Press.

Evans, John G.
　1978 *An Introduction to Environmental Archaeology*. Ithaca, NY: Cornell University Press.

Felgenhauer, Fritz
　1951 Aggsbach: Ein Fundplatz des späten Paläolithikums in Niederösterreich. *Mitteilungen der*

Prähistorischen Kommission der Österreichischen Akademie der Wissenschaften, Band 5, Teil 6.

1956–59 Willendorf in der Wachau. Monographie der Paläolith-Fundstellen I–VII. *Mitteilungen der Prähistorischen Kommission der Österreichischen Akademie der Wissenschaften,* Band 8/9, Teil 1, Text; Band 8/9, Teil 2, Inventar; Band 8/9, Teil 3, Abbildungen.

1962 Das niederösterreichische Freilandpaläolithikum. *Mitteilungen der Österreichischen Arbeitsgemeinschaft für Ur- und Frühgeschichte* 13:1–16.

Feustel, Rudolf, Klaus Kerkmann, Elisabeth Schmid, Rudolf Musil, and Helga Jacob
1971 Der Bärenkeller bei Königsee-Garsitz, eine jungpaläolithische Kulthöhle. (I). *Alt-Thüringen* 11:81–130.

Flint, Richard Foster
1971 *Glacial and Quaternary Geology.* New York: Wiley.

Frayer, David F.
1984 Biological and Cultural Change in the European Late Pleistocene and Early Holocene. In *The Origins of Modern Humans: A World Survey of the Fossil Evidence,* edited by Fred H. Smith and Frank Spencer, pp. 211–250. New York: Alan R. Liss.

Freeman, Leslie G.
1978 The Analysis of Some Occupation Floor Distributions from Earlier and Middle Paleolithic Sites in Spain. In *Views of the Past: Essays in Old World Prehistory and Paleoanthropology,* edited by Leslie G. Freeman, pp. 57–116. The Hague, The Netherlands: Mouton.

Frison, George C., and Lawrence C. Todd
1986 *The Colby Mammoth Site: Taphonomy and Archaeology of a Clovis Kill in Northern Wyoming.* Albuquerque: University of New Mexico Press.

Gábori, M.
1964 Beiträge zum Paläolithikum des Donauknie-Gebietes. *Acta Archaeologica Academiae Scientiarum Hungaricae* 16(3–4):171–186.

1965 Der zweite paläolithische Hausgrundriss von Ságvár. *Acta Archaeologica Academiae Scientiarum Hungaricae* 17:111–127.

1970 25 Jahre Paläolithforschung in Ungarn (1945–1969). *Acta Archaeologica Academiae Scientiarum Hungaricae* 22:351–364.

Gábori, M., and V. Gábori
1959 Der erste paläolithische Hausgrundriss in Ungarn. *Acta Archaeologica Academiae Scientiarum Hungaricae* 9(1–4):19–34.

Gábori-Csánk, V.
1970 C-14 Dates of the Hungarian Palaeolithic. *Acta Archaeologica Academiae Scientiarum Hungaricae* 22:3–11

1984 Die Behausungsspuren von Dömös. In *Jüngpaläolithische Siedlungsstrukturen in Europa,* edited by Hubert Berke, Joachim Hahn, and Claus-Joachim Kind, pp. 251–256. Urgeschichtliche Materialhefte 6. Tübingen, Germany: Archaeologica Venatoria.

1986 Spuren des Jungpaläolithikums in Budapest. *Acta Archaeologica Academiae Scientiarum Hungaricae* 38(1–2):3–12.

Gale, Stephen J., and Peter G. Hoare
1991 *Quaternary Sediments: Petrographic Methods for the Study of Unlithified Rocks.* New York: Halsted Press.

Gamble, Clive
1983 Culture and Society in the Upper Palaeolithic of Europe. In *Hunter-Gatherer Economy in Prehistory: A European Perspective,* edited by Geoff N. Bailey, pp. 201–211. Cambridge: Cambridge University Press.

1986 *The Palaeolithic Settlement of Europe.* Cambridge: Cambridge University Press.

1991 An Introduction to the Living Spaces of Mobile Peoples. In *Ethnoarchaeological Approaches to Mobile Campsites,* edited by Clive S. Gamble and William A. Boismier, pp. 1–23. International Monographs in Prehistory, Ethnoarchaeological Series 1. Ann Arbor, MI: International Monographs in Prehistory.

Gamble, Clive S., and William A. Boismier (editors)
1991 *Ethnoarchaeological Approaches to Mobile Campsites.* International Monographs in Prehistory, Ethnoarchaeological Series 1. Ann Arbor, MI: International Monographs in Prehistory.

Gamble, Clive, and Olga Soffer (editors)
1990a *The World at 18 000 BP, Volume 2: Low Latitudes.* London: Unwin Hyman.

Gamble, Clive, and Olga Soffer
1990b Introduction. Pleistocene Polyphony: The Diversity of Human Adaptations at the Last Glacial Maximum. In *The World at 18 000 BP, Volume 1: High Latitudes,* edited by Olga Soffer and Clive Gamble, pp. 1–23. London: Unwin Hyman.

Gaussen, Jean
1980 *Le paléolithique supérieur de plein air en Périgord.* XIVe Supplément à Gallia Préhistoire. Paris: CNRS.

Gearing, Fred
1962 *Priests and Warriors: Social Structures for Cherokee Politics in the 18th Century.* American Anthropological Association, Memoir 93.

Good, I.J.
1969 Some Applications of the Singular Decomposition of a Matrix. *Technometrics* 11(4):823–831.

Gordon, Bryan C.
 1988 *Of Men and Reindeer Herds in French Magdalenian Prehistory*. BAR International Series 390. Oxford, England: British Archaeological Reports.

Gould, Peter
 1970 Is *Statistix Inferens* the Geographical Name for a Wild Goose? *Economic Geography* 46(2)(supplement):439–448.

 1981 Letting the Data Speak for Themselves. *Annals of the Association of American Geographers* 71(2):166–176.

Gould, Stephen J.
 1977 *Ever Since Darwin: Reflections in Natural History*. New York: Norton.

Grayson, Donald K.
 1984 *Quantitative Zooarchaeology: Topics in the Analysis of Archaeological Faunas*. Orlando: Academic Press.

Haesaerts, Paul
 1985a *Étude stratigraphique preliminaire du gisement paléolithique de Grubgraben (Basse Autriche)*. Manuscript.

 1985b Les loess du Pléistocène supérieur en Belgique; comparaisons avec les séquences d'Europe centrale. *Bulletin de l'Association française pour l'étude du Quaternaire* 2(3):105–115.

 1990a Nouvelles Recherches au Gisement de Willendorf (Basse Autriche). *Bulletin de l'Institut Royal des Sciences Naturelles de Belgique, Sciences de la Terre* 60:203–218.

 1990b Stratigraphy of the Grubgraben Loess Sequence. In *The Epigravettian Site of Grubgraben, Lower Austria: The 1986 and 1987 Excavations*, edited by Anta Montet-White, pp. 15–35. ERAUL 40. Liège, Belgium: ERAUL.

Hahn, Joachim
 1973 Eine Gravettien-Industrie von Krems-Hundssteig (Niederösterreich). *Homo* 72(1–2):81–89.

 1976 Das Gravettien im westlichen Mitteleuropa. In *Périgordien et Gravettien en Europe*, edited by Bohuslav Klíma, pp. 100–120. UISPP Congrès IX, Colloque XV, Nice. Paris: CNRS.

 1977 *Aurignacien, das ältere Jungpaläolithikum in Mittel- und Osteuropa*. Fundamenta, Reihe A, Band 9. Köln: Böhlau.

 1981a Abfolge und Umwelt der jüngeren Altsteinzeit in Südwestdeutschland. *Fundberichte aus Baden-Württemberg* 6:1–27.

 1981b Zur Abfolge des Jungpaläolithikums in Südwestdeutschland. *Kölner Jahrbuch* 15:52–67.

 1983 Das Gravettien im westlichen Mitteleuropa. In *Aurignacien et Gravettien en Europe*, Fascicule I, pp. 241–253. ERAUL 13. Liège, Belgium: ERAUL.

 1984 *Die steinzeitliche Besiedlung des Eselsburger Tales bei Heidenheim (Schwäbische Alb)*. Forschungen und Berichte zur Vor- und Frühgeschichte in Baden-Württemberg, Band 17. Stuttgart: Konrad Theiss.

 1987 Aurignacian and Gravettian Settlement Patterns in Central Europe. In *The Pleistocene Old World*, edited by Olga Soffer, pp. 251–261. New York: Plenum.

 1988a Das Jungpaläolithikum in Württemberg. In *Archäologie in Württemberg. Ergebnisse und Perspektiven archäologischer Forschung von der Altsteinzeit bis zur Neusteinzeit*, edited by Dieter Planck, pp. 41–54. Stuttgart: Konrad Theiss.

 1988b *Die Geißenklösterle-Höhle im Achtal bei Blaubeuren I: Fundhorizontbildung und Besiedlung im Mittelpaläolithikum und im Aurignacien*. Forschungen und Berichte zur Vor- und Frühgeschichte in Baden-Württemburg, Band 26. Stuttgart: Konrad Theiss.

 1993 *Erkennen und Bestimmen von Stein- und Knochenartefakten: Einführung in die Artefaktmorphologie*. 2nd edition. Archaeologica Venatoria, Band 10. Tübingen, Germany: Archaeologica Venatoria.

Hahn, Joachim, and Wighart von Koenigswald
 1977 Die steinzeitlichen Funde und die spätglaziale Nagetierschicht aus der Kleinen Scheuer am Hohlenstein im Lonetal. *Fundberichte aus Baden-Württemberg* 3:51–75.

Hammond, Allen L.
 1976 Paleoclimate: Ice Age Earth Was Cool and Dry. *Science* 191(4226):455.

Harpending, Henry, and Trefor Jenkins
 1973 Genetic Distance Among Southern African Populations. In *Methods and Theories of Anthropological Genetics*, edited by Michael H. Crawford and Peter L. Workman, pp. 177–199. Albuquerque: University of New Mexico Press.

Harpending, Henry, and Alan Rogers
 1985 *ANTANA: A Package for Multivariate Data Analysis*. Version 1.2. 1 February 1985.

Hayden, Brian
 1982 Interaction Parameters and the Demise of Paleo-Indian Craftsmanship. *Plains Anthropologist* 27(96):109–123.

Heinrich, Wolfgang
 1973 Das Jungpaläolithikum in Niederösterreich. Unpublished dissertation, Salzburg, Austria.

1974–75 Paläolithforschung in Österreich—Ein Rückblick auf die letzten 25 Jahre. *Mitteilungen der Österreichischen Arbeitsgemeinschaft für Ur- und Frühgeschichte* 25:1–40.

Hemingway, M.F.
1980 *The Initial Magdalenian in France.* BAR International Series 90. Oxford, England: British Archaeological Reports.

Hill, Matthew E., Jr.
1993 *The Quartz Artifacts from Grubgraben.* Manuscript.

Hillebrand, Jenö
1934 Vorläufiger Bericht über die Ausgrabungsresultate der Ságvárer Lößjägerstation bei Siófok in Ungarn. *Mannus* 26:321–325.

Horn, Roger A., and Charles R. Johnson
1985 *Matrix Analysis.* Cambridge: Cambridge University Press.

Hughes, T.J., G.H. Denton, B.G. Andersen, D.H. Shilling, J.L. Fastook, and C.S. Lingle
1981 The Last Great Ice Sheets: A Global View. In *The Last Great Ice Sheets*, edited by George H. Denton and Terence J. Hughes, pp. 263–317. New York: Wiley.

Jaguttis-Emden, Martin
1983 Die Radiocarbondatierung der Ausgrabung Petersfels. In *Naturwissenschaftliche Untersuchungen an Magdalénien-Inventaren vom Petersfels, Grabungen 1974–1976*, edited by G. Albrecht, H. Berke, and F. Poplin, pp. 47–57. Tübinger Monographien zur Urgeschichte 8. Tübingen, Germany: Archaeologica Venatoria.

Jelinek, Arthur J.
1982 The Tabun Cave and Paleolithic Man in the Levant. *Science* 216(4553):1369–1375.

Jochim, Michael A.
1976 *Hunter-Gatherer Subsistence and Settlement: A Predictive Model.* New York: Academic Press.

1981 *Strategies for Survival: Cultural Behavior in an Ecological Context.* New York: Academic Press.

1983 Palaeolithic Art in Ecological Perspective. In *Hunter-Gatherer Economy in Prehistory: A European Perspective*, edited by Geoff N. Bailey, pp. 212–219. Cambridge: Cambridge University Press.

1987 Late Pleistocene Refugia in Europe. In *The Pleistocene Old World*, edited by Olga Soffer, pp. 317–331. New York: Plenum.

1991 Archeology as Long-Term Ethnography. *American Anthropologist* 93(2):308–321.

Jones, George T., Donald K. Grayson, and Charlotte Beck
1983 Artifact Class Richness and Sample Size in Archaeological Surface Assemblages. In *Lulu Linear Punctated: Essays in Honor of George Irving Quimby*, edited by Robert C. Dunnell and Donald K. Grayson, pp. 55–73. Ann Arbor, MI: Anthropological Papers, Museum of Anthropology, University of Michigan, No. 72.

Julien, Michele
1988 Organisation de l'espace et fonction des habitats magdalénien du Bassin Parisien. In *De la Loire à l'Oder: les civilisations du paléolithique final dans le nord-ouest européen*, edited by Marcel Otte, pp. 85–119. BAR International Series 444(i). Oxford, England: British Archaeological Reports.

Keeley, Lawrence H.
1980 *Experimental Determination of Stone Tool Uses: A Microwear Analysis.* Chicago: University of Chicago Press.

1982 Hafting and Retooling: Effects on the Archaeological Record. *American Antiquity* 47(4):798–809.

1987 Hafting and "Retooling" at Verberie. In *La Main et l'Outil*, edited by Danielle Stordeur, pp. 89–96. Lyon: Maison de l'Orient.

Kelly, Robert L.
1992 Mobility/Sedentism: Concepts, Archaeological Measures, and Effects. *Annual Review of Anthropology* 21:43–66.

1995 *The Foraging Spectrum: Diversity in Hunter-Gatherer Lifeways.* Washington, DC: Smithsonian Institution Press.

Kendall, Sir Maurice G.
1980 *Multivariate Analysis.* 2nd edition. London: Charles Griffin.

Kießling, Franz
1918 Die Aurignacienstation im Gruebgraben bei Kammern in Niederösterreich. *Mitteilungen der Anthropologischen Gesellschaft in Wien* 48:229–246.

1934 Das Lößaurignacien im Gruebgraben bei Kammern. In *Beiträge zur Ur-, Vor- und Frühgeschichte von Niederösterreich und Südmähren*, by Franz Kießling, pp. 72–75. Vienna: Roland, Verein nied.-österr. Altertumsfreunde.

Kind, Claus-Joachim
1985 *Die Verteilung von Steinartefakten in Grabungsflächen: Ein Modell zur Organisation alt- und mittelsteinzeitlicher Siedlungsplätze.* Urgeschichtliche Materialhefte 7. Tübingen, Germany: Archaeologica Venatoria.

Kintigh, Keith W.
1984 Measuring Archaeological Diversity by Comparison with Simulated Assemblages. *American*

Antiquity 49(1):44–54.

1990 Intrasite Spatial Analysis: A Commentary on Major Methods. In *Mathematics and Information Science in Archaeology: A Flexible Framework,* edited by Albertus Voorrips, pp. 165–200. Bonn: Holos.

Kintigh, Keith W., and Albert J. Ammerman
1982 Heuristic Approaches to Spatial Analysis in Archaeology. *American Antiquity* 47(1):31–63.

Klein, Richard G., and Kathryn Cruz-Uribe
1984 *The Analysis of Animal Bones from Archeological Sites.* Chicago: University of Chicago Press.

Koetje, Todd A.
1987 *Spatial Patterns in Magdalenien Open Air Sites from the Isle Valley, Southwestern France.* BAR International Series 346. Oxford, England: British Archaeological Reports.

Kozlowski, Janusz K.
1972–73 The Origin of the Lithic Raw Materials Used in the Palaeolithic of the Carpathian Countries. *Acta Archaeologica Carpathica* 13:5–19.

1980 Technical and Typological Differentiation of Lithic Assemblages in the Upper Palaeolithic: An Interpretation Attempt. In *Unconventional Archaeology: New Approaches and Goals in Polish Archaeology,* edited by Romuald Schild, pp. 33–55. Wroclaw: Zaklad Narodowy im. Ossolinskich.

1983 Le Paléolithique supérieur en Pologne. *L'Anthropologie* 87:49–82.

1986 The Gravettian in Central and Eastern Europe. *Advances in World Archaeology* 5(3):131–200.

1989 Le Magdalénien en Pologne. In *Le Magdalénien en Europe,* edited by J.-Ph. Rigaud, pp. 31–37. ERAUL 38. Liège, Belgium: ERAUL.

1990 Northern Central Europe c. 18 000 BP. In *The World at 18 000 BP, Volume 1: High Latitudes,* edited by Olga Soffer and Clive Gamble, pp. 204–227. London: Unwin Hyman.

1991a Le Gravettien du bassin Rhenan et du haut Danube: Contribution au probleme des relations entre le Perigordien occidental et le Gravettien oriental. In *Les bassins du Rhin et du Danube au paléolithique supérieur: environnement, habitat et systèmes d'échange,* edited by Anta Montet-White, pp. 76–90. ERAUL 43. Liège, Belgium: ERAUL.

1991b Raw Material Procurement in the Upper Paleolithic of Central Europe. In *Raw Material Economies Among Prehistoric Hunter-Gatherers,* edited by Anta Montet-White and Steven Holen, pp. 187–196. Lawrence, KS: University of Kansas, Publications in Anthropology 19.

Kozlowksi, Janusz K., and Krzysztof Sobczyk
1987 *The Upper Palaeolithic Site of Kraków-Spadzista Street C2. Excavations 1990.* Warszawa-Kraków: Pan'stwowe Wydawnictwo Naukowe.

Kroll, Ellen M., and T. Douglas Price (editors)
1991 *The Interpretation of Archaeological Spatial Patterning.* New York: Plenum.

Krzanowski, W.J.
1988 *Principles of Multivariate Analysis: A User's Perspective.* Oxford: Clarendon Press.

Kukla, G.J.
1975 Loess Stratigraphy of Central Europe. In *After the Australopithecines: Stratigraphy, Ecology, and Culture Change in the Middle Pleistocene,* edited by Karl W. Butzer and Glynn Ll. Isaac, pp. 99–108. The Hague, The Netherlands: Mouton.

1977 Pleistocene Land-Sea Correlations, I. Europe. *Earth Science Review* 13:307–374.

Kúrten, Björn
1968 *Pleistocene Mammals of Europe.* London: Weidenfeld and Nicolson.

Lang, Gerhard
1962 Vegetationsgeschichtliche Untersuchungen der Magdalénienstation an der Schussenquelle. *Veröffentlichungen des Geobotanischen Institutes der Eidg. Techn. Hochschule, Stiftung Rübel* 37:129–154.

Laplace, Georges
1970 L'industrie de Krems-Hundssteig et le problème de l'origine des complexes aurignaciens. In *Frühe Menschheit und Umwelt I,* edited by Karl Gripp, Rudolf Schütrumpf, and Hermann Schwabedissen, pp. 247–297. Fundamenta, Reihe A, Band 2. Köln: Böhlau.

Leader-Williams, N.
1988 *Reindeer on South Georgia: The Ecology of an Introduced Population.* Cambridge: Cambridge University Press.

Lee, Richard B.
1968 What Hunters Do for a Living, or How to Make Out on Scarce Resources. In *Man The Hunter,* edited by Richard B. Lee and Irven DeVore, pp. 30–48. Chicago: Aldine.

Lenoir, Michel
1988 Le Magdalénien ancien en Gironde: Conditions de gisement, variabilité typologique et technique. In *Upper Pleistocene Prehistory of Western Eurasia,* edited by Harold L. Dibble and Anta Montet-White, pp. 397–410. Philadelphia, PA: The University Museum, University of Pennsylvania.

Leonard, Robert D., and George T. Jones (editors)
1989 *Quantifying Diversity in Archaeology.* Cambridge: Cambridge University Press.

Leroi-Gourhan, André (editor)
1976a *Les structures d'habitat au paléolithique supérieur.* UISPP Congrès IX, Colloque XIII, Nice. Paris: CNRS.

Leroi-Gourhan, André
1976b L'habitat au paléolithique supérieur. In *Les structures d'habitat au paléolithique supérieur,* edited by André Leroi-Gourhan, pp. 85–92. UISPP Congrès IX, Colloque XIII, Nice. Paris: CNRS.

1983 Une tête de sagaie à armature de lamelles de silex à Pincevent (Seine-et-Marne). *Bulletin de la Société Préhistorique Française* 80(5):154–156.

1984 *Pincevent: Campement magdalénien de chasseurs de rennes.* Paris: Ministere de la Culture.

Leroi-Gourhan, André, and Michel Brézillon
1966 L'habitation magdalénienne no. 1 de Pincevent près Montereau (Seine-et-Marne). *Gallia Préhistoire* 9:263–385.

1972 Fouilles de Pincevent: Essai d'analyse ethnographique d'un habitat magdalénien (La section 36). *Gallia Préhistoire,* supplément 7.

Lindly, J.M., and G.A. Clark
1990 Symbolism and Modern Human Origins. *Current Anthropology* 31(3):233–261.

Logan, Brad
1990a The Hunted of Grubgraben: An Analysis of Faunal Remains. In *The Epigravettian Site of Grubgraben, Lower Austria: The 1986 and 1987 Excavations,* edited by Anta Montet-White, pp. 65–91. ERAUL 40. Liège, Belgium: ERAUL.

1990b "The Changing Game: Gravettian-Epigravettian Hunting Strategies in the Middle Danube". Paper presented at the International Symposium "La Chasse dans la Préhistoire", Treignes, Belgium, October 1990.

Long, Austin, and Bruce Rippeteau
1974 Testing Contemporaneity and Averaging Radiocarbon Dates. *American Antiquity* 39(2):205–215.

Malina, Jaroslav
1970 Die jungpaläolithische Steinindustrie aus Mähren, ihre Rohstoffe und ihre Patina. *Acta Praehistorica et Archaeologica* 1:157–173.

Mania, Dietrich, and Volker Toepfer
1973 *Königsaue.* Halle, Germany: Veröffentlichungen des Landesmuseums für Vorgeschichte, Band 26.

Manly, Bryan F.J.
1986 *Multivariate Statistical Methods: A Primer.* London: Chapman and Hall.

May, Fabienne
1986 *Les sépultures préhistoriques: Étude critique.* Paris: CNRS.

Merton, Robert K.
1948 Discussion of "The Position of Sociological Theory" by Talcott Parsons. *American Sociological Review* 13:164–168.

1968 *Social Theory and Social Structure.* 3rd edition. New York: Free Press.

Mohr, Erna
1971 *The Asiatic Wild Horse.* [Translation of *Das Urwildpferd* by Daphne M. Goodall]. London: J.A. Allen.

Mohr, Erna, and Jirí Volf
1996 *Das Urwildpferd: Equus przewalskii.* 3rd edition. Magdeburg, Germany: Westarp Wissenschaften.

Montet-White, Anta (editor)
1990a *The Epigravettian Site of Grubgraben, Lower Austria: The 1986 and 1987 Excavations.* ERAUL 40. Liège, Belgium: ERAUL.

Montet-White, Anta (editor)
1991c *Les bassins du Rhin et du Danube au paléolithique supérieur: Environnement, habitat et systèmes d'échange.* ERAUL 43. Liège, Belgium: ERAUL.

Montet-White, Anta
n.d.a *Grubgraben and Kamegg. Preliminary Report for the 1985 Field Season.* Manuscript.

n.d.b *The 1989 Excavations at Grubgraben. Preliminary Report.* Manuscript.

1984 Palaeoecology and Palaeolithic Settlements in the Great Plains of Europe. Review of "Préhistoire de la Grande Plaine de L'Europe". *Quarterly Review of Archaeology* 5(2):14–15.

1988a Raw-Material Economy Among Medium-Sized Late Paleolithic Campsites of Central Europe. In *Upper Pleistocene Prehistory of Western Eurasia,* edited by Harold L. Dibble and Anta Montet-White, pp. 361–373. Philadelphia, PA: The University Museum, University of Pennsylvania.

1988b Recent Excavations at Grubgraben: A Gravettian Site in Lower Austria. *Archäologisches Korrespondenzblatt* 18:213–218.

1990b Introduction. In *The Epigravettian Site of Grubgraben, Lower Austria: The 1986 and 1987 Excavations,* edited by Anta Montet-White, pp. 1–6. ERAUL 40. Liège, Belgium: ERAUL.

1990c The Archaeological Layers: Features and Spatial Distribution. In *The Epigravettian Site of Grubgraben, Lower Austria: The 1986 and 1987 Excavations,* edited by Anta Montet-White, pp. 47–64. ERAUL 40. Liège,

Belgium: ERAUL.

1990d The Artifact Assemblages. In *The Epigravettian Site of Grubgraben, Lower Austria: The 1986 and 1987 Excavations,* edited by Anta Montet-White, pp. 133–157. ERAUL 40. Liège, Belgium: ERAUL.

1991a Un Epigravettien en Basse Autriche. In *Les bassins du Rhin et du Danube au paléolithique supérieur: Environnement, habitat et systèmes d'échange,* edited by Anta Montet-White, pp. 62–74. ERAUL 43. Liège, Belgium: ERAUL.

1991b Lithic Acquisition, Settlements and Territory in the Epigravettian of Central Europe. In *Raw Material Economies Among Prehistoric Hunter-Gatherers,* edited by Anta Montet-White and Steven Holen, pp. 205–219. Lawrence, KS: University of Kansas, Publications in Anthropology 19.

1994 Alternative Interpretations of the Late Upper Paleolithic in Central Europe. *Annual Review of Anthropology* 23:483–508.

Montet-White, Anta, and Djuro Basler
1977 L'industrie gravettienne de Kadar en Bosnie du Nord (Yougoslavie). *Bulletin de la Société Préhistorique Française* 74:531–544.

Montet-White, Anta, and Steven Holen (editors)
1991 *Raw Material Economies Among Prehistoric Hunter-Gatherers.* Lawrence, KS: University of Kansas, Publications in Anthropology 19.

Montet-White, Anta, and Alfred E. Johnson
1976 Kadar: A Late Gravettian Site in Northern Bosnia, Yugoslavia. *Journal of Field Archaeology* 3:407–424.

Montet-White, Anta, and Jeff T. Williams
1992 "A Reindeer Hunters' Winter Camp During the Last Glacial Maximum". Paper presented at the 57th Annual Meeting of the Society for American Archaeology, Pittsburgh, PA.

1994 Spatial Organization at a Winter Campsite of the Last Glacial Maximum: The Case of Grubgraben AL1. *Journal of Anthropological Archaeology* 13:125–138.

Montet-White, Anta, Paul Haesaerts, and Brad Logan
1990 The Epigravettian of Grubgraben: An Overview of the 1986/87 Excavations. In *The Epigravettian Site of Grubgraben, Lower Austria: The 1986 and 1987 Excavations,* edited by Anta Montet-White, pp. 159–162. ERAUL 40. Liège, Belgium: ERAUL.

Moss, Emily H.
1983 *The Functional Analysis of Flint Implements. Pincevent and Pont d'Ambon: Two Case Studies from the French Final Paleolithic.* BAR International Series 177. Oxford, England: British Archaeological Reports.

Moss, E.H., and M.H. Newcomer
1981 Reconstruction of Tool Use at Pincevent: Microwear and Experiments. *Studia Praehistoria Belgica* 2:289–312.

Murdock, George Peter
1967 *Ethnographic Atlas.* Pittsburgh, PA: University of Pittsburgh Press.

Musil, Rudolph
1969 Die Pferde der Pekarna-Höhle. Ein Beitrag zur Problematik der Evolution von Equiden. *Zeitschrift für Tierzüchtung und Züchtungsbiologie* 16(2):147–193.

Nuytten, Phil
1993 Money from the Sea. *National Geographic Magazine* 183(1):108–117.

Oakes, Jillian E.
1991 *Copper and Caribou Inuit Skin Clothing Production.* Canadian Ethnology Service Mercury Series Paper No. 118. Quebec, Canada: Canadian Museum of Civilization.

Obermaier, Hugo
1908 Die am Wagramdurchbruch des Kamp gelegenen niederösterreichischen Quartärfundplätze. *Jahrbuch für Altertumskunde* 2:49–85.

Obermaier, Hugo, and Henri Breuil
1908 Die Gudenushöhle in Niederösterreich. *Mitteilungen der Anthropologischen Gesellschaft in Wien* 38:277–294.

O'Connell, J.F.
1987 Alyawara Site Structure and its Archaeological Implications. *American Antiquity* 52:74–108.

Odum, Eugene P.
1971 *Fundamentals of Ecology.* 3rd edition. Philadelphia, PA: Saunders.

Oliva, Martin
1989 La cabana des chasseurs de mammouth de Milovice (Moravie du sud). *L'Anthropologie* 93(4):887–892.

Olive, Monique
1988 *Une habitation magdalénienne d'Étiolles: L'Unité P15.* Mémoires de la société préhistorique française, Tome 20. Paris: Société préhistorique française.

Olive, Monique, and Yvette Taborin (editors)
1989 *Natur et Fonction des Foyers Préhistoriques.* Mémoires du Musée de Préhistoire d'Ile de France, No. 2. Nemours: A.P.R.A.I.F.

Orlove, Benjamin S.
1980 Ecological Anthropology. *Annual Review of Anthropology* 9:235–273.

Orquera, Luis Abel
1984 Specialization and the Middle/Upper Paleolithic

Transition. *Current Anthropology* 25(1):73–98.

Oswalt, Wendell H.
1973 *Habitat and Technology: The Evolution of Hunting.* New York: Holt, Rinehart and Winston.

1976 *An Anthropological Analysis of Food-getting Technology.* New York: Wiley.

Otte, Marcel
1981 *Le Gravettien en Europa Centrale.* Dissertationes Archaeologicae Gandensis, Vol. XX. Brugge, Belgium: De Tempel.

1990 The Northwestern European Plain Around 18 000 BP. In *The World at 18 000 BP, Volume 1: High Latitudes,* edited by Olga Soffer and Clive Gamble, pp. 54–68. London: Unwin Hyman.

1991 Revision de la Sequence de Willendorf. In *Les bassins du Rhin et du Danube au paléolithique supérieur: environnement, habitat et systèmes d'échange,* edited by Anta Montet-White, pp. 46–59. ERAUL 43. Liège, Belgium: ERAUL.

Pawlikowski, Maciej
1990a Morphological and Mineralogical Analysis of Loess Samples. In *The Epigravettian Site of Grubgraben, Lower Austria: The 1986 and 1987 Excavations,* edited by Anta Montet-White, pp. 37–46. ERAUL 40. Liège, Belgium: ERAUL.

1990b The Origin of Lithic Raw Materials. In *The Epigravettian Site of Grubgraben, Lower Austria: The 1986 and 1987 Excavations,* edited by Anta Montet-White, pp. 93–119. ERAUL 40. Liège, Belgium: ERAUL.

Peterkin, Gail L., Harvey Bricker, and Paul Mellars
1993 *Hunting and Animal Exploitation in the Later Palaeolithic and Mesolithic of Eurasia.* Archaeological Papers of the American Anthropological Association, No. 4. Washington, D.C.: American Anthropological Association.

Pielou, E.C.
1975 *Ecological Diversity.* New York: Wiley.

1977 *Mathematical Ecology.* 2nd edition. New York: Wiley.

Platt, John R.
1964 Strong Inference. *Science* 146(3642):347–353.

Plog, S. and M. Hegmon
1993 The Sample Size-Richness Relation: The Relevance of Research Questions, Sampling Strategies, and Behavioral Variation. *American Antiquity* 58(3):489–496.

Press, William H., Brian P. Flannery, Saul A. Teukolsky, and William T. Vetterling
1989 *Numerical Recipes in Pascal: The Art of Scientific Computing.* Cambridge: Cambridge University Press.

Pye, Kenneth
1987 *Aeolian Dust and Dust Deposits.* London: Academic Press.

Raab, L. Mark, and Albert C. Goodyear
1984 Middle-Range Theory in Archaeology: A Critical Review of Origins and Applications. *American Antiquity* 49(2):255–268.

Read, Dwight W.
1985 The Substance of Archaeological Analysis and the Mold of Statistical Method: Enlightenment Out of Discordance? In *For Concordance in Archaeological Analysis: Bridging Data Structure, Quantitative Technique, and Theory,* edited by Christopher Carr, pp. 45–86. Kansas City, MO: Westport.

Rensink, E., J. Kolen, and A. Spieksma
1991 Patterns of Raw Material Distribution in the Upper Pleistocene of Northwestern and Central Europe. In *Raw Material Economies Among Prehistoric Hunter-Gatherers,* edited by Anta Montet-White and Steven Holen, pp. 141–159. Lawrence, KS: University of Kansas, Publications in Anthropology 19.

Renfrew, Colin
1987 An Interview with Lewis Binford. *Current Anthropology* 28(5):683–694.

Rhode, David
1988 Measurement of Archaeological Diversity and the Sample-Size Effect. *American Antiquity* 53(4):708–716.

Riek, Gustav
1973 *Das Paläolithikum der Brillenhöhle bei Blaubeuren (Schwäbische Alb). Teil I.* Forschungen und Berichte zur Vor- und Frühgeschichte in Baden-Württemberg, Band 4/I. Stuttgart: Müller and Gräff.

Rigaud, Jean-Philippe
1976 Les civilisations du paléolithique supérieur en Périgord. In *La Préhistoire Française,* edited by Henry de Lumley, pp. 1257–1270. Paris: CNRS.

Rigaud, Jean-Philippe, and Jan F. Simek
1990 The Last Pleniglacial in the South of France (24 000–14 000 Years Ago). In *The World at 18 000 BP, Volume 1: High Latitudes,* edited by Olga Soffer and Clive Gamble, pp. 69–86. London: Unwin Hyman.

Rindos, David
1985 Darwinian Selection, Symbolic Variation and the Evolution of Culture. *Current Anthropology* 26(1):65–88.

1986 The Genetics of Cultural Anthropology: Toward a Genetic Model for the Origin of the Capacity for Culture. *Journal of Anthropological Archaeology* 5(1):1–38.

1989 Diversity, Variation and Selection. In *Quantifying Diversity in Archaeology,* edited by Robert D. Leonard and George T. Jones, pp. 13–23. Cambridge: Cambridge University Press.

Ringrose, T.J.
1993 Bone Counts and Statistics: A Critique. *Journal of Archaeological Science* 20:121–157.

Ruddiman, W.F., and J.C. Duplessy
1985 Conference on the Last Deglaciation: Timing and Mechanism. *Quaternary Research* 23:1–17.

Sackett, James R.
1988 The Neuvic Group: Upper Paleolithic Open-Air Sites in the Perigord. In *Upper Pleistocene Prehistory of Western Eurasia,* edited by Harold L. Dibble and Anta Montet-White, pp. 61–84. Philadelphia, PA: The University Museum, University of Pennsylvania.

Schacherl, Gustav
1893 Gobatsburg, Gobelsburg. In *Topographie von Niederösterreich, Band III,* pp. 480–486. Vienna: Verein für Landeskunde von Niederösterrich.

Schiffer, Michael B.
1975 Factors and "Toolkits": Evaluating Multivariate Analyses in Archaeology. *Plains Anthropologist* 20:61–70.

1976 *Behavioral Archeology.* New York: Academic Press.

1985 Review of "Working at Archaeology" by Lewis R. Binford. *American Antiquity* 50(1):191–193.

Schild, Romuald
1980 Introduction to Dynamic Technological Analysis of Chipped Stone Assemblages. In *Unconventional Archaeology: New Approaches and Goals in Polish Archaeology,* edited by Romuald Schild, pp. 57–85. Wroclaw: Zaklad Narodowy im. Ossolinskich.

Schmider, Béatrice
1990 The Last Pleniglacial in the Paris Basin (22 500 – 17 000 BP). In *The World at 18 000 BP, Volume 1: High Latitudes,* edited by Olga Soffer and Clive Gamble, pp. 41–53. London: Unwin Hyman.

Scott, Katherine
1980 Two Hunting Episodes of Middle Paleolithic Age at La Cotte de Saint-Berlade, Jersey. *World Archaeology* 12:137–152.

Seitl, Ludek, Jirí Svoboda, Vojen Lozek, Antonín Prichystal, and Helena Svobodová
1986 Das Spätglazial in der Barová-Höhle im Mährischen Karst. *Archäologisches Korrespondenzblatt* 16:393–398.

Sheehan, Michael S.
1995 Cultural Responses to the Altithermal or Inadequate Sampling? *Plains Anthropologist* 40(153):261–270.

Shott, Michael J.
1989 Diversity, Organization, and Behavior in the Material Record: Ethnographic and Archaeological Examples. *Current Anthropology* 30(3):283–315.

Simán, Katalin
1990 Population Fluctuation in the Carpathian Basin from 50 to 15 Thousand Years BP. *Acta Archaeologica Academiae Scientiarum Hungaricae* 42(1–4):13–19.

Simek, Jan F.
1984 *K-means Approach to the Analysis of Spatial Structure in Upper Paleolithic Habitation Sites: Le Flageolet I and Pincevent Section 36.* BAR International Series 205. Oxford, England: British Archaeological Reports.

Smalley, Ian J. and José G. Cabrera
1970 The Shape and Surface Texture of Loess Particles. *Geological Society of American Bulletin* 81(5):1591–1596.

Snedecor, George W., and William G. Cochran
1980 *Statistical Methods.* 7th edition. Ames, IA: The Iowa State University Press.

Soffer, Olga (editor)
1987a *The Pleistocene Old World.* New York: Plenum.

Soffer, Olga
1985 *The Upper Paleolithic of the Central Russian Plain.* San Diego: Academic Press.

1987b Upper Paleolithic Connubia, Refugia, and the Archaeological Record from Eastern Europe. In *The Pleistocene Old World,* edited by Olga Soffer, pp. 333–348. New York: Plenum.

1987c Upper Paleolithic Hunter-Gatherers in Europe: Studies of Subsistence Practices and Settlement Systems 1986–1990. In *Le Paléolithique supérieur européen,* edited by Marcel Otte, pp. 321–340. ERAUL 24. Liège, Belgium: ERAUL.

1990 The Russian Plain at the Last Glacial Maximum. In *The World at 18 000 BP, Volume 1: High Latitudes,* edited by Olga Soffer and Clive Gamble, pp. 228–252. London: Unwin Hyman.

Soffer, Olga, and Clive Gamble (editors)
1990 *The World at 18 000 BP, Volume 1: High Latitudes.* London: Unwin Hyman.

de Sonneville-Bordes, Denise
1960 *Le paléolithique supérieur en Périgord.* Bordeaux, France: Delmas.

1963 Le Paléolithique supérieur en Suisse. *L'Anthropologie* 67(3–4):205–268.

1966 L'évolution du paléolithique supérieur en Europe occidentale et sa signification. *Bulletin de la Société Préhistorique Française* 63:3–34.

de Sonneville-Bordes, Denise, and Jean Perrot
1954–56 Lexique typologique du paléolithique supérieur: Outillage lithique. *Bulletin de la Société Préhistorique Française* 51:327–335; 52:76–79; 53:408–412, 547–549.

Spaulding, Albert C.
1954 Reply To Ford. *American Antiquity* 19(4):391–393.

1960 The Dimensions of Archaeology. In *Essays in the Science of Culture: In Honor of Leslie A. White*, edited by Gertrude E. Dole and Robert L. Carneiro, pp. 437–456. New York: Thomas Y. Crowell.

1977 On Growth and Form in Archaeology: Multivariate Analysis. *Journal of Anthropological Research* 33(1):1–15.

Speth, John D.
1983 *Bison Kills and Bone Counts: Decision Making by Ancient Hunters*. Chicago: University of Chicago Press.

Spieksma, A.T.
1989 *A Study on the Distribution of Non-local Raw Materials During the Early Upper Palaeolithic in Central Europe*. Unpublished thesis, University of Leiden, Netherlands.

Spiess, Arthur E.
1979 *Reindeer and Caribou Hunters: An Archaeological Study*. New York: Academic Press.

Spöttl, Ignaz
1889 Die Resultate der diesjährigen Ausgrabungen in Niederösterreich. *Mitteilungen der Anthropologischen Gesellschaft in Wien* 19:201–202.

1890 Resultate der Ausgrabungen für die Anthropologische Gesellschaft in Niederösterreich und in Mähren im Jahre 1889. *Mitteilungen der Anthropologischen Gesellschaft in Wien* 20:59–100.

Stapert, Dick
1989 The Ring and Sector Method: Intrasite Spatial Analysis of Stone Age Sites, with Special Reference to Pincevent. *Palaeohistoria* 31:1–57.

1992 *Rings and Sectors: Intrasite Spatial Analysis of Stone Age Sites*. Dissertation, Rijksuniversiteit Groningen, The Netherlands.

Stapert, Dick, and Thomas Terberger
1989 Gönnersdorf Concentration III: Investigating the Possibility of Multiple Occupations. *Palaeohistoria* 31:59–95.

Stewart, Andrew, and Michael Jochim
1986 Changing Economic Organization in Late Glacial Southwest Germany. In *The End of the Paleolithic in the Old World*, edited by Lawrence G. Straus, pp. 47–62. BAR International Series S284. Oxford, England: British Archaeological Reports.

Straus, Lawrence G.
1987 Hunting in Late Upper Paleolithic Western Europe. In *The Evolution of Human Hunting*, edited by Matthew H. Nitecki and Doris V. Nitecki, pp. 147–176. New York: Plenum.

1991 Human Geography of the Late Upper Paleolithic in Western Europe: Present State of the Question. *Journal of Anthropological Research* 47(2):259–278.

Straus, L., and C. Heller
1988 Explorations of the Twilight Zone: The Early Upper Paleolithic of Vasco-Cantabrian Spain and Gascony. In *The Early Upper Paleolithic: Evidence from Europe and the Near East*, edited by John F. Hoffecker and Cornelia A. Wolf, pp. 97–133. BAR International Series 437. Oxford, England: British Archaeological Reports.

Straus, Lawrence G., Berit V. Eriksen, Jon M. Erlandson, and David R. Yesner (editors)
1996 *Humans at the End of the Ice Age: The Archaeology of the Pleistocene–Holocene Transition*. New York: Plenum.

Sturdy, Derek A.
1975 Some Reindeer Economies in Prehistoric Europe. In *Palaeoeconomy*, edited by Eric S. Higgs, pp. 55–95. London: Cambridge University Press.

Svoboda, Jiří
1983 Raw Material Sources in Early Upper Paleolithic Moravia: The Concept of Lithic Exploitation Areas. *L'Anthropologie* 21(2):147–158.

1985 Neue Grabungsergebnisse von Stránská skála, Mähren, Tschechoslowakei. *Archäologisches Korrespondenzblatt* 15:261–268.

1990 Moravia During the Upper Pleniglacial. In *The World at 18 000 BP, Volume 1: High Latitudes*, edited by Olga Soffer and Clive Gamble, pp. 193–203. London: Unwin Hyman.

1991 Neue Erkenntnisse zur Pékarna-Höhle im Mährischen Karst. *Archäologisches Korrespondenzblatt* 21(1):39–43.

Taborin, Yvette
1993 Shells of the French Aurignacian and Périgordian. In *Before Lascaux: The Complex Record of the Early Upper Paleolithic*, edited by Heidi Knecht, Anne Pike-Tay, and Randall White, pp. 211–227. Boca Raton, FL: CRC Press.

Teichert, Manfred
 1971 Die Knochenreste aus der Wildpferdjägerstation Bad Frankenhausen. *Alt-Thüringen* 11:227–234.

Testart, Alain
 1982 The Significance of Food Storage Among Hunter-Gatherers: Residence Patterns, Population Densities, and Social Inequalities. *Current Anthropology* 23(5):523–537.

Thieme, Hartmut
 1991 Frieden (Leine). Jungpaläolithische Station. In *Ur- und Frühgeschichte in Niedersachsen*, edited by Hans-Jürgen Häßler, pp. 423–424. Stuttgart: Konrad Theiss.

Thomas, David H.
 1978 The Awful Truth About Statistics in Archaeology. *American Antiquity* 43(2):231–244.

Todd, Lawrence C.
 1987 Analysis of Kill-Butchery Bonebeds and Interpretation of Paleoindian Hunting. In *The Evolution of Human Hunting*, edited by Matthew H. Nitecki and Doris V. Nitecki, pp. 225–266. New York: Plenum.

Torrence, Robin
 1989 Retooling: Towards a Behavioural Theory of Stone Tools. In *Time, Energy, and Stone Tools*, edited by Robin Torrence, pp. 57–66. Cambridge: Cambridge University Press.

Tukey, John W.
 1977 *Exploratory Data Analysis*. Reading, MA: Addison-Wesley.

Tukey, John W., and M.B. Wilk
 1970 Data Analysis and Statistics: Techniques and Approaches. In *The Quantitative Analysis of Social Problems*, edited by Edward R. Tufte, pp. 370–390. Reading, MA: Addison-Wesley.

Tyler, Stephanie J.
 1972 The Behaviour and Social Organization of the New Forest Ponies. *Animal Behaviour Monographs* 5(2):87–196.

Urbanek, Martin
 1990 A Review of Archaeological Research at the Grubgraben Prior to 1980. In *The Epigravettian Site of Grubgraben, Lower Austria: The 1986 and 1987 Excavations*, edited by Anta Montet-White, pp. 7–13. ERAUL 40. Liège, Belgium: ERAUL.

Valoch, Karel
 1968 Das Jung- und Spätpaläolithikum in der Kulna-Höhle im Mährischen Karst. *Germania* 46:110–118.

 1975 Paleolitická stanice v Konevove ulici v Brne. *Archeologické rozhledy* 27(1):3–17.

 1980 La fin des temps glaciaires en Moravie (Tchécoslovaquie). *L'Anthropologie* 84(3):380–390.

 1987 Raw Materials Used in the Moravian Middle and Upper Palaeolithic. In *Proceedings of the International Conference on Prehistoric Flint Mining and Lithic Raw Material Identification in the Carpathian Basin, Budapest–Sümeg 1986*, edited by K.T. Bíró, pp. 263–268. Budapest: Magyar Nemzeti Múzeum.

 1989 Osídlení a Klimatické Zmeny v Poslední Dobe Ledové na Morave. [Settlement and Climatic Changes in the Last Ice Age in Moravia]. *Acta Musei Moraviae* 74:7–34.

van Andel, T.H.
 1990 Living in the Last High Glacial—An Interdisciplinary Challenge. In *The World at 18 000 BP, Volume 1: High Latitudes*, edited by Olga Soffer and Clive Gamble, pp. 24–38. London: Unwin Hyman.

Vértes, László
 1962 Ausgrabungen der altsteinzeitlichen Siedlung von Arka 1960–61. *Acta Archaeologica Academiae Scientiarum Hungaricae* 14(3–4):143–157.

 1964/65 Das Jungpaläolithikum von Arka in Nord-Ungarn. *Quartär* 15/16:79–132.

 1966 The Upper Palaeolithic Site on Mt. Henye at Bodrogkeresztúr. *Acta Archaeologica Academiae Scientiarum Hungaricae* 18:3–14.

Vierra, Robert K.
 1975 *Structure Versus Function in the Archaeological Record*. Ph.D dissertation, Department of Anthropology, University of New Mexico, Albuquerque. Ann Arbor, MI: University Microfilms.

Vierra, Robert K., and David L. Carlson
 1981 Factor Analysis, Random Data, and Patterned Results. *American Antiquity* 46(2):272–283.

Vörös, István
 1982 Faunal Remains From the Gravettian Reindeer Hunters' Campsite at Ságvár. *Folia Archaeologica* 33:43–71.

Vogel, J.C., and H.T. Waterbolk
 1972 Groningen Radiocarbon Dates X. *Radiocarbon* 14(1):6–110.

Watson, Patty Jo, Steven A. LeBlanc, and Charles L. Redman
 1984 *Archeological Explanation: The Scientific Method in Archeology*. 2nd edition. New York: Columbia University Press.

Weniger, Gerd-C.
 1981 Aktivitätsspezifische Differenzierungen zwischen Siedlungsplätzen des südwestdeutschen Magdalénien. *Archäologisches Korrespondenzblatt* 11:293–300.

1982 *Wildbeuter und ihre Umwelt: Ein Beitrag zum Magdalénien Südwestdeutschlands aus ökologischer und ethno-archäologischer Sicht.* Archaeologica Venatoria 5. Tübingen, Germany: Archaeologica Venatoria.

1987a Magdalenian Settlement Pattern and Subsistence in Central Europe: The Southwestern and Central German Cases. In *The Pleistocene Old World*, edited by Olga Soffer, pp. 201–215. New York: Plenum.

1987b Magdalenian Settlement and Subsistence in South-west Germany. *Proceedings of the Prehistoric Society* 53:293–307.

1989 The Magdalenian in Western Central Europe: Settlement Pattern and Regionality. *Journal of World Prehistory* 3(3):323–372.

1990 Germany at 18 000 BP. In *The World at 18 000 BP, Volume 1: High Latitudes*, edited by Olga Soffer and Clive Gamble, pp. 171–192. London: Unwin Hyman.

1991 Überlegungen zur Mobilität jägerischer Gruppen im Jungpaläolithikum. *Saeculum* 42(1):82–103.

West, Dixie L.
1995 *Epigravettian Hunting Strategy and Animal Use in the Middle Danube*. Ph.D dissertation, Department of Anthropology, University of Kansas, Lawrence. Ann Arbor, MI: University Microfilms.

West, Dixie, and Anta Montet-White
1990 Raw Material Use. In *The Epigravettian Site of Grubgraben, Lower Austria: The 1986 and 1987 Excavations*, edited by Anta Montet-White, pp. 121–131. ERAUL 40. Liège, Belgium: ERAUL.

Wetzel, Robert
1958 *Die Bocksteinschmiede*. I. Teil. Stuttgart: W. Kohlhammer.

Whallon, Robert
1973a Spatial Analysis of Occupation Floors I: The Application of Dimensional Analysis of Variance. *American Antiquity* 38(3):266–278.

1973b Spatial Analysis of Palaeolithic Occupation Areas. In *The Explanation of Culture Change*, edited by Colin Renfrew, pp. 115–130. London: Duckworth.

1974 Spatial Analysis of Occupation Floors II: The Application of Nearest Neighbor Analysis. *American Antiquity* 39(1):16–34.

1978 The Spatial Analysis of Mesolithic Occupation Floors: A Reappraisal. In *The Early Postglacial Settlement of Northern Europe: An Ecological Perspective*, edited by Paul Mellars, pp. 27–35. London: Duckworth.

1982 Comments on 'Explanation'. In *Ranking, Resource, and Exchange: Aspects of the Archaeology of Early European Society*, edited by Colin Renfrew and Stephen Shennan, pp. 155–158. Cambridge: Cambridge University Press.

1984 Unconstrained Clustering for the Analysis of Spatial Distributions in Archaeology. In *Intrasite Spatial Analysis in Archaeology*, edited by Harold J. Hietala, pp. 242–277. Cambridge: Cambridge University Press.

White, J.P.
1968 Fabricatoirs, outils écaillés or scalar cores? *Mankind* 6:658–666.

White, J. Peter, and David Hurst Thomas
1972 What Mean These Stones? Ethno-taxonomic Models and Archaeological Interpretations in the New Guinea Highlands. In *Models in Archaeology*, edited by David L. Clarke, pp. 275–308. London: Methuen.

White, Leslie A.
1949 *The Science of Culture: A Study of Man and Civilization*. New York: Farrar, Straus & Giroux.

White, Randall
1982 Rethinking the Middle/Upper Paleolithic Transition. *Current Anthropology* 23(2):169–192.

1987 Glimpses of Long-Term Shifts in Late Paleolithic Land Use in the Périgord. In *The Pleistocene Old World*, edited by Olga Soffer, pp. 263–277. New York: Plenum.

1993 Technological and Social Dimensions of "Aurignacian-Age" Body Ornaments across Europe. In *Before Lascaux: The Complex Record of the Early Upper Paleolithic*, edited by Heidi Knecht, Anne Pike-Tay, and Randall White, pp. 277–299. Boca Raton, FL: CRC Press.

Whitelaw, Todd
1983 People and Space in Hunter-Gatherer Camps: A Generalising Approach in Ethnoarchaeology. *Archaeological Review from Cambridge* 2(2):48–66.

1989 *The Social Organisation of Space in Hunter-Gatherer Communities: Some Implications for Social Inference in Archaeology*. Ph.D dissertation, Faculty of Archaeology and Anthropology, University of Cambridge, Cambridge, England.

1991 Some Dimensions of Variability in the Social Organisation of Community Space Among Foragers. In *Ethnoarchaeological Approaches to Mobile Campsites*, edited by Clive S. Gamble and William A. Boismier, pp. 139–188. International Monographs in Prehistory, Ethnoarchaeological Series 1. Ann Arbor, MI: International Monographs in Prehistory.

Whitney, Patsy L.

1992 *A Faunal Analysis of Grubgraben AL1: The 1989 Excavations*. Unpublished Master's thesis, Department of Anthropology, University of Kansas, Lawrence.

Williams, Jeff T.
1988 *Middle-Range Research in Archaeology: Science or Science-Fiction?* Unpublished Master's thesis, Department of Anthropology, University of Kentucky, Lexington, KY.

Winkler, Eike-Meinrad
1987 Paläolithische Stein- und Knochenartefakte aus dem Bereich der Gudenushöhle in Nöhagen, Niederösterreich. *Fundberichte aus Niederösterreich* 26:173–178.

Wobst, H. Martin
1990 Afterword. Minitime and Megaspace in the Palaeolithic at 18 K and Otherwise. In *The World at 18 000 BP, Volume 1: High Latitudes*, edited by Olga Soffer and Clive Gamble, pp. 331–343. London: Unwin Hyman.

Wright, H.E. Jr.
1993 Environmental Determinism in Near Eastern Prehistory. *Current Anthropology* 34(4):458–469.

Wright, H.E. Jr., J.E. Kutzbach, T. Webb III, W.F. Ruddiman, F.A. Street-Perrott, and P.J. Bartlein
1993 *Global Climates Since the Last Glacial Maximum*. Minneapolis: University of Minnesota Press.

Wurmbrand, G. Graf
1879 Über die Anwesenheit des Menschen zur Zeit der Lössbildung. *Denkschriften der kaiserlichen Akademie der Wissenschaften. Mathematisch-naturwissenschaftliche Classe*. Band 39, Abteilung 2, pp. 165–186.

Yellen, John E.
1977 *Archaeological Approaches to the Present: Models for Reconstructing the Past*. New York: Academic Press.

www.ingramcontent.com/pod-product-compliance
Lightning Source LLC
Chambersburg PA
CBHW040949020526
44116CB00039B/2977